THE 23 MOST COMMON MISTAKES IN PUBLIC RELATIONS

Also by Alec Benn

The 27 Most Common Mistakes in Advertising (AMACOM 1978)

THE

23

MOST COMMON MISTAKES
IN PUBLIC RELATIONS

ALEC BENN

amacom American Management Associations

Library of Congress Cataloging in Publication Data

Benn, Alec.
    The 23 most common mistakes in public relations.

    Includes index.
    1. Public relations. I. Title. II. Title: Twenty-
three most common mistakes in public relations.
HM263.B387   659.2   82-71316
ISBN 0-8144-5715-0   AACR2

First Printing

Dedicated to the memory of an unusual teacher of English,
Mrs. Van Wagner,
and my fellow pupils in Yonkers Public School #5

ACKNOWLEDGMENTS

This book could not have been written without the generous help of a number of people experienced in public relations and communications. I am particularly grateful to those who read drafts of the manuscript and contributed valuable comments: Joseph B. Smith, Stephen Fenichell, William A. MacDonough, Caroline M. Benn, Julie Connelly, and Gerald J. Voros.

Many thanks also to the following, who contributed valuable information, commented on sections of the manuscript, or helped in other ways: Andrew R. Paul, Barbara A. Keebler, Harry L. Darling, Elias Buchwald, Amelia Lobsenz, Harold Burson, Amos Landman, Lee Seabolt, John DeFrancesco, Mark Appleman, Gerald Tolle, Paul A. Wagner, Herbert L. Corbin, D. L. Jeka, Heidi Kane, Amanda Sherwin, Leo Floros, Robert H. Gersky, Barry Polsky, Richard H. Truitt, Robert Wood, Roy G. Foltz, DeWitt C. Morrill, Michael R. Murasko, Carol Sloan, and David Morris. My thanks also to the many people who sent me case histories that for one reason or another, often similarity, were not included.

Special thanks to my editor, Eric Valentine, for his always cheerful help in a number of ways, particularly a fundamental suggestion regarding the tone and direction of this book.

I appreciate the kind permission of the Industrial Communication Council to include facts from their *Case Studies in Organizational Communication* for the case histories on "the large chemical company," Standard Oil of California, and Mississippi Management, Inc.

Finally, thank you William H. McElnea, Jr., and Jenkin Lloyd Jones for permission to reprint the two speeches in the Appendix.

READ THIS BOOK IF YOU'RE

a member of top management of a corporation

It will show you how better public relations can increase sales, reduce costs, minimize regulation, and improve your stock's price–earnings ratio.

a corporate executive or other businessperson

Anyone in business who spurns public relations cannot get far in today's world. In addition, no matter how well you communicate now, this book will improve your ability to inform, persuade, and get action both orally and in writing.

an association executive

You will get the same benefits as a corporate executive, and perhaps even more.

a public relations professional

Not only will you expand your knowledge and your communications capabilities, but you'll see how to better convince others of the soundness of your recommendations.

hoping to be a public relations professional

This book will give you a comprehensive knowledge of public relations, show you how to solve public relations problems, and enable you to write or otherwise produce any public relations communication faster and better.

in a nonprofit or political organization

While this book concerns itself principally with public relations for corporations, the techniques for other organizations are virtually identical. And some topics covered—such as getting the cooperation of volunteers, fund raising, and influencing legislation—are directly applicable to your needs.

otherwise curious about how the most skilled public relations practitioners control and change group attitudes and actions

You'll read how public relations can and does affect the laws we live under, the taxes and prices we pay, the common stocks we buy, and how well we like our jobs.

CONTENTS

SECTION TWO: A NEW, COMPLETE, PRACTICAL THEORY OF PUBLIC RELATIONS COMMUNICATION

SECTION THREE: HOW TO INFLUENCE SPECIFIC PUBLICS

CASE HISTORIES

INTRODUCTION: BETTER PUBLIC RELATIONS ARE NEEDED TODAY

"I am your adversary"—that's how a young reporter began the interview with a corporate executive of excellent reputation. Such open antagonism is rare, but there is little doubt that today more reporters and editors are, if not hostile, more distrustful of business than ever before.

Osborn Elliot, dean of the Graduate School of Journalism at Columbia University, said in 1981: "Too often these days reporters bring too much suspicion to their jobs—suspecting that anyone in a position of power is there for some ulterior motive."

That's one reason—and only one of many—why public relations policies and practices that once were acceptable are no longer sufficient today.

Not only has the attitude of the media changed, but so has the attitude of people generally. They're more skeptical. Perhaps because of such events as Vietnam, Watergate, Abscam, and publicized bribery of foreign politicians by American businessmen. Perhaps because the population is older; the median age reached 30 in 1980. Perhaps because the standard of living of many has not improved as much as anticipated, or has even regressed. Perhaps simply because the general public knows more about economics and business than ever before. Actions of the Federal Reserve System, once banished to the back pages of the business section, are now often front-page news. Terms formerly used only by economists, such as *gross national product* and *leading economic indicators*, are now familiar to the masses. The newspaper with the largest daily circulation in the United States is no longer a general newspaper but *The Wall Street Journal*.

While becoming more skeptical and more knowledgeable, people generally have become more easily bored. Most people in the United States today have been exposed to television for several hours every day since birth. They're accustomed to receiving information quickly and vividly, by pictures and spoken words. They're impatient with printed, wordy explanations that fail to come to the point in a stimulating way. This means that when only words are used—and words alone will continue to be the most common public relations communications tools for years to come—the message must be better written than ever before.

Just as radio made it necessary to improve recordings (hi-fidelity, long playing) and television stimulated improvements in motion pictures (wide screens, better scripts, bigger budgets), so television also makes it necessary for public relations communications—news releases, annual reports and other booklets, speeches, company newspapers, letters—to capitalize more fully on their individual unique advantages.

Besides changing in character, the publics that most corporations need to influence have also increased in number and importance.

Government regulations are all-pervasive today; consequently, many chief executives, particularly those of large companies, spend much more time worrying about what a government—federal, state, or local—will do next or what the reaction of government officials and voters will be to a contemplated change. Opening or closing a factory or store, for example, can be a traumatic experience.

The most significant issue in the United States today may be how to improve productivity. The attitude of employees and those who supervise employees can make a big difference. It's one reason corporations in resource-poor Japan can produce automobiles and cameras that are less expensive and of better quality, in the opinion of many Americans, than American companies can.

Investors need to be courted as never before—and differently. Efficient plants and equipment count even more than worker attitude in improving productivity, yet much of America's plants are old and obsolete. Inflation has made the tax-deductible reserves set aside for replacement insufficient, and the new high-technology equipment costs more anyway. Consequently, not only growing companies but many that are established need to raise additional capital in sizable quantities at reasonable rates.

Paradoxically, inflation has also made the enduring assets of some companies, such as land, worth much more. When these values are not reflected in the price of a corporation's common stock, the company becomes a tempting takeover target.

At the same time that influencing investors has become more important, the nature of the investment community has changed. Pension funds and other institutional investors dominate the securities markets, making fuller disclosure by more expert investor relations people essential. Conversely, companies whose stocks are not suitable for institutional investment may have difficulty reaching and influencing individual investors if they stick to traditional ways.

Opportunities to influence all these audiences, especially members of the general public in their roles as customers and voters, have increased almost bewilderingly. Many newspapers have expanded their business sections, as well as their entertainment and travel sections, and created new sections on food, science, furnishings, and other subjects. A new, specialized magazine is launched every day, it seems. Cable TV has further increased the possibilities for TV exposure—and may have even more profound effects. In fact, cable TV may have as great an effect on broadcast TV as broadcast TV had on other media. By 1990, it is estimated, more than half the country will have cable TV.

Yesterday's public relations policies, methods, and levels of competence cannot successfully influence today's less trusting, more knowledgeable, multiple audiences accustomed to absorbing information without effort and reachable in a variety of ways, often through reporters with an antibusiness bias. Not only do executives with public relations titles need to expand their knowledge and capabilities, but more corporate executives from the chief executive on down need to devote increased time and attention to public relations. How the executives of a corporation talk and write to government officials, investors, employees, the general public as customers and voters, and the media largely determines the attitudes these publics will have toward the corporation.

Specific solutions will vary from corporation to corporation, depending on size, relative importance of the different publics, previous history, attitudes of top management, and a variety of other factors. It is clear, however, that not only public relations executives but all corporate executives with ambition need the following:

1. *A method for solving any solvable public relations problem.* The diversity and changing nature of today's public relations audiences, means of communication, and objectives make past practices of limited use. (Even though, of course, the more an executive knows about what has succeeded in the past, the better.) No doctor knows all there is to know about medicine, but competent doctors know how to diagnose, how to judge whether they know enough, and which specialist to call in. Like doctors, lawyers, and engineers, executives faced with public relations problems need a methodology.

2. *Knowledge of what makes a communication effective.* Ideally, every executive should be able to communicate clearly and convincingly to any audience, no matter what the form of communication or other conditions. Today there are too many different kinds of public relations communications for any executive to master them all—and new forms are emerging. An executive should, however, be able to judge the likely effectiveness of any public relations communication and improve it by editing. And an executive considered a public relations professional should be able to write and speak in as many forms, to as many different audiences, under as many different conditions as possible.

3. *Better salesmanship for appropriate public relations mea-*

sures. It's not enough for an executive to know what to do, he or she must be able to convince fellow executives, directors, and the chief executive officer of the best course of action. This is seldom easy, partly because public relations is not as simple as many executives trained in other disciplines believe it to be and partly because the instincts of many executives concerning public relations are often wrong. The public relations salesperson needs to know what mistakes are commonly made, why they are made, and how to convince others to avoid them.

4. *A clear concept of public relations morality*. Not needed: a namby-pamby code of ethics that will be given only lip service. People engaged in public relations need hardheaded morality that will make top management feel they are as devoted to the company's interests as any lawyer. At the same time, however, this morality must cause those engaged in public relations to be proud of what they do.

This book aims to fill all four of these needs and more.

SECTION ONE

HOW TO MAKE THE MEDIA
NOT AN ENEMY
BUT AN ALLY

HOW TO FIGURE OUT
WHAT TO DO—ESPECIALLY TO
COUNTER
BAD PUBLICITY

When Henry Ford II was accused of using corporate funds for his personal benefit and taking kickbacks from suppliers, he called a press conference and vigorously denied the charges. By holding the conference a few days after the accusation was first published, Ford gave the media basis for another damaging story that would not otherwise have appeared. What is more, those who had seen or listened to the first story were reminded of the accusation, so they remembered it better. Henry Ford II was guilty of **Common Mistake #1: Giving additional publicity to bad news by attempting to rebut it.**

This mistake results from failure to differentiate between mass communication and one-to-one communication. In one-to-one communication, a meaningful dialog is possible because each participant can hear everything the other says. In mass communication, not only is the communication generally one way, but only some of the audience sees or hears any particular message. The readers of newspapers and magazines, the viewers of television, and the listeners to the radio are like a passing parade. They are not all the same people on successive days—and those who are the same don't read, see, or listen to everything every day. Only part of the audience who sees a story on a certain subject one day will see the follow-up story the next day. And only some of those who see the story the second day will have seen the original. The percentage of readers who see both an original story and its rebuttal depends, of course, largely on how dominantly or obscurely both versions are treated. However, even when both versions are given considerable coverage by a publication, the overlap can be less than 25 percent of the total audience. More than 75 percent will see only one version.

Common Mistake #1 results from a second, more fundamental public relations mistake. Some people who make this next common mistake have little sense of what interests the press and what does not. Some don't comprehend how independent, even willful, the media can be. Some don't know that on days when news is light otherwise undeserving stories are printed and broadcast, and on days when news is heavy, some otherwise deserving stories must be left out. As a consequence of their lack of understanding, these executives may direct a public relations person to promptly place a particular story in a specific publication and expect a reporter to write the story the way they'd like it written. They confuse public relations with paid advertising. They make **Common Mistake #2: Establishing an unrealistic public relations objective.**

Henry Ford II probably said something like, "I want everyone to believe I couldn't possibly be guilty of using corporate money for my personal benefit. I'm going to call a press conference." This was an unrealistic public relations objective. The best any public relations effort could have accomplished was to *minimize* the effect of the accusation. When the mass media slings mud, some always sticks.

Henry Ford II was not an incompetent executive—far from it. As a young man, he took over a failing company and by judicious choice of executives and intelligent policies made the Ford Motor Company not only a highly profitable operation but also one of the largest and most productive corporations in the world.

American corporate executives are the most competent doers of any kind, anytime, anywhere, yet the polls show that American business is held in low regard. The reason: Most American businesspeople know little about how to influence mass audiences—and don't realize how dangerous a little knowledge can be. Often they pay insufficient attention to deciding what should be done. They react instead of planning.

Sometimes what needs to be done is obvious, but more often extensive analysis based on experience and knowledge is necessary. It is not enough to hold a meeting during which otherwise competent executives with little experience in public relations make suggestions. And it especially cannot be a meeting in which public relations professionals are simply told what to do. (Henry Ford had at his command some of the country's most highly paid professional public relations people. Did they voice what they thought? Were they heeded?)

The forms of communication that can be used in public relations are unlimited and increasing. They include press releases, letters, telephone calls, speeches, slide presentations, videotapes, motion pictures, meetings of all kinds, public service announcements, booklets, posters, video cassettes and discs, and TV channels with answer-back facilities. Some may be used to communicate to hundreds, thousands, or millions of people; some to only one key person who in turn can influence a mass audience. Each form has its advantages and disadvantages—some of which are not obvious to inexperienced people. Which form should be used depends on the circumstances.

Sometimes formulating a feasible public relations plan requires research. When public officials and business and labor leaders in the state of Washington faced the possibility that the state tax on gasoline would be repealed, research gave them the fundamental theme they needed to convince voters that the tax was necessary. The revenues from the tax were used to repair roads; research revealed that the cost of driving over bad roads was higher than what each owner was asked to pay in taxes. (A full case history appears in Chapter 12.)

When two unions tried to organize a Rockwell International plant, an early step recommended by their public relations agency, Ketchum, MacLeod & Grove, was to survey plant management and supervisors to get at the reasons for the employee unrest. As a consequence, the public relations successfully focused on the points of discontent.

The purpose of the owner of Harbor Point, a condominium, was to sell apartments (see the case history in Chapter 5). The public relations plan was determined only after thorough analysis of the condominium and the market for its apartments.

In deciding what to do, a competent executive asks two questions: Can public relations accomplish the objective? How? The two are interrelated. The first cannot be answered without tentatively answering the second.

There are nine conditions that determine the best way to accomplish a public relations objective. This chapter will briefly describe all nine and also discuss how to counter and prevent negative publicity. We've already discussed one condition—the form of communication. Another is the purpose. Defeating a legislative proposal calls for different techniques than does helping paid advertising sell dog food.

The source of the communication is often very important. Is the corporation part of the wave of the future in the eyes of the press? Or is it a tired has-been? What's the chief executive officer like? There's little sense in calling a press conference if the chief executive is a dud at handling reporters. It would be a mistake to arrange for an appearance on TV by an executive who doesn't have the necessary presence and won't take the training.

Gulf Oil recognized that the most important source of information about the company in each local community where it had a facility was the local district manager. So the company instituted a public relations training program for its managers. (This program is in Chapter 2.)

Sometimes selecting and properly utilizing the right source is the solution to a problem. Here's a case history.

HOW CONFIDENCE WAS RESTORED IN THE NEW YORK STATE LOTTERY

The year before the New York City–headquartered public relations agency of Lobsenz-Stevens Inc. was retained for the New York State Lottery, all operations had been suspended following charges of mismanagement, alleged fraud, unsold winning tickets, duplicate tickets, and computer errors. The press, the public, and the vendors had all lost confidence in the lottery—a big obstacle to the sale of lottery tickets.

The governor of New York State selected John D. Quinn, former deputy commissioner of the Michigan Lottery, to be director of the to-be-revived lottery. Lobsenz-Stevens analyzed Quinn—his personality, character, how he interacted with people—and based on that analysis formulated a public relations plan that would help restore confidence in the state lottery.

Quinn's task was to personally visit publishers and editors in major cities in New York State and project the true picture of the new lottery—honest, efficient, and vital to the financial health of the education program of New York State. He told publishers and editors about the security and management methods he had instituted to make sure the mismanagement of the old regime would not be repeated. He told them how the lottery was to be run; he gave them all the facts.

How well he did was proved in record time. When a series of public drawings was scheduled a few weeks later to pay unpaid prizes from the old lottery, there were favorable stories in print and on radio and TV throughout the state. And a press conference held at the World Trade Center a couple of weeks later was even more successful.

If the nature of the source—John D. Quinn—had been different, then a different plan would have been needed.

A fourth determinant of the public relations plan is the subject— the information that is to be communicated. Is it simple or complicated, concrete or abstract? How inherently interesting is it? It's much easier to communicate interesting, concrete information—for example, the delights of a new toy—than to explain that profits were lower because the Federal Reserve raised interest rates by tightening the money supply. The degree of difficulty and interest may affect the choice of the communication's form. Complicated, abstract information cannot, for example, be adequately communicated by telephone.

Recognizing subject interest is what counts most in getting

publicity. An immense amount of information is often available to an executive concerned with public relations within a company. Of critical importance is that person's ability to select the particular activities and accomplishments that will interest reporters, editors, and other audiences. What is more, the executive must match up the audiences with the items. Trade papers, for example, will become excited over a development that would be a waste of time to send to a general newspaper.

Sometimes there is nothing newsworthy to communicate about a subject. When this is true, news can sometimes be manufactured. For example, John D. Rockefeller, Sr., founder of the Rockefeller fortune, was considered one of the outstanding scoundrels of his time. But his image was changed to that of a kindly old gentleman through a dramatic device—by making the philanthropy newsworthy. Rockefeller's public relations people suggested that he personally give dimes to strangers he met. He did so—to every Tom, Dick, and Harry—and was seen doing so in newsreels. A dime was made of silver then and might be worth a dollar today, but the total amount he handed out was small potatoes compared with the millions he gave to organized charities and foundations. Yet his dime-giving—the dramatization of the giving—got the big publicity.

This technique of countering bad publicity is similar to the ploy of the magician who concentrates the audience's attention on something startling, such as the release of a pigeon, while he slips a coin into his pocket. The attention of the audience is diverted away from what the manipulator would like to be ignored. In the case of a news event or series of events that creates a bad public image, a new image is simply established in a dramatic, memorable way. If the new image is strong enough, the audience will concentrate on it. The new image will be associated with the corporation, person, product, or service, and the bad image forgotten.

There are other techniques for remedying a bad image. Which to use depends on the conditions we are considering here. So far we have examined four: purpose, forms, source, and subject.

A fifth determinant of the public relations plan is the audience or audiences. Who is to be influenced directly? Reporters? Security analysts? Employees? Who indirectly? Possible customers? Investors? Members of Congress?

Of utmost importance is the attitude of the audience toward the source. Rightly or wrongly, reporters, editors, and members of regulatory bodies tend to classify a corporation, other organization, or person as either a good guy or a bad guy. Once a bad-guy reputation is established, reversing it is difficult and costly, and may take years. Statements by a good-guy corporation tend to be believed; those of a bad-guy corporation tend to be scoffed at.

Here's a public relations effort that illustrates the importance of, and the interrelationship between, the source, the subject, and the audience as well as some of the other determinants. The corporation was caught in a situation similar to Henry Ford's. The name of the company is fictitious, but otherwise the facts were as stated.

HOW PUBLICITY ABOUT AN ALLEGED VIOLATION OF IMPORT REGULATIONS WAS MINIMIZED

A federal agency considered XYZ Corporation's violation of import regulations as one more example of big business flouting the nation's laws. The company considered it a mere technicality. There was substance to the arguments on both sides.

The initial reaction of the corporation's top executives and their lawyers to the impending announcement of the corporation's guilt was to issue a press release telling their side of the story. If this had been done, the result would have been similar to that in the Henry Ford situation. More people would have known about the violation than if only the original story had appeared and those who had read the first story would have had the memory reenforced.

The company executives and lawyers were concentrating on influencing the general public and ignoring the reporters. XYZ's public relations agency recommended that the reporters be made the primary audience—not all reporters, however, only those who were likely to have covered or received a release from the federal agency—and that the method of influencing the reporters be telephone calls made immediately. This was done. The reporters were told the corporation's side of the story. Some decided not to use the story at all when they realized it was not as significant as the federal agency tried to make it out to be. And those who used the story also included the company's side. Hence, the accusation received no more publicity than if the company had done nothing—in fact, it received less. And the effect on those members of the public who read the story was minimized by their getting both sides of the story at the same time. There was no possibility of hardening an anticompany attitude.

Intrinsic to the success of this effort was the subject of the communication. The company had an argument in its favor that sounded objectively valid. If what was said on the telephone to the reporters had not sounded sensible, but just a lot of hot air, the plan would not have worked. The reporters would have resented the insult to their intelligence, and the story would have reflected their resentment, perhaps subtly, perhaps blatantly. Without a valid-sounding argument,the company would have been better off doing nothing.

Also fundamental to the success of the XYZ plan was the relationship of the audience to the source—that is, the attitude of the reporters toward the corporation. The company did not have a bad reputation. If the company had committed a number of other similar offenses, the press would have disregarded the technical aspects of the violation. The telephone calls would have been a waste of time and would have further damaged the credibility of the corporation and the person making the calls.

Even more important to the success of this plan than the source and the relationship of the source to the audience was a sixth determinant—the public relations professional involved. In this instance the professional was someone from a public relations agency, but the professional may also be anyone within the corporation who acts in this capacity.

The professional in the XYZ case did not just do as he was told—he spoke up. This was to the credit of both the professional and the executives of the corporation. All too often in the past public relations professionals have been treated like stenographers. Today public relations is too vital to a corporation's profits for such a relationship. Professionals who fail to speak up when they know of a better way are not worthy of being called professional public relations people.

In the XYZ instance, the relationship needed to be close enough for rapid action. Deciding what to do and then doing it had to be accomplished in a matter of hours.

The capacity and ability of the public relations professional necessarily may limit the choice of how the purpose is to be carried out. It's foolish and unfair to expect a professional with little knowledge of economics to successfully talk to security analysts, for example.

The credibility of the professional with the audience can make a big difference in what can be accomplished. Some professionals have built up a reputation for reliability, accuracy, and not wasting reporters' time. In difficult and marginal situations, this reputation can make the difference between success and failure.

The seventh determinant of the public relations plan is the authorities—that is, anyone who can arbitrarily negate the plan or require that it be modified. It is seldom today that some authority need not be considered.

Government regulatory bodies are one kind of authority; sometimes they are very important, sometimes not at all. The source— that is, the executive from whom the communication will come—is usually also an authority because of his or her position. And on many occasions the chief executive, and consequently the public relations officer, must consider the views and attitudes of certain members of the board of directors, regardless of how reasonable or unreasonable, helpful or obstructive, the directors may be. In fact, one experienced corporate public relations man who revolutionized a leading bank's previously stodgy public relations says, "Getting the board of directors on your side is half the battle."

Let's summarize the determinants we've covered so far:

Form	Audience
Purpose	Professional
Source	Authorities
Subject	

These seven factors affect not only every part of the public relations plan but all the tools created to carry out the plan, right down to the choice of words.

Two more determinants usually affect only the planning itself. One is the budget. Spending a hundred thousand dollars on an industrial motion picture may be desirable, but only a few thousand dollars may be available. Not everyone has Rockefeller's millions. The other is the time allowed. In the XYZ import violation case, the need to respond immediately made telephone calls the only possible form to use.

In sum, a public relations plan describes what is to be communicated for what corporate *purpose* on what *subject* in what *form* to what *audiences* from what *source*, usually with the aid of a public relations *professional*, and within the mandates of *authorities*, a certain *budget*, and a certain period of *time*. These nine determinants are all an executive need consider when faced with a public relations problem or when public relations is to be used to achieve or help achieve any corporate purpose. How well they are implemented depends on the ingenuity, experience, and other capabilities of the executives or professionals concerned. Every public relations problem is different. The purpose of this book is to provide readers with methods and knowledge that will enable them to use public relations effectively to achieve corporate goals and to solve any solvable public relations problem.

Analysis of the situation in terms of the nine determinants usually reveals that one or two determinants are key. Most often it is the relationship of the audience, either the media or the ultimate audience, to one of the other conditions. Here is a case history where all that mattered was changing the media's attitude toward the subject.

HOW CREDIBILITY WAS OBTAINED FOR A FOOD PRODUCT CRITICIZED BY THE PRESS

Key food critics and editors had publicly stated that table or vintage wines were preferable to cooking wines for use in food preparation. One critic had gone so far as to say that cooking wines ruined food! At Holland House, the nation's leading producer of cooking wines for the consumer market, members of top management were clearly upset. Having conducted their own taste preference tests hundreds of times using various recipes, they knew that these claims were totally false. Objective testing had repeatedly confirmed that cooking wines test out very favorably in comparison with table wines and are often preferred in blind taste tests. Cooking wines have two other advantages for the consumer—a longer shelf life and a lower price than comparable table wines.

The problem still existed. Kanan, Corbin, Schupak & Aronow, Inc., was retained by Holland House to contend with this public relations problem. The agency immediately pointed out to Holland House officials that the best way to sway public opinion would be to convince leading cooking experts and tastemakers that cooking wines are as good or better than vintage varieties. Although taste preference tests had previously been conducted, it was suggested that major studies be conducted again—this time at major universities with hotel administration or home economics programs, including Cornell University, Florida State University, Purdue University, and the City University of New York. In addition to the credibility of the institution, the geographic distribution of the universities was of prime importance, since a local publicity campaign would be launched along with a national publicity effort.

Most important, each university was to submit a written report outlining exactly its testing procedures, the recipes and wines used in testing, and the results.

As Holland House had predicted, the results were very favorable. They were announced at a special press conference for food editors held at New York's famous Laurent Restaurant. While the

19

editors dined on a gourmet meal, in which every course was prepared with cooking wines, the university coordinators announced
and explained the results at their schools.

Of the 977 participants asked for preferences between a recipe
prepared with a Holland House Cooking Wine and the same recipe
prepared with an expensive imported vintage wine, 440 (45 percent)
favored the cooking wine, whereas only 418 (42.8 percent) favored
the table wine. The remaining 119 (12.2 percent) had no preference
between the less expensive cooking wines and the higher priced
table wines. These national findings were summarized in a press kit,
which also included a reproduction of each university's report along
with a comprehensive press release.

As a direct result of the press conference, an enormous amount
of favorable publicity appeared. *Good Housekeeping* magazine du-
plicated the tests with favorable results in the institute's kitchens
and began using the generic term *"cooking wine"* in dozens of its
recipes. *Signature* magazine, which is distributed to Diner's Club
members, did a positive feature story on the taste results. *Harper's
Bazaar* assigned a free-lancer to do her own testing and write an
article on cooking with wine that would include a section on cooking
wines. The Sunday New York *Daily News* began using *cooking
wine* as a generic term in recipes.

The effort didn't stop there. A mailing consisting of the basic
press release, several recipes, and photos of dishes used in the
testing was sent to 1,000 newspaper food editors across the country.
The mailing resulted in several desirable placements.

In addition, local publicity was obtained market by market by
arranging interviews for each professor to talk about the results of
his school's studies. Two of these interviews resulted in syndicated
stories that appeared in major newspapers across the country.

Stories with such headlines as "Cooking Wine Is Best," "Tasters
Prefer Dishes Made with Cooking Wine," and "Professors Prove
Cooking Wine Is Fine" appeared all over the country—in the Mid-
west in Indianapolis, Chicago, Detroit, Toledo; in the South in Jack-
sonville, Tallahassee, Atlanta, Fort Lauderdale; in the Northeast in
New York City, Ithaca, Albany, Boston, Philadelphia.

The attitude of the press had been turned around 180 degrees.

2
WHAT REPORTERS
WANT MOST

The chief executive officer of a corporation, more than any other person, determines the degree of success or failure of a corporation's public relations. Fundamental is the CEO's recognition that in today's society a corporation must continually justify its actions, even its existence, to several publics: consumers, voters, government officials, employees, investors, and those who influence these publics, particularly the media. A corporation failing to do so may have lower sales than it otherwise would, be more restricted by regulations, have less productive employees, pay more for borrowed and equity capital, and perhaps be taken over by another company.

But a chief executive officer's recognition of the importance of public relations in today's world is only the beginning. The next step—actually devoting more time to public relations—may be the toughest.

A chief executive officer has multiple demands on every minute of his or her day. For CEOs immersed in operating their companies, already working as long and as hard as they can, setting aside up to a third of their time for what appears to be unproductive communication may seem impossible.

Often the chief executive officer is the only executive with the knowledge and authority to speak. Sometimes audiences won't be

21

satisfied unless they hear the company's views stated by the CEO. Such audiences include reporters when there is a serious charge against the company, legislators when they are holding a hearing regarding a new law, and security analysts at least once a year. Speeches are much more effective when made by the CEO. Usually only CEOs can get on the most influential television programs. The CEOs must spend more time discussing public relations problems with those who carry on regular communications with their corporations' several publics. They need to reorganize their priorities and attitudes.

Further, except in a very small company, the chief executive cannot carry the public relations ball alone. Other executives also need to devote more time to public relations. And their attitudes, too, need to change.

It's amazing how many businesspeople who know the importance of doing favors for each other don't appreciate the value of cooperating with the media. Sure, reporters often ask when-did-you-stop-beating-your-wife questions. But when they do it, they know they're doing it. They sometimes must, to get executives to respond. The intelligent response to an awkward question is not an indignant angry retort, but a statement that gives the reporter some information and the corporation's viewpoint on the subject at hand. This leads us to **Common Mistake #3: Treating reporters as adversaries, not as people with a job to do.** Just because a reporter adopts an adversary attitude is no reason for an executive to adopt the same attitude. Turning the other cheek is not only virtuous but good public relations.

What a reporter wants above all is a story. Some reporters may have the feeling that what they do will influence the course of history or correct an injustice or otherwise benefit the general public, but even this idealism in a good reporter is usually second to the story itself. So, if an executive doesn't like the angle a reporter is working on, an effective response is not to be silent but to give the reporter a story or concept more suited to the needs and wants of the corporation.

Even worse than saying "No comment" is **Common Mistake #4:**

Not getting back to a reporter promptly. All too often when a corporation is in a ticklish position and top management doesn't want to say anything, secretaries are told to say the executives are not in or not available. At the minimum, an intermediary, such as someone at the corporation's public relations agency, should call the reporter back, get the question, promptly discuss it with the appropriate officers, and get back to the reporter within an hour or so. It is nearly always possible to frame a response that is superior to not calling back at all or saying "No comment."

Perhaps the most important principle in gaining the trust of reporters is this: Never mislead them. All too often a company will put out a news release or make a statement that is factually correct but actually misleads reporters, especially reporters with little knowledge of the subject. If the trust of reporters is to be gained, the public relations person or other executive needs to make sure that reporters correctly understand what is being communicated to them. All too often executives who never lie to reporters but who mislead them with partial truths wonder why reporters are so vindictive.

Sometimes when the situation is ticklish, the principles of not misleading and not saying "no comment" can be sustained by talking off the record to a reporter. Most reporters understand the necessity for this and can be trusted not to break a confidence.

Sometimes poor public relations results not from executives not knowing better, but from the way the communications function of the corporation is organized. Here are some examples:

• Calling back is delayed for hours, overnight, or even days simply because the public relations person is required or feels obligated to check with so many executives.

• An officer of the company makes a statement. Later another executive makes an apparently contradictory statement. As a result, future statements of the company are received skeptically. The fault may not lie with the executives individually—each statement might have stood by itself.

• Advertising to investors and the financial community is deemed necessary by the financial vice president, but because all

23

advertising is controlled by the marketing department, the vice president cannot get any money, and even if he or she could, the company would not get the kind of advertising it needs.

Organizing the communications function is a difficult problem. Usually one executive is in charge of advertising, reporting perhaps to the marketing director, and another is in charge of public relations, reporting to the chief executive. Graphic design people may report to either. Responsibility for in-house publications and the annual report may lie completely outside the public relations domain, or it may be under the public relations director. Sometimes there is one overall communications department, but the functions are still subdivided under advertising and public relations.

The chief problems when the communications function is organized by techniques and forms often are:

Who is responsible for product publicity? (It's obviously public relations but performs a marketing function.)

Who is responsible for corporate advertising? (It's clearly advertising, yet its principal purpose may be to influence investors or voters and regulatory officials or prospective employees.)

Who should be responsible for writing the annual report?

Who handles trade shows?

To whom should sales promotion people report?

Compromises and irrational combinations of authority are often the result. **Common Mistake #5: Organizing a corporation's communications function by techniques instead of by purposes and audiences.** The first step in organizing the communications function so as to avoid confusion and delay is deciding who is responsible for influencing which audiences to do what. There are four easily identifiable categories:

Marketing communications. The audiences are customers, prospective customers, and sometimes dealers. The primary purpose is to increase demand for the company's products and/or services. The forms used include those normally associated with product advertising, product publicity, sales promotion, and graphic design.

How is Assurant divided?

Employee communications. The primary purpose is to maintain and improve productivity. The forms are the company magazine or newspaper, bulletins, and any other communications to employees.

Legislative communications. The audiences are legislators, regulators, and the general public. The primary purpose is to reduce unjustified interference by such groups as governments, activist organizations, and plant communities—and sometimes to obtain the cooperation of one or more of these groups. The most common communication forms are meetings, telephone calls, letters, publicity, and sometimes advertising.

Financial communications. The audiences are investors, lenders, and other members of the financial community. The primary purpose, often indirect, is usually to maintain or improve the relationship between the stock's price and its earnings, that is, its price–earnings ratio. The forms of communication are primarily meetings, telephone calls, publicity, letters, annual reports, and other specialized forms.

If the chief executive clearly assigns the responsibility for each of these categories—and gives each its own communications budget—the chief executive has considerable flexibility in organizing the rest of the communications function.

In some companies, it may be preferable to funnel all communications to the media through a single executive. This person may be the head of a combined communications department with authority over all four communications categories. Or there may be four separate departments, and the person may be of equal or lower rank than the heads of these departments. In other companies, it may be necessary to authorize dozens, even hundreds, of executives to communicate to the media, as in the case history at the end of this chapter.

In any case, any executive communicating to the media will know what people to check with. To get the answer to an awkward question, the executive will usually need to make only one phone call and can get back to the reporter fast with information that will be consistent with other statements by the corporation. The executive won't inadvertently mislead the reporter.

As with other functions of a corporation, the more clearly the responsibilities for communications are assigned and the more the official description coincides with what really goes on in the company, the more efficiently the function will be implemented.

Getting fair treatment in today's media is not difficult if the correct policies and procedures are followed with great care. One misstep, however—misleading a reporter once or not getting back to him or her promptly—will sour the relationship for a long, long time.

In this chapter we have discussed how media relations can be damaged by:

1. Executives not setting aside sufficient time to deal with public relations.
2. Executives having the wrong attitude toward the media.
3. The communications function being poorly organized.

Media relations also suffer if communications to the media do not meet certain specific standards. These are discussed in the next two chapters. Meanwhile, to illustrate the points in this chapter, here are two case histories. One shows what happened to a long-established, highly ethical firm with old-fashioned public relations attitudes and practices; the other shows how a corporation adapted its public relations to the times.

HOW A LEADING INVESTMENT BANKING FIRM DAMAGED ITS REPUTATION BY COMMITTING MISTAKES #1, #2, and #3

(All names in this case history are fictitious; otherwise it is completely accurate.)

Conglomerate, Inc., retained Proud Partnership, an investment banking firm, to help it acquire Target Products Corporation. Proud Partnership knew a lot about Target Products. In fact, too much. Nine months previously, Proud had obtained confidential information from Target Products. Now Proud faced this dilemma: If it communicated the information to Conglomerate, Inc., it would be violating its implicit promise to Target to keep the information confidential. On the other hand, if Proud did not tell Conglomerate, it would be guilty of withholding pertinent information from its client.

Proud couldn't ask Target to be released from its promise of confidentiality for a number of reasons. One was that Target would probably say, "No, we want the information kept confidential," thus intensifying the dilemma.

Two law firms advised Proud to give the confidential information to Conglomerate, Inc., and Proud did so. Conglomerate, Inc., included the confidential information in a filing it was required to make to the Securities and Exchange Commission. The filing was routinely made public. An alert *Wall Street Journal* reporter spotted the confidential information and decided to investigate. He called Proud and asked a number of questions.

Proud had committed Common Mistake #3 even before this incident began. Proud had consistently had a haughty attitude toward the press. Other investment firms gain favor with the press by continually helping reporters with information and comments; Proud did not. So Proud, while highly regarded for its integrity and competence, was not well liked by reporters.

Proud's response to *The Wall Street Journal*'s questions regarding the confidentiality of the information obtained from Target Products Corporation was consistent with Proud's previous policies: "No comment." The reporter, therefore, acting on the only information he had, wrote a story stating that Proud may have compromised its integrity.

The reaction from Proud was explosive. A long letter stating Proud's position was sent to *The Wall Street Journal* with the request that the paper print all of the letter or none of it.

In sending the letter, Proud was committing Common Mistake #2—establishing an unrealistic public relations objective. *The Wall Street Journal* naturally refused the conditions. Proud was also about to make Common Mistake #1—giving additional publicity to damaging information in an effort to rebut it. The *Journal*'s refusal almost saved Proud from this mistake, but the partners were so incensed that they paid for a full-page advertisement in the *Journal* featuring the letter.

Not only did the advertisement inform the people who hadn't known about the possible breach of confidentiality and remind those who did, it raised the matter to a higher level. *Institutional Investor*, a highly regarded magazine for professional investors, decided to publish an article on the matter. This time Proud did the right thing but in the wrong way. Proud decided to cooperate with *Institutional Investor*, but the managing partner who was interviewed was accompanied—and apparently prepared—by a lawyer. In justification of Proud's action, a legal response was given—that there was no written confidential agreement with Target. Obviously, Proud did not mean to convey the implication of that remark—that Proud could only be depended on to keep information confidential when there was an agreement in writing. It was a legal defense, acceptable in the courtroom, unacceptable outside. An investment banker who cannot be relied on to keep information confidential won't stay in business very long. What is more, in the investment world, oral agreements are considered as binding as written ones. Otherwise the financial community could not function with the necessary speed.

Note that no firm suffered in this whole incident except Proud Partnership. Target Products Corporation was acquired at a price that pleased the management, the board of directors, and most stockholders. Conglomerate, Inc., made a desirable acquisition. The SEC had no quarrel with anyone's activities. *The Wall Street Journal* and the *Institutional Investor* benefited from the articles they published. Only Proud suffered by having its alleged breach of confidentiality widely known—and it suffered, not because it had done anything ethically or legally wrong, but only because its management had no public relations sense.

While Proud made a number of mistakes, the entire incident could have been minimized if Proud had simply responded to *The Wall Street Journal*'s first query with a simple statement, "Yes, we supplied the information about Target to Conglomerate, Inc., on the advice of counsel. Two law firms advised us that we had no choice in the matter." The *Journal's* story might never have appeared. If it had, not only would it have contained Proud's justification, but even better, it would have been deflated and boring. And there would have been no subsequent publicity in *Institutional Investor*.

HOW A GIANT OIL COMPANY IMPROVED THE WAY THE PRESS REPORTED ITS ACTIVITIES

Traditionally, all public relations at Gulf Oil had been handled by executives in Gulf's headquarters office in Pittsburgh, even problems that arose in Europe and South America. Only headquarters personnel were involved in handling problems with the media and local pressure groups.

In the early 1970s, the chairman decided that Gulf's over 200 middle- and upper-level managers, located all over the world, should be responsible for the communications function. Few if any had had any public relations experience or training. The public relations agency of Burson-Marsteller was retained to supply that lack.

Burson-Marsteller began with a six-week, nationwide research effort to determine the kinds of problems faced by Gulf managers and to gauge the managers' abilities to perform the communications function. The result of the research tour was a recommendation for a day-long management training seminar that would travel around the country and reach all targeted managers within the Gulf organization. "Crisisport—the 365th Day" was the name of the seminar, which was eventually attended by more than 1,300 Gulf U.S. managers.

At the same time, the Gulf situation in Europe and South America was investigated, and Crisisport (the name of a fictitious city) was adapted to fit the needs in those locations. Europa was the fictitious country in which the Europeans learned the community relations lessons; Petroport was the name of the Gulf country in South America.

Implementation was as follows:

1. *Script book development.* This included everything from the

29

moderator's remarks to descriptions of the fictitious locations, to mock television interviews, to lists of critique points for each problem covered during the day's events. The book became the bible of the seminar faculty, which was made up of agency personnel, Gulf experts in particular parts of the business, and outside experts, such as news media personnel.

2. *Invitation.* Gulf managers were invited to attend the seminar with a letter from the chairman indicating that they were being transferred for a day to the fictitious city. Along with the invitation, they received a detailed dossier on the city and the Gulf facilities there.

3. *Cocktail party.* The night before the seminar, attendees from the given region met each other over cocktails and began initial discussions about the city of Crisisport.

4. *Introduction.* A multimedia presentation set the stage for the day's events, showing all the kinds of problems Gulf might face in the future at the community level. The city of Crisisport was also introduced visually.

5. *Team sessions.* Newspaper girls rushed into the meeting room, delivering the *Crisisport Post.* Each of the five editions of the paper contained a different anti-Gulf article as the lead story on the front page. Topics included a reported layoff at the plant, a unionization threat, a negative story on offshore drilling, a negative story quoting a fired employee, and a negative story charging that the company tried to block a new bus route proposal. The audience was divided into five teams, and each team had to deal with a different edition of the paper. The teams had 45 minutes to agree on two things: What they, as senior Gulf representatives in the community, should do right now about the negative story, and what they should have been doing for the past year to keep the story from ever appearing in print. After the 45-minute work session, a captain from each team presented the team's recommendations. Each presentation was followed by a detailed discussion and critique by a panel of experts. The critique included Gulf's policy on the issue, public relations guidelines, and examples of how similar problems had been handled by the corporation in the past.

6. *Lunch*. Outside speakers addressed the audience at lunch and told the Gulf executives what they liked least about dealing with business in general and Gulf in particular. The segment was designed to give managers the chance to hear firsthand what some of their opponents had to say about them. Included among the speakers were members of the press, environmentalists, politicians, and minorities.

7. *Consumerism*. An audiovisual presentation launched the afternoon portion of the program and showed the audience the kinds of poor treatment a Gulf customer could get from Gulf service station or corporate personnel. A discussion of how to handle complaints followed.

8. *Civil rights*. Two black actors traveled with the seminar and played the roles of militants who wanted to meet with Gulf Crisisport officials. The audience had to decide if, when, and where to meet with these militants, then actually acted out the confrontation. The actors were well versed in the facts and figures of Gulf's minority hiring and advancement record. Following the role-playing exercise, the panel critiqued the performance of the Gulf personnel and discussed Gulf's overall record and policy.

9. *Pollution*. A radio announcement told the group that the city of Crisisport was considering an antipollution referendum that would be damaging to the company and announced a public hearing on the subject. The participants had to decide if they should attend the hearing and, if so, who should attend. Then they acted out the hearing, with agency and staff personnel playing the hostile town councilmen. Following the role-playing exercise, Gulf and agency personnel critiqued the performance and reviewed Gulf's overall position on pollution.

10. *Handling an emergency*. In the final segment of the day, an explosion was simulated at a Gulf refinery. Managers had to respond to the disaster as it unfolded. People were killed in the blast; the city was threatened. The managers had to take the information on the explosion as it was presented to them and deal with employees' families, the press, and city officials. The exercise concluded with a press conference in which real members of the local

press questioned Gulf managers on the disaster. Agency and staff experts critiqued the press conference and gave overall emergency guidelines to the audience.

The most tangible results came in subsequent tough situations faced by Gulf managers in their communities. A mining death was handled extremely well, the manager saving the company hundreds of thousands of dollars by communicating promptly and accurately with the media and avoiding a mine shutdown for an official investigation. A number of minor oil spills were handled "better than ever in the past," according to Gulf management. Media treatment improved at a dramatic rate in Gulf cities across the United States.

3

NEWS RELEASES
REPORTERS APPRECIATE

The printed news release continues to be the most common form for communicating news about a company to the media. The form has changed little over the years, partly because of its familiarity. Even radio and television reporters are used to the form. They are comfortable with it. It's easy for them to rewrite a release according to their own styles and the requirements of their medium.

Another, more important reason for the news release's durability is this: The old-style press release is organized according to fundamental principles for communicating news in any medium. The style for other than print media is different. Long sentences need to be broken up. The sounds of words need to be considered. Repetition may be necessary when the words are spoken so relationships between ideas are not lost. (Readers can always go back if they don't understand; listeners can't.) And on TV the words may need to be coordinated with pictures. But the order of ideas is the same regardless of the medium.

The news outline is one of the three or four key outlines every public relations person needs to know thoroughly. Knowledge of these key outlines will enable (a) a public relations professional to quickly and competently write any kind of communication and (b) any executive to judge and improve by editing any kind of public relations communication. This chapter will discuss the news story outline; the other outlines will be covered in Section Two.

Legend has it that the way news stories are written today originated in the Civil War, when war correspondents for the first time in world history transmitted their stories by telegraph. Because the telegraph was new—and perhaps because of enemy action as well—the telegraph lines would often go dead, and stay dead for hours.

Consequently, so the legend goes, newspapermen developed the habit of putting the most important part of their news first. They then added details in descending order of importance. Suppose, for example, that the editor of a northern newspaper received the following telegram:

ON JULY ONE SEVERE FIGHTING BEGAN BETWEEN TROOPS LED
BY GENERAL ROBERT E. LEE OF THE CONFEDERATE ARMY
AND GENERAL GEORGE C. MEADE . . .

The suspense would be great, but neither the editor nor the readers of his newspaper would know the most important facts. In the same number of words, the war correspondent could have sent the following message:

LEE DEFEATED AT GETTYSBURG X RETREATS BEHIND
POTOMAC X TWENTY THOUSAND CONFEDERATE DEAD X IN A
THREE DAY BATTLE COMMENCING JULY ONE GENERAL
GEORGE C MEADE . . .

The legend concludes that newspaper reporters have never been able to shake the habit of writing this way.

There's another popular explanation for the order in which ideas are presented in a newspaper story. This one is based on the mechanics of publishing a newspaper.

At the time a reporter sits down to write, there is no way to tell how much space there will be in the newspaper for the story. The final length is decided by the makeup editor after all the stories have been printed on preliminary galleys. The makeup editor cuts each story in accordance with its relative importance. If there is considerable important news competing for space, a reporter's story will be cut short. If there is little competing news, the story may run for several columns.

So any professional newspaper reporter writes so that the story can be cut just about anywhere after the first paragraph without confusing the reader.

This may be factually true—and the Civil War legend may also be true—but both would have long been forgotten if they didn't serve as dramatic, memorable guidelines for neophyte reporters. Newspaper stories are written the way they are because the order of ideas most precisely suits the newspaper audience and the purpose of a news story.

In scanning a newspaper page, readers first want to know whether any event of overwhelming significance has occurred since they last saw a newspaper. Next they want to know whether any event of significance has occurred in fields that interest them specifically. Therefore, each page is crowded with headlines, giving the significance of individual events.

When a headline, such as "37 percent of paved roads in state are 'deficient,'" catches their interest, readers want to know more. They want the headline clarified. In this specific instance, they're particularly interested in the basis for the statement. They want to know *who* said so, *when*, *where* the roads are deficient, *why* they are considered deficient, and *how* they are so judged. The first paragraphs therefore state the essence:

OLYMPIA (AP)—Of Washington State's 23,000 miles of paved main roads, 37 percent are deficient and cost an average of $129 per driver, claims a study done for road builders and highway construction interests.

The study, released today, says the deficient roads include 5,226 miles rated "fair" and 3,317 miles considered "poor" by inspection standards adhered to in all states.

This may be all some readers want to know. Others will want to know more with varying degrees of interest. Thus, the story is not

35

written so as to heighten suspense by building to a climax. Instead, additional facts are presented in more or less descending order of importance, with the intention of pleasing the maximum number of readers without making them conscious of the way the story is written.

The broad outline of a news story is therefore as follows:

1. The significance (headline)—Why the event is important.
2. The essence (lead)—Who? What? When? Where? And sometimes why and how?
3. The details (tail).

Note: A news story always describes an event—in this case, the publication of the findings of the study. A news story has no definite end. The third part is usually the longest by far. And a news story should be perceived by a majority of the audience as objective—not slanted in any way.

From time to time, different forms of communicating news have been experimented with. Marshall Field, Jr., for example, spent millions of dollars and collected some of the best brains in journalism to develop a different kind of newswriting. The name of the newspaper founded on his theory—*P.M.*—is now only dimly remembered by aged journalists and has left no impression on the form of the news story.

The civil legend and logic of how news stories came to be written the way they are and the undue emphasis on makeup editors' requirements were unwittingly based on the concept that the form is the principal determinant. In actual fact, the form is comparatively unimportant in determining how news is best communicated. Newspaper stories are organized just about the way news is best communicated in any form. On radio and television, for example, the announcer gives the bare facts, which indicate the significance of the story, then fills out with the essence—that is, who, what, where, why, when, and how—and then enlarges upon the essence with details.

A media release is little more than a news story with some

additional obvious information added: who is sending the release and when the information can be published. Yet three mistakes are continually made by intelligent, knowledgeable people.

People with a little, dangerous knowledge about newspapers know that reporters don't write the headlines, so they make **Common Mistake # 6: Not putting a headline on a news release.** They feel it is redundant. Not so. Most reporters receive an enormous number of press releases each day. To get a day's work done, they must swiftly assess each release to see if it's worth paying attention to. The headline on the release gives them the indication they need. In those rare instances when a headline is not suitable, as may be the case with a feature of some kind, public relations professionals put a quick summary at the top. A release without a headline not only irritates but is more likely to be ignored.

Even worse is **Common Mistake #7: Failing to put the news in the headline and lead.**

It's difficult to understand why this mistake is made so often, but here are some thoughts: The executive doesn't really want to communicate the news. Or the executive, accustomed to being polite, shrinks from the abruptness that is appropriate for a news story. Or the executive doesn't really understand what is news and what is not. Or the executive, concerned about some people's reaction to the news, is confused about whether he or she wants publicity or not.

Common Mistake #8: Not tailoring a communication to the specific interests of its audience. Editors of local newspapers are most interested in news that relates to their cities, counties, or other areas they serve. Most get huge quantities of national releases that they ignore. Consequently, the more a release is made pertinent to the local audience, the more likely it is to be used. If a company has a plant or a sales office in the area or if an officer who resided there at one time is being promoted, that fact belongs in the news release headline.

Similarly, editors of trade papers are more likely to use a release that is tailored to their interests. The Globe-Amerada Glass Co. case history, which appears in Chapter 5, includes a general release and one on the same subject aimed at architectural magazines.

When time permits, studying the kind of stories a columnist or a magazine uses and slanting the release accordingly may make the difference between the story being used or discarded.

As the number of specialized media increases, it will become more and more difficult to avoid this mistake, especially when the budget is too small or the time is too short to allow for extensive rewriting. Usually, however, something can be done. One solution is to attach a note to a local editor that simply states, for example, "ABC company has a plant in your area."

In the "Stop 348" case history in Chapter 12, it would have been desirable to write a press release for each city and town in Washington. This was not feasible, but a sheet was attached to the release that listed *by locality* the road work that would not be done if the initiative were passed.

Rewriting press releases to suit radio or TV is seldom necessary except when the information, as in the case of a public service announcement, is to be broadcast precisely as is. The key difference in writing for radio is that the news cannot be reread as it can when it is printed. The information must be clearly and easily understood the first time. The essence cannot be packed into one long sentence; it must be broken up. While repetition may appear clumsy in print, it can be helpful in radio. In both print and oral news, short, concrete, familiar words of Anglo-Saxon origin are generally preferable to long, abstract, unfamiliar words with Latin roots, and on radio the former style is virtually mandatory. (A sample public service announcement is included in the Harbor Point case in the next chapter.)

The art of writing a press release consists of primarily reconciling its ostensible purpose—to help reporters and editors—with its real purpose—usually to gain favorable publicity for the employer. To a degree, the release can be slanted toward the employer, but if done in an obvious way, this may backfire. An attempt to bury the bad news down in the fourth or fifth paragraph may cause a reporter to retaliate by rewriting the press release in as damaging a way as possible. On the other hand, a release that puts the appropriate emphasis on the bad news and attaches ameliorating circumstances to it may appeal to the fair-mindedness of the reporter and be published with the same emphasis.

Much can be accomplished if the rules for objective writing are followed: use very few adjectives and no loaded ones, put all opinions in quotes, and substantiate them with facts.

Some examples of successful press releases are included in Chapters 4, 5, and 12.

4

OTHER WAYS
OF COMMUNICATING
WITH THE MEDIA

To meet the need for better public relations, corporations have expanded their public relations staffs. Consequently, reporters are getting more releases than ever before—and they were getting plenty before the public relations revolution.

Most reporters still like to get releases, but some prefer phone calls, some letters, and some a combination of two or three forms. Sometimes, however, it is not possible or worthwhile to find out in advance what forms or combination of forms a reporter prefers. Then the best procedure is to send the release and follow it up with a telephone call.

Common Mistake #9: Failing to follow up a news release with a telephone call. Reporters don't want to be bothered with unnecessary phone calls, but they know they have difficulty weeding out the important releases from those that are unimportant. They welcome the chance to talk to a public relations person who calls to make sure they got an important release. If they already received it, they may have some questions. If a release is important and may be received close to a reporter's deadline, it is not amiss to call ahead to tell the reporter that it is coming and then call later to make sure it arrived.

Half the battle with a press release is making sure that the right person at a publication receives it. It is doubtful that the release will be forwarded to an interested reporter. Why should the reporter who gets an inappropriate release do the work of the public relations professional?

Sometimes, of course, assignments are shifted, causing the wrong reporter to get the release. This is an additional reason for following up with a phone call. The mistake can be promptly corrected.

A telephone call also enables the public relations person to sell the release. If an inexperienced reporter fails to see right away why a certain release should be used, an experienced public relations person may be able to convince the reporter.

The two-way nature of the telephone call makes this form uniquely suited to dealing with reporters' antipathies and objections. What's bothering an individual reporter can be unearthed and dealt with. Putting out a release that tries to answer negative attitudes only gives broader coverage to those attitudes (Mistake #1). The disadvantage of using only a telephone call is lack of permanency, because it is oral. The telephone call therefore is usually used in conjunction with one or more other, written forms.

In getting people to act, a letter has other advantages over the telephone call in addition to permanency. More can be said. The reader is given time to consider and therefore may be less likely to give a quick refusal. Together the letter and telephone call make a powerful combination.

In getting someone on a radio or television show, a letter that opens with why the person will make an outstanding guest is usually essential, but the follow-up telephone call is even more important.

In placing a story with a magazine, it is not unusual to telephone first to see if the writer or editor is interested, then follow up with a letter that has full information, and then follow up further by phone to see if the writer or editor has any questions or would like more information.

When the corporation has news to announce that is obviously of widespread importance, the press conference becomes an excellent public relations tool. The reporters stimulate each other to ask questions, and the attendance of the reporters themselves helps to make the occasion more important and exciting.

One disadvantage of a press conference is that it takes up more of the reporters' time than the simpler forms of communication. It is therefore vital that a press conference be called only when the information that will be presented at the conference is really newsworthy.

The other disadvantage is that the principal speaker at the press conference is put in the position of answering questions. The character and abilities of this person (the source) must be carefully considered before a press conference is included in the public relations plan. Is he or she good at answering questions? Will he or she devote the time to prepare adequately for the press conference? President John F. Kennedy was so smooth at press conferences because he was very well rehearsed. His public relations people and other advisors would pepper him with questions, asking tougher questions than the reporters would. If Kennedy's answer wasn't top grade, they all went over it till it was.

Like the telephone call, the press conference is oral, and therefore printed material should also be supplied. Sometimes a release is sufficient. More often a press kit is handed out. It is designed to give reporters as much information as they want in a usable form. A press release is almost always included, but the other items may vary depending on the situation. Possible items include a biography and photograph of the principal speaker, a fact sheet on the subject (that is, a summary of the pertinent facts for easy reference), a booklet, an annual report, and a history of the new company or other organization.

Here's a case history of a successful press conference.

HOW AN EXOTIC SERVICE FOR INSTITUTIONAL INVESTORS OBTAINED PUBLICITY THAT INCREASED SALES

Only security analysts and other professional investors with similar training have any interest in the *Quality of Earnings Report*, published twice monthly. Its staff delves deeply into reports filed with the Securities and Exchange Commission, annual reports, and other public documents and arrives at some startling conclusions regarding the earnings of certain corporations. For example, the reported earnings may imply a healthy, fast-growing company, but the *Quality of Earnings Report* may show that earnings in later years were boosted by reductions in research expenditures and fortuitous gains made in foreign exchange.

The service does not make any recommendations as to which stocks to sell. Users of the report are told that other information needs to be considered before a conclusion can be confidently reached. However, it seemed to the authors of the report that stocks they criticized did go down sooner or later. They therefore commissioned an economics professor to see if this was statistically true. He made the study and determined it was.

Benn & MacDonough, the *Report*'s public relations and marketing agency, was asked how best to capitalize on the professor's findings. A press conference was recommended for the following reasons:

1. The findings (the subject) were worth this kind of attention.
2. A press conference would enable the authors of the *Report* and the professor to answer questions.
3. The physical presence of the professor would make the objectivity of the findings even more impressive.
4. Reporters who did not ask questions for fear of exposing their ignorance would benefit from the questions asked by the more knowledgeable and less self-conscious. In addition, they could be talked to informally before and after the press conference.

The press conference was held at a club in midtown New York City at noon. Cocktails were served before the conference, a buffet luncheon afterward. Members of the financial press were invited by telephone, followed up by a confirmation note, then called again the day before.

The press kit handed out at the conference included a press release (which follows), a photograph of the two principal authors of the *Quality of Earnings Report*, a single sheet with the professor's

FOR IMMEDIATE RELEASE

From: Benn & MacDonough, Inc.   Contact: Alec Benn
   111 Broadway   (212) 267-6900
   New York, NY 10006

For: Quality of Earnings Report   Robert A. Olstein
   Published by: Co-author of Quality
   Reporting Research Corporation of Earnings Report
   560 Sylvan Avenue   (201) 568-6586
   Englewood Cliffs, New Jersey 07632

69% OF STOCKS CITED BY QUALITY OF EARNINGS REPORT

UNDERPERFORM STANDARD & POOR'S INDEX

NEW YORK, June 21, 1977--The Quality of Earnings Report is not a sell recommendation service, says its co-authors Robert A. Olstein and Thornton L. O'Glove, yet the results of an analysis conducted by Dr. Frank J. Fabozzi of Hofstra University showed that 69% of the 549 stocks negatively critiqued by the Report in a six year period underperformed the Standard & Poor's Industrial Index 12 months after each critique.

When the analysis period was extended from 12 months to 24 months, Dr. Fabozzi found the percentage of stocks underperforming the market increased to 74%.

The Quality of Earnings Report is a twice monthly service for institutional investors which aims to alert subscribers to deteriorations in the quality of corporate earnings and/or disclosure practices before these deteriorations become apparent to the mass of investors.

"The significance of the results are more far reaching than just the value of the service," said Fabozzi. "This analysis contradicts the efficient market theory which has led to the increasing use of indexing as the current craze in portfolio management."

Olstein added, "The results give credence to the loser's game theory, expounded by Charles Ellis of Greenwich Research Associates, which theorizes that the way to better performance in portfolio management is to avoid the big losers."

(Subsequent pages of release not shown)

findings, two booklets (one on the *Report* in general, one on the professor's study and its implications), and an issue of the *Quality of Earnings Report.*

A story with a headline stretching halfway across the back page (see the following pages) appeared in *The Wall Street Journal*—a result that alone would have been worth the cost and time of the conference. Other newspapers and magazines also ran stories, some with the picture.

Additional subscriptions resulted, some directly traceable to the publicity and some from an enhanced direct mail program that immediately followed the press conference.

—Your Money Matters—

How Professional Nay-Sayers Attempt to Find Hidden Flaws in the Highfliers on Wall Street

By Donald Moffitt

Staff Reporter of The Wall Street Journal.

NEW YORK— Thornton O'Glove and Robert A. Olstein don't get tossed out of Wall Street's best saloons, but they don't win the neighborhood's nice-guy contests, either. They pay the rent and keep potatoes on the table by debunking corporate financial statements in a publication called the Quality of Earnings Report. For the mere price of a subscription, $12,000 a year, you get to watch them pick apart the per-share earnings of your favorite highfliers. As Levitz Furniture was taking a nosedive from $60.50 a share to $1.50 a few years back, Messrs. O'Glove and Olstein may have been the first securities analysts to spot real trouble in the company.

Mr. O'Glove, 45 years old, and Mr. Olstein, 35, disdain Wall Street's conventional wisdom, although both have worked in the past as conventional securities analysts. For one thing, most securities analysts carefully cultivate their sources in corporate management. Messrs. O'Glove and Olstein boast that they *never* talk to management. Well, hardly ever. When they do, it's usually when an enraged executive phones to complain about an O'Glove-Olstein hatchet job on his company's earnings.

Messrs. O'Glove and Olstein believe that most $300,000-a-year executives aren't paid to produce anemic-looking financial statements, that "generally accepted accounting principles" applied by management-hired auditors may shelter some very strange critters and that securities analysts are re-

luctant to write negative reports on companies whose pension funds the analysts' firms may manage or hope to manage Wall Street, they say, is always over optimistic. "We're accused of being overly negative," Mr. Olstein says. "But there's a dearth of really critical 'sell' advice on Wall Street, and we have to be overly negative to help balance things."

Where to Look

"Management has a vested interest in putting the best foot forward," Mr. Olstein adds. "And auditors aren't that independent. They hide behind generally accepted accounting principles, and an auditor's certificate doesn't deal with whether the financial statement reflects a real situation. Only when an industry gets into trouble do the accountants do what they should have done in the first place and impose realistic accounting." Real-estate investment trusts, land-development companies and franchisers, he says, have been prime examples of tardy accounting reform.

Messrs. O'Glove and Olstein try to find hidden weaknesses in corporate financial reports in order to alert their 100 clients to securities that may wind up big losers. They list the critical source documents, in order of importance, as these:

1) The Form 10-K, a yearly filing with the Securities and Exchange Commission that often provides more information on a company's business and finances than the annual report. The 10-K can be obtained from the SEC or from any of several commercial services. Many corporations will provide copies of their own 10-K at a nominal charge.

2) The annual report, which most companies will provide free, and the annual meeting proxy statement.

3) The prospectus, issued when a company sells new securities.

4) Form 10-Q, a quarterly SEC filing, ss detailed but more current than the early 10-K.

5) Quarterly shareholder reports.

6) Company press releases.

Burroughs' Decline

Some examples best show how O'Glove and Olstein glean nuggets from this forbidding mass of material. In March 1976, Burroughs Corp. shares were selling at a yearly high of $108.50. Late in the month, Messrs. O'Glove and Olstein took a close look at a preliminary prospectus Burroughs had issued in connection with the sale of $100 million in notes. The analysts also studied Burroughs' 1975 and 1974 annual reports. For the year 1975, Burroughs had reported an increase in earnings to $4.14 a share from $3.38 a share in 1974. For the fourth quarter of 1975, the company had reported an increase to $1.73 a share from $1.37 a share in the like quarter of 1974.

Messrs. O'Glove and Olstein found nine items that contributed $1.43 a share to Burroughs's 1975 full-year earnings and 54 cents a share to fourth quarter earnings—figures that exceeded the 76-cent and 36-cent increases in earnings reported for these periods. The biggest single item involved translating overseas debt from foreign currencies into dollars. Under a 1975 accounting change required by the Financial Accounting Standards Board, the company valued its debt and other foreign-currency accounts at current exchange rates rather than at the rates in effect when the obligations or assets were incurred.

This affected earnings in several ways. For one, fourth quarter 1974 earnings originally had been reported as $1.58 a share.

The change in accounting created restated earnings of only $1.37 a share, which made fourth quarter 1975 earnings look even better by comparison. For the full year 1975, gains on foreign currency because of exchange-rate changes amounted to 13 cents a share, in contrast to a 38-cent-a-share loss in 1974. The difference, or "swing," equaled 51 cents a share, or 67% of the gain in 1975 per-share earnings. The comparison with 1974 was also favorably affected by reductions in the costs of sales, rentals and service of Burroughs products and lower depreciation.

Red Flag? Or Dead Horse?

None of this means that Burroughs' accounting was misleading. But to Messrs. O'Glove and Olstein, at least, it suggested that the company might have trouble bettering its earnings in the future. Other folks apparently were thinking along the same lines. From its high of $108.50 in March, Burroughs slid steadily downward to $83 near year-end. Although Burroughs again reported increased year-to-year earnings for the fourth quarter and full year of 1976, the gains weren't as convincing as many analysts had expected them to be, and the analysts quickly began slashing their 1977 earnings estimate for Burroughs. The stock if now selling around $63 a share.

The validity of O'Glove-Olstein analysis, in the view of some financial executives, is questionable. One arguable case involves

5

GETTING
FAVORABLE PUBLICITY

Often getting a product, service, person, or corporation favorably mentioned in newspapers and magazines and on radio and television is routine and easy. A new chief executive officer is elected, for example. The public relations professional need only write a release, enclose a picture, send them to the appropriate media, and follow up with telephone calls. The principal difficulties may be internal and mostly matters of tact: how the departure of the previous chief executive officer is explained, how the career of the incoming CEO is described, and whether the shift implies different policies for the company.

Getting favorable publicity for a product can be even easier if, for example, it will make life happier for millions of housewives. Women's service magazines such as *Good Housekeeping* are eager to print this kind of information. If a company has thousands of free booklets available, the magazine will encourage its readers to send for them. And there are a number of daytime radio and television shows catering to housewives with voracious appetites for the new and useful.

In any case, competent professionals first decide what publications and shows will be interested in the product, service, person, or corporation. They avoid **Common Mistake #10: Continually sending reporters, writers, editors or producers information in which they have**

no interest. There's little excuse for the amount of mail dumped on editors', reporters', and producers' desks that just wastes their time. Because it's easy to figure out what will interest each.

Ideally, a public relations professional studies every publication and every columnist to see the kinds of stories they use and regularly tunes in to every radio and television show. This is obviously impossible, but there are publications that give this information. Bacon's *Publicity Checker* is most commonly used for newspapers and magazines, for example. In actual practice, the professional studies those media of greatest importance and depends on publicity aids, and perhaps the advice of colleagues, for those of lesser importance.

When in doubt, it is of course sensible to send a release, write a letter, or make a telephone call. But there's a difference between a story, idea, or person being close to the mark—which media people understand—and being wide of the mark. Companies and agencies that continually bother media people with items of no interest make them impatient. As a consequence, the media people may not listen long enough or otherwise pay enough attention to a marginally worthwhile story from the same source to recognize its worth.

The next step after preparing the media list is to write the letter or release or both and decide what to say in the telephone call. Which forms are best to use depends partly on the intermediary audience and partly on the time available. A release is usually right for newspaper reporters; a letter best for radio and television producers; and either or both for magazine editors. For print people, a telephone call follows when possible. For radio and television producers, a follow-up call is an absolute must. Candace Caruthers, contributing producer of "Good Morning, America!," advises stating in the letter that the writer will telephone.

"That makes me stop and think right then about whether we are interested or not," she says. When she gets the call, she is thus better prepared to say yes, no, or maybe, and to discuss the maybe.

A letter to a publication or show is designed to get action and therefore follows the principles of an action-getting letter (established in the next chapter).

To get favorable publicity, a public relations person must make

49

it easy for the reporter, writer, editor, or producer to do his or her job. This means supplying information that is accurate down to the last detail, in plenty of time for rewriting and editing. Not calling a reporter near a deadline (except in an emergency), but instead knowing the best time to call, which differs for different publications. For example, writers at *Time* are very busy Thursday afternoon and Friday morning; reporters on the *American Banker* give short shrift to public relations people who call near five o'clock.

A competent public relations person knows the subject thoroughly so that a reporter's or editor's questions can be answered quickly. In trying to sell a feature in person or by telephone, it is vital to know not only the publication's needs but also what has appeared in it recently so as to avoid suggesting something that has just been done.

The ease with which information can be used can often make the difference between success and failure. That's why setting publicity material in type can be very successful in obtaining publicity for certain products in certain kinds of publications. These clipsheets are particularly successful, especially when combined with illustrations, when sent to smaller newspapers that are understaffed and eager for material that will fill up space and also interest their readers. (An example of a clipsheet appears in this chapter.)

Even when the public relations professional does everything right and even though the event, person, or idea is worthy of publicity, failures sometimes occur. There will always be reasons impossible for a public relations professional to anticipate that will cause a specific publication not to use a story. Every experienced professional recalls with pleasure the times a marginal news story received a big play and represses the horrible memories of worthy stories that failed to appear or received little display. The reason in both instances is often the same: the amount of other news on that particular day. How this happens can be seen by comparing the front pages of a newspaper on consecutive days. Sometimes relatively insignificant stories get big headlines, and sometimes stories that would normally make the front page are pushed to the inside by a big volume of sensational stories. These stories in turn push other stories right out of the paper. This fact—that the amount of news affects the likelihood of any specific news story appearing—while obvious, is accepted with difficulty by many executives, especially when they are told that a story that did not appear will never appear because the next day it is no longer news.

Sometimes when major news shunts a worthy story aside, an ingenious public relations person can dig up some new information, rewrite the story, and release it with success. But these are necessarily exceptions, and their success may make it difficult for the public relations person to convince others that he or she can't do it every time.

Other principal reasons for a worthy story not being used are that the publication or show used a similar story or concept recently and that the policy at the publication or show has changed.

Sometimes the reasons are within the control of the public relations professional or other executives involved. One is not getting the story to the publication early enough. There are only so many hours in the day. The later a story is received, the less likely it is to be used. Often, as discussed in Chapter 3, the information is not slanted to the needs of the recipient.

Most often there is a combination of reasons: Internal problems make it difficult to write the release as well as it could be; the release reaches the reporter near the deadline; there is an abundance of news that day; and a new reporter is on the job who fails to recognize the importance of the news in the release.

Human nature being what it is, executives and professionals concerned often believe a story or idea to be more worthy of publication or broadcasting than it really is. We all live in a world that revolves around ourselves. Some corporate executives have difficulty in distinguishing what is significant for their corporations and what is significant for society. If a corporation is large enough, with millions of customers and many thousands of stockholders, news about the corporation may be significant for society, but for smaller corporations an event may need to be indicative of a broader trend. Professionals seeking publicity for a small solar heating company had little success in 1970, but a bonanza in 1980.

Most often, a publicity effort is neither an obvious big success nor an obvious failure. Then the question must be asked: Was it worth the cost?

The amount of publicity obtained can sometimes be measured. If the objective is to place a story in a few publications, it's easy to get copies of the publications and see. But if the objective is to get national publicity in a large number of newspapers, magazines, radio stations, and television stations, measuring the volume is much more difficult.

There are two services that do about as good a job as can be done economically in collecting clippings—Burrelle's Press Clipping Service and Luce Press Clippings—but neither claims to come close to finding all the times a story, a subject, or a name appears in every publication. When both are used, about a quarter of the clippings are duplications, although individual experiences vary widely. This means that one service alone finds 57 percent of the clippings that both would find (100 percent divided by 175 percent). And there's no way of knowing what percentage the total that both find is of all the clippings that resulted from a national news story. The actual number of appearances may be anywhere from two to ten times the number of clippings received. Further, there is no economical way to monitor the appearances of news items on radio and television on a broad scale. It is too costly for nearly all public relations plans. (A tape of a single important show can always be obtained.)

When the clippings are received, somebody must judge whether the stories are favorable or unfavorable. This is generally easier than obtaining a reading on the number of clippings, but not always. A large corporation in the public eye is continually reported on. Some stories are favorable, some unfavorable, some mixed. For, say, a $40,000 executive to read them all would be uneconomical.

AT&T has established an elaborate system for measuring the effectiveness of its public relations. Clips are obtained from all over the country and then classified by people specially trained for this work. They go through a course and have a manual to follow. Periodically, AT&T executives test their consistency by mathematical correlation. Clippings are classified by individual Bell company, by subject matter, by whether they are positive, negative, or mixed, and in other ways. By plotting the results, members of management can tell whether AT&T is getting more favorable or less favorable treatment from the press from year to year. They can tell what aspects of Bell are getting the most criticism—and perhaps remedy what is wrong. And, by ranking individual Bell companies by the kind of publicity each receives, they provide an incentive for the laggards to do better.

Public relations professionals face their biggest challenge when there are no events connected with the product, service, person, or corporation that are newsworthy. Sometimes nothing can be done, but sometimes ingenuity and the use of other communications tools in addition to the press release, letter, and telephone call can gain considerable publicity.

One successful method is to promote consumer protection with the product or other subject seeming to benefit more or less by coincidence. Here's an example.

HOW PUBLICITY INCREASED SALES OF HIGHER-PRICED SUNGLASSES DESPITE INTENSE COMPETITION

In 1970 there was a bursting forth of sunglass styles. In tune with the times, sunglasses were being offered in hundreds of shapes and hues. When there is so much quantity, plus an emphasis on fashion, the quality appeal of a product stands in danger of getting lost among consumers. This was the problem faced by Bausch & Lomb, makers of the fine quality line of Ray-Ban sunglasses.

Bausch & Lomb asked its public relations agency, Ruder & Finn, to make consumers aware of what they should be looking for when they purchase a pair of sunglasses, that there *is* a difference in quality, and that the higher-priced Ray-Ban glasses are well worth the difference in price. In other words, Bausch & Lomb wanted the agency to help defend its market. This task was given almost wholly to public relations; there was very little advertising support.

The Ray-Ban line was under attack on at least two fronts: attempts by other manufacturers to weaken Ray-Ban's market position by emphasizing style as the most important sunglass feature and attempts to capture a share of Ray-Ban's market by implying that lower-priced glasses were just as good.

To offset these attacks, the public relations program concentrated on two major activities: consumer education and product publicity for the Ray-Ban line, plus product publicity only for Bausch & Lomb's line of "funglasses" known as Fashion Eyewear. In the case of this latter product, Bausch & Lomb felt that in those instances where consumers wanted mainly high style, it was necessary to educate them about how *sun*glasses and *fun*glasses differed and to convince them to purchase Bausch & Lomb's Fashion Eyewear products if the emphasis was on *fun* rather than on *sun*.

The heart of the consumer education campaign for the Ray-Ban line was the preparation of "Sunglasses and Your Eyes," a public service consumer guide on sunglass selection and use. More than 100,000 copies were distributed to interested consumers in just the first few months of the campaign. The brochure was also used as the basis for national magazine, television, and newspaper publicity that reached more than 18 million consumers with the *sun*glass and *fun*glass education story.

An important audience of community opinion leaders was also contacted by mailing the brochure, with a personal letter, to 350 federal, state, and top city officials in consumer affairs, health, and education departments plus private individuals and organizations concerned with consumer education and protection. Many complimentary letters were received from these sources congratulating Bausch & Lomb on its positive role in consumer education and protection.

From product publicity alone, close to 24 million people saw, read, and heard about Bausch & Lomb's Ray-Ban sunglasses and Fashion Eyewear collections in the first six months of 1971. The spread of publicity was complete, covering newspapers, outdoor and sporting magazines, fashion magazines, and TV and radio. Tie-in promotions also were worked out with ski, motorcycle, and fashion manufacturers on behalf of specific styles in the Ray-Ban and Fashion Eyewear collections.

Product publicity combined with consumer education brought the following results:

- More than 42 million people learned about Ray-Ban sunglasses and Fashion Eyewear between January and June 1971.
- Sales of the Ray-Ban line continued to rise, despite strong advertising and promotion by competitors.
- Retailers were supplied with the arguments and materials they needed to educate sunglass purchasers as to *why* they should pay more for Ray-Ban products.

Another way, perhaps the most common way, of getting publicity when there is nothing new is to tie in the product or other subject with an event that will occur anyway. One popular way to do this is by sponsoring sports events, but it can be accomplished also without paying any fees, as the following example shows.

HOW PUBLICITY IS OBTAINED ANNUALLY FOR A FOOD PRODUCT ABOUT WHICH THERE IS NOTHING NEW

Food publicity featuring recipes inundates food editors of major newspapers. They will carry news of new products, but throw out 95 percent of the rest they receive, or, sad to relate, they will run the recipes without the brand names.

Selz, Seabolt & Associates, Inc., public relations agency for La Choy Food Products, found an answer to this problem. The agency built publicity around the Chinese New Year. This holiday is traditionally celebrated in cities with large Chinese populations but receives little attention elsewhere.

The agency produces a special kind of press release—a clipsheet—that is a large printed sheet resembling a newspaper food page. The clipsheet (see example on the opposite page) features recipes utilizing La Choy products and is distributed to food editors across the country. Mastheads of these printed pages carry artwork symbolic of the particular Chinese New Year. In 1980, these clipsheets resulted in full pages of publicity in 65 major newspapers.

GUNG HOY FET TOY !

HAPPY CHINESE NEW YEAR 4677!

CHINESE "YEAR OF RAM" BEGINS JAN. 28

A festive dish for celebrating Chinese New Year is spicy Lemon Chicken, roasted chicken pieces covered with a sauce rich with ginger, lemon, green pepper and bamboo shoots. La Choy home economists suggest serving Lemon Chicken with egg rolls, rice or chow mein noodles and a Chinese vegetable such as pea pods.

新年快樂

This spells Happy New Year in Chinese.

CHINESE LEMON CHICKEN SPARKS NEW YEAR FEAST

According to the ancient Chinese lunar calendar, the Year of the Ram begins on Saturday, January 28. It will be the year 4677.

We can be sure of uncertainty during Ram years, the Chinese tell us, particularly in finance and politics—but we can expect all to end well. The fine arts—painting, sculpture, music, drama—are favored during the Year of the Ram.

Children born in the Year of the Ram are elegant, polite, wise—and passionate. A Ram child may be timid and shy, yet he or she can be expected to find success in the arts, say Oriental lore experts at La Choy Food Products. While Ram people may not feel great wealth, they are sure of a comfortable living.

In the old days, Chinese New Year was marked by a month of festivities. Now the celebration is concentrated into a few days, but wherever there are Chinese communities it is still the occasion for parades, exchanging gifts, visiting friends, setting off firecrackers and good eating.

If you'd like to welcome the Year of the Ram with your own celebration, center it around a Chinese-influenced feast. The meal begins with a traditional New Year delicacy, egg rolls, available frozen and ready to heat and serve with bottled Chinese Hot Mustard and Sweet and Sour Sauce. The main dish is spicy Lemon Chicken, made from a recipe developed by La Choy home economists for the holiday celebration. Stir-fried vegetables such as Chinese pea pods, available frozen, can complete the festival dinner.

LEMON CHICKEN
(6 Servings)

1 whole frying chicken, about 3 pounds
1/2 cup water
1 tablespoon sugar
1/2 tablespoon La Choy Soy Sauce
Cooking oil
2 tablespoons shredded lemon rind
1/2 cup shredded fresh ginger
1/2 cup shredded green pepper
1/2 cup shredded La Choy Bamboo Shoots
3 tablespoons cooking oil
2 1/2 tablespoons sugar
2 teaspoons salt
1 1/2 cups chicken broth, cooled to room temperature, divided
2 tablespoons cornstarch
1/2 cup lemon juice
2 tablespoons grated lemon rind

Note to Editors:
Black and white glossy photos are available free of charge from Seiz, Seabolt & Associates, 221 S. LaSalle St., Chicago, Ill. 60601.

Rinse and dry chicken, putting giblets aside for another use. Place chicken in large bowl. Heat water, sugar and soy sauce together in small saucepan; pour over chicken. Let stand, turning occasionally, 15 minutes. Drain chicken; place breast side down on rack in shallow roasting pan and roast in 400-degree oven for 20 minutes. Turn breast side up and brush with oil. Roast 35 to 40 minutes longer, basting with drippings, until chicken is browned and juices run clear.

Using poultry shears, cut off chicken wings at joints. Remove and disjoint legs and thighs. Remove backbone; split breast lengthwise and cut each half crosswise into three pieces. Arrange chicken pieces on deep platter and keep warm.

Combine shredded lemon peel, ginger, green pepper and bamboo shoots. Heat oil in large saucepan. Add vegetables and cook, stirring for 2 minutes. Stir in sugar and salt. Add 1 1/2 cups chicken broth and bring to boil. Mix remaining 1/2 cup broth with cornstarch; blending well. Stir into sauce and boil 1 minute more. Stir in lemon juice and grated rind. Pour sauce over chicken pieces and serve.

1. Marinate chicken in soy sauce mixture for 15 minutes. Drain. Roast breast side down, basting with oil, 20 minutes. Turn breast side up and roast 35 to 40 minutes longer, basting with drippings.

3. Shred ginger, pepper, bamboo shoots and lemon rind for sauce. Grate enough additional lemon rind to make 1 tablespoon and squeeze 1/3 cup of juice. Measure remaining ingredients and keep ready.

2. With poultry shears remove wings and legs, separating drumsticks from thigh. Split along backbone as breastbone and cut each breast half into three pieces. Arrange chicken pieces on platter; keep warm.

4. Heat oil in saucepan. Add shredded vegetables. Cook, stirring, 2 minutes. Add seasonings and broth. Combine broth and cornstarch; stir into boiling sauce. Add lemon juice and grated rind, pour over chicken.

On Saturday, January 28, 1979

On Saturday, January 28, 1979, there'll be a second chance for a happy New Year. On that day, the world will leave the Year of the Horse and enter the Year of the Ram, which is also the year 4677 in the Chinese tradition.

Although the Chinese many years ago officially changed to the Gregorian calendar—the one we use—they still celebrate festivals based on their ancient moon calendar, such as New Year.

In Chinese communities in this country, everyone shares a share in the fun of the New Year festival, whether the celebration takes the form of firecrackers in the street, a parade, a night at the theater watching old legends retold, or a family reunion.

The date of Chinese New Year changes every year, but always falls between January 21 and February 19. It arrives with the second new moon after the winter solstice (the shortest day of the year).

The Year of the Ram, which starts January 28, follows the tradition of naming the years after constellations of the Zodiac in 12-year cycles. In order after the Ram are the constellations of Monkey, Rooster, Dog, Boar, Rat, Ox, Tiger, Rabbit, Dragon, Serpent and Horse.

The Chinese say that if you were born in the Year of the Ram, you will be wise and gentle and elegant and passionate Ram people, the Chinese tell us, tend to be shy and often passionate. They are talented in the arts, and they can expect to achieve a comfortable living.

For the rest of us, Goat years promise political and financial uncertainty, but all can be expected to end well. It will be a good year, the Chinese say, for art, music and theater.

Nowadays the celebration of the New Year is condensed into a few days. In days gone by, according to Oriental lore experts at La Choy Food Products, preparations began a month in advance and festivities lasted a full month after New Year's Day, from new moon to full moon.

Weeks before the New Year, villages bustled with housecleaning activity, befitting the New Year as a time of renewal. Men in masks and warrior costumes symbolically chased pestilence out of the town. A villager, garbed as a sorcerer, ran through the streets with an ax in hand driving out evil spirits. All debts were to be paid before the old year ended.

Products, preparations began a month in advance and festivities lasted a full month after New Year's Day, from new moon to full moon.

Weeks before the New Year, villages bustled with housecleaning activity, befitting the New Year as a time of renewal.

Food is a welcome New Year's gift, and oranges are especially favored. For members of one's own family, ornaments or fabrics, especially silks, are preferred. Children and servants receive small packets of money wrapped in red paper.

The old year is finished with visits to relatives and, for the women, cooking. All food preparation must be finished on the last day of the year, since using a kettle or any sharp instrument on New Year's Day is thought to cut the coming year's luck patterns.

The final hours of New Year's Eve are devoted to family worship of the gods and to remembering ancestors. After the feast, family members join in a feast. All their quarrels must by now be forgiven.

Fireworks and good wishes at midnight hail the new year. At midnight, cries of "Gung Hoy Fet Toy" (Happy New Year) and "La Choy" (good luck) ring through the household. Before dawn, the glow of worship may be repeated.

On New Year's Day, and often the few days following, families remain at home. Shops close, streets are empty, and behind closed doors, each family enjoys feasting and unaccustomed leisure. The days following are for still more feasts and visiting friends.

The official ending of the New Year holidays is the Feast of Lanterns, celebrated on the 15th of the first month. The colorful and elaborate lanterns are hung over household doors to attract prosperity and longevity.

OFFER ORIENTAL RECIPE BOOKLET

"The Wonderful World of Oriental Cookery," a full-color recipe booklet featuring 40 recipes for American dishes with an Oriental flavor and authentic Far Eastern dishes, is now from La Choy Food Products.

The booklet includes menu suggestions, a description of Oriental cooking techniques with helpful how-to photos, and recipes for appetizers, soups, sandwiches, main dishes, vegetables and desserts. Also included is a section on authentic Oriental creations.

To order a copy of "The Wonderful World of Oriental Cookery," send 50¢ for each copy with your name and address to: La Choy Oriental Recipes, P.O. Box 47342, Dallas, Texas 75247.

CELEBRATE CHINESE NEW YEAR WITH ORIENTAL DELICACIES

It's Christmas, New Year's Day and the first day of spring all rolled into one. And it's everyone's birthday, too.

What is it?

It's Chinese New Year, the biggest and most important holiday on the Chinese calendar. It's celebrated with feasting, gift-giving, firecrackers and parades.

The exact date of the Chinese New Year varies annually, depending on phases of the moon. In 1979, Chinese New Year falls on January 28. It will be the Year of the Ram, known as year 4677. The Ram is one of 12 animals that has given its name to a lunar calendar year. Legend has it that Buddha called all the animals to his kingdom together but only 12 came: the rat, tiger, hare, dragon, serpent, horse, sheep, monkey, rooster, dog and boar. To honor them, Buddha named the years after the animals in the order that they arrived at his kingdom.

Children born this year, say Oriental lore experts at La Choy Food Products, will be wise, gentle, elegant and passionate.

If you'd like to join in the Chinese New Year fun, celebrate on January 28 with a Chinese feast. La Choy home economists have developed recipes for Chinese Steak with Mushrooms and Shrimp & Sprout Puffs. Prepared for the meal with even less fuss, available in frozen and concentrated form in supermarkets, hot cooked rice and tea.

If you'd like to join in the Chinese New Year fun, celebrate on January 28 with an Oriental feast. Recipes developed for the holiday by La Choy home economists are Chinese Steak with Mushrooms and Shrimp & Sprout Puffs. Serve them with won ton soup, available in frozen, concentrated form of supermarkets, hot cooked rice and tea.

SHRIMP & SPROUT PUFFS
(60 Puffs)

4 medium potatoes, peeled
3 green onions (7" of top left on)
1 1/2 cups cooked shrimp, cut into bite-size pieces

1 1/3 cups La Choy bean sprouts, drained and coarsely chopped
2 eggs, beaten
2 cups flour
1 tablespoon baking powder
1 tablespoon salt
1 teaspoon dill weed
2 eggs, separated
1 tablespoon La Choy Soy Sauce

Put potatoes and onions together through medium-fine blade of food grinder. Mix with shrimp and bean sprouts. Stir flour, salt and baking powder together and add to potato-shrimp mixture, blending well. Mix in still well. Heat oil to 365 degrees. Drop up a few units until golden. Fold in beaten egg whites. Drop batter by heaping teaspoonfuls into hot oil, frying a few at a time. Fry 10 minutes or until golden brown. Serve with additional soy sauce.

CHINESE STEAK WITH PEA PODS AND MUSHROOMS
(6 Servings)

1 1/2 lbs. boneless sirloin steak, cut into 1/2 inch cubes
2 cloves garlic, minced
3 tablespoons La Choy Soy Sauce
1 tablespoon dry sherry
1 teaspoon sugar
1 teaspoon ground ginger
1/4 teaspoon ground pepper
3 tablespoons cooking oil
1/4 lb. sliced fresh mushrooms
1/2 cup sliced La Choy Bamboo Shoots
1 8-oz. pkg. La Choy Chinese Pea Pods, thawed
2 green onions, cut into 2-inch lengths
1 cup oil
1 teaspoon sugar
1 tablespoon cornstarch
3 tablespoons water

Pound steak cubes lightly with plain edge of kitchen knife. Combine garlic, soy sauce, sherry, 1 tablespoon sherry, 1 teaspoon sugar and ginger. Pour over meat and mix well; let aside 30 minutes. Heat oil in wok or large skillet. Add steak cubes, cooking and stirring over high heat about two minutes. Remove steak and drain. Pour off all but 3 tablespoons oil.

From: LA CHOY FOOD PRODUCTS, Archbold, Ohio 43502   By: Seiz, Seabolt & Associates, 221 N. LaSalle St., Chicago, Ill. 60601

Exposure on television is also obtained by sending a letter like the one shown here offering four slides featuring Chinese food. A reply card makes it easy for the station to ask that the slides be sent. Publicity on more than 55 TV stations resulted in 1980.

Clipsheets are based on the principle that the easiest way to get people to do something for you is to make it as easy as possible for them to do it. An electronic version of the clipsheet is the Video News Release. Grumman Aerospace, for example, sent a special crew to photograph the return of the carrier *Nimitz* from the Far East. By controlling the filming, Grumman was able to have the planes identified as Grumman-made.

"The problem with a Video News Release is cost," says Robert Harwood, public relations manager for Grumman Aerospace Corporation. "For about $10,000, we got the *Nimitz* story in the 20 major markets where we were most anxious to get coverage. We were pleased, but with the other demands on our budget, we can't do that often. Much more cost-effective is to simply send out filmed shots of our aircraft with a note that they are for the TV station's library."

A spectacular way to get publicity when there is no news is to make news. Here's an example.

HOW MAKING NEWS SOLD OUT A FAILING 742-UNIT CONDOMINIUM IN ONE AND A HALF YEARS

Three years after Harbor Point, a Chicago condominium, was built, only 35 percent of the apartments had been sold, even though the Chicago real estate market had bounced back from a recession. Real estate taxes and interest on the construction loan were costing the building millions of dollars a year. A new sales agency, Sudler & Company, was retained, which in turn retained Daniel J. Edelman, Inc., as the public relations agency.

Edelman analyzed the situation and decided that, though the problem was partly Harbor Point itself (the subject), it was mostly the way the audiences (prospective buyers and those who influence prospective buyers) perceived Harbor Point.

SELZ, SEABOLT & ASSOCIATES, INC.

International
Public Relations Counsel

221 North LaSalle Street
Chicago, Illinois 60601
Phone (312) 372-7090

Dear Most Honorable Broadcaster:

The Year of the Ram, according to the ancient Chinese calendar,
will butt in on Sunday, January 28. That will be the first
day of the year 4677.

Chinese New Year is like Christmas,
the Fourth of July, and everyone's birthday, all rolled into
one big holiday. Whether you're
Chinese or not, it's a good day for
a celebration.

To welcome the Year of the Ram,
home economists of La Choy Food
Products have created a festive
New Year dish. Chinese Lamb with
Green Onions, flavored with soy,
garlic and ginger, is a perfect
main dish for the holiday.

To let your viewers in on this
exciting new recipe, fill out
the enclosed return card ordering
the four-slide, 3-minute
presentation.

If your audience will want recipes, let us know how many you'll
need and we'll send them along.

Gung Hoy Fet Toy! (Happy New Year!)

Cordially,

Jill Cleary
Account Executive

JC:as
encl.

Harbor Point was large and impersonal. It was not a prestigious address. It was isolated on the lakefront. There was no sense of community among the residents. And possible buyers felt the apartments were high priced, both in terms of purchase price and monthly costs.

Some of the negatives were real, but most were caused by a lack of a positive image of Harbor Point, a lack of information, or misinformation. (Harbor Point condominiums were competitively priced.)

The public relations objectives were therefore defined as:

1. To reposition Harbor Point in the minds of prospective buyers and those who influence prospective buyers.
2. To develop a sense of community at Harbor Point (thus not only improving the subject but also changing for the better the attitude of a very influential group).
3. To help generate on-site traffic.
4. To attract prestige groups and prospects to the building.

Not enough would be happening to make strong, continuing publicity with the right tone possible. It was necessary to dig deep for facts that could be turned into news and to create newsworthy events.

A survey of residents was conducted that provided useful background information for the agency. (The survey itself and one of the highly successful press releases that resulted follow this case history.)

At the beginning, events were created that had as their primary objective establishing a sense of community among residents. They not only made Harbor Point more attractive but stimulated present owners to recommend Harbor Point to friends and acquaintances. In October 1976 a Vagabond Clown party was sponsored. Residents and their children were entertained by a traveling troupe and shown how to apply clown makeup.

The next month, residents were sent a cordial letter saying that each would receive as a gift a 20-pound Thanksgiving turkey. At

Christmastime, owners of Harbor Point condominiums were given a supply of attractively designed holiday cards featuring a picture of Harbor Point.

Next came the major special event of the program. This not only generated considerable favorable publicity and increased resident pride but, most important, caused hundreds of people to visit Harbor Point. It was the Great Chicago Memorabilia Auction. Plans for the event began early in 1977. A search was made for a suitable nonprofit organization to benefit from the auction. A plausible appropriate tie-in was found in the ArchiCenter, a minimuseum that serves as a showcase for the city's great architecture.

Although officials of the ArchiCenter were willing to cosponsor the event and to lend their impressive mailing lists of supporters for the invitations roster, they were short on volunteers to do the work. It was the public relations agency's responsibility not only to conduct a massive publicity effort but to organize a city-wide search for donations and make all the arrangements for invitations, auctioneer, guest celebrities, and room setup. Contributions to the auction were solicited by letter, telephone calls, and publicity over three and a half months. (Included at the end of this case history are a typical letter asking for a donation of an article to be auctioned, a letter to public service directors of radio and television stations, and the public service announcement that was enclosed.) The 150 donated auction items included 1929 opera house signs, a Frank Lloyd Wright–designed window, and a massive mahogany-framed watercolor of Chicago's South Side in the early 1900s.

The auction put Harbor Point in the news frequently through March, April, and May 1977 and drew 500 spectators to the building. And the raising of $4,500 for the ArchiCenter further improved the image of Harbor Point.

The next event was stimulated by the installation of a flagpole in front of the Harbor Point building in the spring. Research revealed that no one in Chicago had organized an official ceremony for Flag Day, June 14, which that year was the two-hundredth anniversary of the American flag. So the agency organized the event. The Fort Sheridan Band was asked to perform and did so. Great Lakes Naval

Sea Cadets raised the U.S. flag, and naval signal pennants spelled out "Harbor Point." A representative of the mayor presided. All three Chicago newspapers carried photos (front-page coverage in two), and four television stations showed the event and mentioned Harbor Point on the evening news.

Now the created events moved more directly to selling. In August a luncheon was held for real estate brokers. In September two wine-and-cheese parties were held to which residents were asked to come and bring guests who might be interested in living in Harbor Point. By October 1977, 90 percent of the apartments had been sold. So a thank-you dinner with entertainment was held for the Chicago press—but the public relations did not end. In November Harbor Point was used as the setting for a Buick television commercial. In December Santa Claus arrived by lift truck to show that the absence of chimneys presented no obstacle, and residents were invited to participate in a holiday apartment decorating contest. By February 1978 the building was 100 percent sold, and a sales success dinner was held to which just the insiders, not the press, were invited.

Betty Kalahar, sales director of Harbor Point, said, "Public relations was the turning point for us. It changed the image of the building and brought people to us. Harbor Point was publicized so expertly that prospects became confident in making purchases here . . . whenever a major story had appeared on Harbor Point our traffic increased 50–55 per cent."

DANIEL J. EDELMAN, INC. • Public Relations

221 NORTH LA SALLE STREET • CHICAGO, ILLINOIS 60601 • AREA CODE 312-368-0400

Dear Harbor Point Homeowner:

Would you please take a few minutes to answer the questions
in the attached survey we are conducting.

This questionnaire explores your reasons for purchasing a
Harbor Point condominium, what you like best about your new
lifestyle, your use of the building's amenities and those
of the surrounding neighborhood.

Your answers will be helpful in advising management as to
your special interests, coordinating building events and
activities and generally publicizing the interesting aspects
of living at Harbor Point.

If you would like to sign your name, please feel free to do
so. Be assured that all this information will be held in
confidence.

Thank you for your help. We look forward to your reply.
For your convenience, we have enclosed a stamped, self-addressed
envelope.

Sincerely,

Louise A. Palvig
P.R. Counsel to Harbor Point

HARBOR POINT HOMEOWNER SURVEY

1. How did you first learn about Harbor Point?

   _____ Newspaper ads   _____ Worked in area
   _____ Sales pavilion   _____ Lived in neighborhood
   _____ Friends/relatives   _____ Other:_____
   _____ Passed building

2. What features most attracted you to Harbor Point? (rank in order if more than one)

   _____ Location   _____ Convenience to transportation
   _____ Condominium lifestyle   _____ Convenience to work
   _____ Size/layout of units   _____ Prestigious address
   _____ Building atmosphere   _____ Benefits of owning vs. renting
   _____ Amenities/recreational   _____ Security system
         aspects   _____ Other:_____
   _____ View

3. Which Harbor Point recreational amenities do you like/use? (rank if more than one)

   _____ Pool   _____ Crafts room
   _____ Exercise room   _____ Social rooms
   _____ Sauna   _____ Racquetball/handball courts
   _____ Whirlpool   _____ Other:_____
   _____ Game room

4. Where did you live before moving to Harbor Point?

   _____ City   _____ Another state
   _____ Suburbs   _____ Another country

5. If city, was it:

   _____ Immediate neighborhood   _____ Outlying neighborhood
   _____ North side

6. If suburb, was it:

   _____ North
   _____ West
   _____ South

7. Did you:

   _____ Own
   _____ Rent

8. Was it a:

   _____ High-rise apartment   _____ Townhouse
   _____ Low-rise apartment   _____ Condominium
   _____ Single family house

9. How long have you lived at Harbor Point?

   _____ 1-6 months   _____ 1-1½ years
   _____ 6 months - 1 year   _____ Over 1½ years

10. Do you own a car?

   _____ Yes
   _____ No

   If yes, how often do you use it?

   _____ 1-2 times a week   _____ weekends only
   _____ 3-4 times a week   _____ nights only
   _____ 5 or more times a week

   Do you use your car for:

   _____ Business   _____ Necessities (i.e. grocery
   _____ Pleasure   shopping, etc.)

11. Do you own a boat?

_____ Yes
_____ No

If yes, how often do you use it? _____
_____

Can you see your boat from your apartment?

_____ Yes
_____ No

Do you use your boat for:

_____ Business   _____ Transportation
_____ Recreation

12. Occupation:

Husband:_____
Wife: _____

13. Are you self-employed?

Husband:_____Yes   Wife:_____Yes
_____No   _____No

14. Which age bracket do you best fit into?

_____ 20's   _____ 50's
_____ 30's   _____ 60's
_____ 40's   _____ 70's or over

15. How would you describe yourself? (can check more than one)

_____ Emptynesters   _____ Couple with children
_____ Single man   _____ Couple without children
_____ Single woman
_____ Divorced   If children, ages living with you:
_____ Widowed   _____ boy   _____ girl
_____ Retired   _____   _____
                              School they attend:_____

16. Is Harbor Point your first experience owning a condominium?

_____ Yes   If "no," why did you decide to purchase
_____ No   another:_____
_____

17. If "yes," would you buy another condominium?

_____ Yes   Please explain:_____
_____ No   _____

18. What nearby neighborhood amenities do you most utilize? (rank if more than one)

_____ Shops   _____ Opera
_____ Restaurants   _____ Grant Park
_____ Nightclubs and theaters _____ Harbor and lake
_____ Art Institute   Other: _____

19. Interesting, unusual hobbies or collections: _____
_____

20. Interesting, unusual condominium changes or decorating: _____
_____

21. Do you have a lake view apartment?

_____ Yes
_____ No

22. Do you have a telescope?

_____ Yes
_____ No

23. Building events that interest you: (rank those that apply)

_____ Happy hours   _____ Holiday events
_____ Exercise classes   _____ Craft sales
_____ Dance classes   _____ Auctions
_____ Sports lessons   _____ Special events
_____ Sports competitions   Other: _____
_____ Art/Photo exhibits   _____
_____ Lectures

24. Comments/Suggestions: _____
_____
_____

25. Name/Address if you wish:

Name: _____

Condominium # _____

FROM: DANIEL J. EDELMAN, INC.   FOR: HARBOR POINT
      221 North LaSalle Street   155 North Harbor Drive
      Chicago, Illinois 60601   Chicago, Illinois 60601
      Phone: 312/368-0400

For further information contact Louise Palvig or
                          Barbara Keebler

SINGLE WOMEN CATCH UP TO MEN IN CONDOMINIUM PURCHASES

Chalk one up for the single women of the world, as one category of homebuyers rapidly catching up with the single male. A recent survey trend indicates the single woman is only one percent behind the single man in condominium purchases.

A survey conducted by Sudler & Company polling homeowners at Harbor Point, a major Chicago lakefront highrise, indicated the single woman represented 17 percent of the purchasers, only one point behind the single man representing 18 percent of the ownership of the building.

Howard Bouton, Vice President of the Woman's Division of The First National Bank in Chicago was not surprised at the figures: "It has been apparent for a long time that women are becoming more and more sophisticated in financial matters."

House & Home magazine recently reported "singles" as a whole are buying more homes--the result of both an economic and emotional decision that's triggering an expanding new market. They want a tax break and a chance to build equity. It is also a matter of "a sense of acquiring one's own piece of turf."

And, from turf to town seems to be yet another trend. Thirty percent of the total homebuyers polled were from suburban areas. Of that percentage, suburban residents were divided proportionately between the West, North and South suburban areas.

But, the majority of the condominium buyers did come from the city. Four fifths of the purchasers came from the North side or the immediate area, indicating a liking for the central city location.

Sixty-two percent of Harbor Point buyers were renters prior to their purchase. For many buyers, their purchase was a "step up in life" since 45 percent indicated that they previously lived in a single-family

-more-home or in a low-rise apartment.

Interestingly, the age groups of the residents were evenly distributed. The majority of the buyers spanned three decades--from the 30's to the 50's, although the largest single group of homeowners is in the 30-year bracket. A significant number (16%), however, are in their 20's, which appears to indicate that many young buyers have elected to make a condominium their first home.

The most prevalent buyer is the couple without children, representing the largest single ownership group, and numbering two to one over couples with children.

The physical location of a building appears to be the major attraction of their purchase--in finding the building and as a primary reason for purchasing. Benefits of owning versus renting and the convenience to work ranked second and third.

Homeowners cited pools, racquetball/handball courts and whirlpools as the top three amenities used in the condominium building. The amenity package seems often to be a selling factor in condominium complexes.

A majority of the homeowners showed strong interest in planned building activities. Highest ranking were the Happy Hours--community social gatherings held every other Friday evening; next in order of popularity were lectures, holiday events and sports lessons.

As far as neighborhood amenities, shopping and restaurants ranked as favorites. However, Chicago's cultural facilities and the lakefront were also ranked highly, indicative of the lifestyle where people live, work and play in the same area.

Planned communities seem to be working in our part of town. Harbor Point's "vertical neighborhood" is just one example. High-rise condominium sales are booming across the nation and their market seems to have expanded to include a wide variety of purchasers.

All figures were compiled from the findings of 184 Harbor Point respondents to a four-page survey by Sudler & Company. Copies available upon request.

Daniel J. Edelman, Inc.   221 north LaSalle street Chicago, Illinois 60601 phone 312. 368 0400

EDELMAN

public relations   April 6, 1977

Dan Hoffman
Midwest Regional Manager
Cleveland Wrecking Company
3801 N. Milwaukee
Chicago, Illinois

Dear Mr. Hoffman:

One cannot think of wrecking companies without "Cleveland" coming first to mind.
The reason I am writing you today is because we are aware that you are one of
the largest wrecking companies and are involved in demolishing many Chicago
area buildings.

Perhaps at times wrecking companies are criticized for tearing down certain buildings.
That, of course, is silly; it is merely your job -- and not your decision which
buildings come down. I offer you now the opportunity to show your goodwill to
the Chicago area and your appreciation of fine architecture.

May 8-14 is national Building Preservation Week. The Chicago School of Architecture Foundation and Harbor Point Condominium high-rise are planning a
"Chicago Memorabilia" auction as a gala nostalgia event during the week. All
proceeds will benefit CSAF's ArchiCenter architectural exhibit and tour center
on 111 South Dearborn.

Knowing that you might have mementos and various items of nostalgia (i.e., signs,
doorknobs, etc.) from various buildings of the past, I ask you to participate in
our auction plans with a donation.

Naturally, all items are tax deductible. We also plan on making this a big publicity event -- you, of course, would be credited in all releases and in the auction
program, for your contribution.

I've enclosed a Chicago Tribune article about our upcoming event and other information sheets. I'll give you a call in the near future to see if you might be able
to participate.

Thank you so much!

Sincerely,

Louise Palvig
Account Executive

Daniel J. Edelman, Inc.   221 north LaSalle street Chicago, Illinois 60601 phone 312. 368 0400

EDELMAN

public relations   April 12, 1977

Dear Public Service Director:

Attached is a public service announcement regarding an upcoming auction to benefit the Chicago School of Architecture's ArchiCenter.

Titled "The Great Chicago Memorabilia Auction," the event is being sponsored by Harbor Point in conjunction with The Chicago School of Architecture Foundation and has been scheduled as part of this city's observation of national Historic Preservation Week.

The ArchiCenter, 111 South Dearborn Street, is a free-admission architectural exhibit, lecture and tour center that began as a Bicentennial activity and has been sustained by donations. Last year 50,000 people representing 45 states and 40 different countries visited this mini-museum to better understand Chicago's past and present architectural greatness.

Your support is appreciated...please let me know if you need any additional materials.

Sincerely,

Barbara Keebler

Barbara Keebler
Vice President

BK:rs

attach.

FROM: DANIEL J. EDELMAN, INC.   FOR: ARCHICENTER
       221 North La Salle Street   111 S. Dearborn
       Chicago, Illinois 60601   Chicago, Illinois

For further information contact   HARBOR POINT
Louise Palvig or Barbara Keebler   155 N. Harbor Drive
                                                  Chicago, Illinois 60601

Public Service Announcement: 60 seconds

"CHICAGO MEMORABILIA" AUCTION

IN RECOGNITION OF NATIONAL BUILDING PRESERVATION WEEK, HARBOR POINT

LAKEFRONT CONDOMINIUM HIGH-RISE IS SPONSORING A "CHICAGO MEMORABILIA"

AUCTION MAY 13 FROM 7-11 PM, TO BENEFIT CHICAGO'S ARCHICENTER.

THE CHICAGO SCHOOL OF ARCHITECTURE FOUNDATION'S ARCHICENTER

IS A FREE-ADMISSION CULTURAL FACILITY AT 111 S. DEARBORN

AIMED AT POINTING OUT THOSE FAMOUS CHICAGO BUILDINGS OF YESTERYEAR AND

TOMORROW. BEGUN AS A BICENTENNIAL EXHIBIT, AT LEAST $60,000 A YEAR NEEDS

TO BE RAISED TO CONTINUE THE ARCHITECTURAL AND TOUR CENTER.

HARBOR POINT IS NOW WELCOMING DONATED ITEMS AND SERVICES FOR THE AUCTION.

ARCHITECTURAL FRAGMENTS, CHICAGO RENDERINGS, RESTAURANT SIGNS, ANTIQUES...

PRACTICALLY ANY ITEM OF NOSTALGIC VALUE QUALIFIES AS "CHICAGO MEMORABILIA."

PLEASE CALL 368-0413 OR WRITE "CHICAGO MEMORABILIA", SUITE 1400,

221 N. LASALLE, CHICAGO, ILL. 60601. YOU CAN HELP THE PAST STAY IN THE

PRESENT.

How do public relations professionals originate ideas like these? Like all creativity, it is difficult to explain and may be impossible to teach, but there seem to be certain fundamentals.

The creative professional considers all nine determinants, concentrating on those that are most pertinent. Most important, the professional has a solid sense of what both the media and the public want and need. It's not enough to have a sense just of what the public is interested in. The professional must know what the various media and their representatives will publish or air.

Basic also is a knowledge of what has been done before. While public relations problems are seldom identical, they are often similar—and similar solutions apply. Here are some common solutions:

1. Make a survey and publicize the findings (as in the Harbor Point case history).
2. Improve the product and publicize the improvement (another technique used in the Harbor Point case history).
3. Give a speech. (This is doubly effective because the speech influences its audience directly and the release on the speech gives wider coverage.)
4. Give an award (generating goodwill as well as publicity).
5. Create an index supplying useful information about the industry in which the corporation is a part.
6. Run a contest (see the case history in Chapter 15).

Sometimes routine treatment will get some publicity, but not enough or as much as is desired. Then consideration may be given to using any of these techniques, but more often a way can be found to make what is already newsworthy more so. The Globe-Amerada case history at the end of this chapter is an example.

Getting publicity can't depend solely on personal friendship with a reporter, editor, or producer. Of course, it helps if the public relations professional has established a reputation for reliability and pertinency. The media people will be more receptive.

However, as helpful as personal relationships with media people can be, no agency, no matter how large, can depend on personal relationships to know what will be of interest. There are too many reporters, writers, editors, and producers—and they are continually changing. Most are young, bright, ambitious, upwardly mobile people. Many get promoted in a year or two, have their assignments shifted, change publications, or go into public relations.

Does the fact that a publication gets advertising revenues from a corporation make that publication more likely to print or air favorable publicity about that corporation? Positively no for top-quality publications, such as *The Wall Street Journal, The New York Times, Forbes,* and *Time.* The worst move a public relations person could make in trying to get a story in publications or on shows of this caliber would be to remind a reporter, editor, or producer how much the corporation advertises in that publication or on that network. The editorial side is jealous of its independence.

Positively yes for some small publications whose publisher acts as both editor and advertising manager and is struggling to make a decent income. Generally speaking, however, if the publicity depends on the corporation paying for advertising, the publicity isn't worth the money and effort.

Common Mistake #11: Canceling advertising in a major publication because of negative publicity.

Chief executive officers who make this mistake confuse placing advertising with giving a supplier an order. Usually there is so much competition between suppliers, and their products are so nearly equal, that changing to a new supplier of, say, nuts and bolts doesn't damage the company. And because American industry is so competitive, the threat of taking away an order will often bring a supplier into line.

Not so with a publication. First, each is distinctly different. If the advertising belonged in the publication in the first place, the marketing of the company will suffer because of the cancellation. Second, canceling the advertising in a major publication will have absolutely no effect on preventing future negative publicity and may even antagonize the editorial side more. Third, and perhaps most important, canceling the advertising eliminates the positive information about the company that would otherwise be communicated to the audience reading the bad publicity.

In setting up a public relations plan to get publicity, then, competent public relations professionals proceed by asking these questions:

1. What publications and shows, what specific writers and reporters, might possibly be interested in this product, service, person, or corporation? (Often the professional will not be able to answer this question out of personal knowledge and experience. He or she will consult colleagues, Bacon's and similar aids, and other plans for similar subjects prepared by the company or agency.)

2. If the publicity is handled in a routine manner, will sufficient publicity result so that the public relations objective will be reached? (If the answer is no, then question 3 must be answered.)

3. How can the subject be made interesting to a sufficient number of editors, writers, and producers so that the public relations objective will be reached? (Some possibilities are to tie in with consumer protection, to tie in with an event that will happen anyway, and to make news.)

Implementing a plan or part of a plan that aims at getting publicity requires:

1. Establishing an up-to-date list of reporters, editors, writers, and producers who might be interested in the product, service, person, or corporation.

2. Communicating with them by press release, letter, telephone, or whatever other forms are appropriate.

HOW CAPITALIZING ON A SINGLE PROMOTIONAL IDEA FOR A TRADE EXHIBIT RESULTED IN POTENTIAL SALES OF $500,000 FOR A GLASS COMPANY

Globe-Amerada Glass Co. is in the highly competitive industry that supplies glass products for a variety of architectural uses. One secret to maintaining a leadership position is innovation of new products responsive to industry needs and aggressive promotion that calls attention to those products. For several years, there had been an increasing demand from the architectural community for thin glass that was still capable of resisting penetration. The need for this material was growing in areas that called for security, such as

73

banks, retail storefronts, mental health facilities, mass transportation vehicles, and especially correctional facilities. The latter application became particularly important because new federal specifications called for glass rather than bars to be used in windows of all newly constructed facilities. Globe-Amerada developed a four-ply glass, SECUR-LITE 4X, to meet the need. These strengthened, laminated panels are resistant to penetration by repeated blows from a wide variety of materials. The company wished to gain immediate and broad recognition for the product among architectural specifiers within the correctional field.

The American Correctional Association Congress, held August 21–25, 1977, in Milwaukee, Wisconsin, was selected as the stage for introduction of the product. Harshe-Rotman & Druck, Inc., the public relations agency, was called upon to dramatize the introduction to generate maximum traffic to the exhibit and to obtain publicity.

The exhibit was set up as follows:

1. What appeared to participants in the trade show as an ordinary pane of glass was framed in an upright position and labeled SECUR-LITE 4X.
2. A check for $1,000 was pasted behind the glass panel.
3. Several baseball bats were placed nearby.
4. A sign said, "Strike it rich. Win $1,000. Break through Globe-Amerada's SECUR-LITE 4X glass."

A female model, in a baseball shirt and with a baseball cap imprinted 4X, distributed throughout the exhibit hall promotional cards that invited participants to take three swings at the glass. If a participant could penetrate it and grab the check, the cards explained, that person kept the $1,000 check; if no one succeeded in getting through the glass, the $1,000 would be donated to Neighborhood House in Milwaukee.

A news release (shown on the opposite page) was hand delivered two days previous to the opening to local and trade media. Representatives from television stations, bureaus of the Associated Press

Glass walls do the job for prison

MILWAUKEE (UPI) —

Glass strong enough to be used for windows in prison cells has been developed by an Illinois firm.

The glass, being shown at the American Correctional Congress at the MECCA center, is a sandwich of four layers of glass and three layers of a plastic material.

"Glass is less threatening than bars, less brutal," said Frederick Moyer, an architect and director of the National Clearinghouse for Criminal Justice Planning and Architecture.

"We have long advocated getting away from much of the tradition in prison design — things like bars, sliding metal doors and screens.

"Of course, there isn't any type of construction that would defy escape," Moyer said. "But court decisions have advocated that prisoners be provided with light and a view. And that isn't obtained in the traditional, zoo-type structure."

GLOBE-AMERADA Glass Co., the firm which developed the glass over the past two years, has been selling it for about eight months. It is being used in the psychiatric section of Walter Reed Hospital in Washington and in the control center of Attica Prison in New York State, according to Richard Miller, vice president of Globe-Amerada.

"The glass is about 50 percent stronger than the force a 200-pound man could exert by running into it in his cell," Miller said. "Even if this glass would be broken, the hole would be so small, no one could escape. And the glass wouldn't shatter, it would be pulverized, so it couldn't be used as a weapon."

A $1,000 check is encased in the window on display at the convention here. The company has offered it to anyone who can get it by breaking the glass with a baseball bat.

By late Monday, a pile of broken bats stood beneath the display. The check was still in the glass.

and United Press International, and local newspapers were invited personally and by telephone to come to the exhibit. A photographer was retained so that photographs would be available for promotional purposes.

When representatives of the media arrived, they were invited to try to break the glass and were given a number of reports by major testing laboratories confirming the strength of the glass, as well as other Globe product literature. Neither the media representatives nor any of the participants succeeded in penetrating the glass and retrieving the check.

The immediate publicity results were:

1. Film clips showing attendees attempting to claim the check appeared on the three principal TV stations in Milwaukee.

2. A front-page article appeared in the *Milwaukee Sentinel*.

3. UPI sent out a wire story.

4. *Chicago Daily News* carried an article based on the UPI story.

5. Radio commentator Paul Harvey used the UPI material and the *Milwaukee Sentinel* article to develop a segment for national broadcast on ABC radio.

6. A radio feature appeared on WOKY in Milwaukee, based on an interview with Globe-Amerada's sales vice president.

Follow-up efforts and results were:

1. When the $1,000 check was presented to Neighborhood House following the event, it was covered by WISN-TV (ABC) and by the *Milwaukee Sentinel*.

2. Copies of the *Sentinel*, *Daily News*, and UPI articles were placed with the commentary editor of the Scripps-Howard newspaper chain in Washington, D.C. As a result, a feature was syndicated to its subscribers, one of which is the Newspaper Enterprises Association (NEA), which in turn distributed the feature to newspapers nationally. Results of the pickup from Scripps-Howard and NEA included use by 85 newspapers in 28 states with circulation over 1 million. Each of the articles credited Globe-Amerada Glass Co. as the producer of security glass for use in correctional institutions.

3. A reprint of clippings was mailed to decision makers in the correctional field, netting more than 300 direct inquiries to the company regarding its product. (A copy of the cover letter and reprints appears at the end of this case history.)

4. Photographs with captions plus an appropriately tailored release (which follow) were distributed to trade publications. Articles appeared in *Auto and Flat Glass Journal, American Glass Review, Architectural Record, U.S. Glass, Metal & Glazing, American Journal of Correction, Glass Digest, Western Construction, Railway Age, Plant Engineering*, and *Mass Transit*, and an additional 1,200 inquiries were received by the firm.

5. Opinion leaders in the correctional field in each of several states were sent clippings from the appropriate state's press, along with a covering letter.

The groundwork laid back in August 1977 had a continuing benefit, not only for the balance of the year but into the next year as well. Additional features about the company and its product appeared in the trade press. Globe-Amerada's management was invited to speak before appropriate audiences, and the public relations agency initiated more speaking engagements. The company further exploited the public relations with a direct mail program. As a direct consequence of this public relations program, according to the company, potential sales of over $500,000 resulted.

GLOBE AMERADA
GLASS CO.

2001 Greenleaf Avenue, Elk Grove Village, Illinois, 60007 • Phone: 312/439-5200

BULLETIN TO CORRECTIONAL PROFESSIONALS

Ask anyone who attended the recent American Correctional Association "Congress,"
and he will tell you he saw something never seen before -- glass that will not
shatter when hit...and hit...and hit again with a baseball bat, and a company
that gave him a "whack" at proving it.

The glass we introduced nationally for high stress applications and penetration
resistance windows is called SECUR-LITE 3X and 4X. These products are made of
3-ply and 4-ply layers of specially strengthened, thin float glass. They are
then laminated with a clear, tough security vinyl interlayer for a strong, stabile
product we warranty for five years.

Our SECUR-LITE 3X and 4X introduction literally "stole" the correctional show with
television interviews, national radio commentary, newspaper stories and on-the-
scene photos. Samples are printed inside. Stacks of broken bats, an unclaimed
$1,000 reward for anyone who could penetrate the product (which was ultimately
donated to a Milwaukee charity), and the undamaged light of SECUR-LITE 4X speak
for themselves!

The 400 ft. lb. test report from Patzig Laboratories prove these products ideal
for high security industrial installations, rapid transit protection, psychiatric
hospitals and for barless windows in all levels of correctional facilities.

Call or write us to discuss your specific glass requirements.

Sincerely,

Richard R. Miller
Vice President

Manufacturers of Automotive and Architectural Glass Products with Distributors in All Major Cities

HARSHE-ROTMAN & DRUCK, INC.
PUBLIC RELATIONS

CHICAGO	NEW YORK	LOS ANGELES	WASHINGTON, D.C.	HOUSTON
444 N. Michigan Ave.	300 E. 44th St.	3345 Wilshire Blvd.	1717 K Street, N.W.	836 Esperson Building
60611	10017	90010	20036	77002
(312) 644-8600	(212) 661-3400	(213) 385-5271	(202) 296-3049	(713) 237-9221

FROM: Carl Oldberg (Chicago Office)   FOR IMMEDIATE RELEASE

FOR: GLOBE-AMERADA GLASS CO.
       2001 Greenleaf Ave.
       Elk Grove Village, Ill. 60007

GLOBE-AMERADA INTRODUCES
GLASS TO REPLACE STEEL

One of the new products to be shown at the American Correctional Congress opening August 21 at the MECCA Center in Milwaukee is an architectural glass strong enough to replace steel bars in correctional institutions.

The glass is called SECUR-LITE 4X and is manufactured by the Globe-Amerada Glass Co. "We have spent almost two years developing this glass," says Richard Miller, Globe-Amerada vice president. "It means that correctional consultants and architects can now specify glass instead of steel for many purposes in their facilities. They can do that without sacrificing security plus gain the important psychological benefits glass provides for those incarcerated."

(Subsequent pages of release not included)

HARSHE-ROTMAN & DRUCK, INC.
PUBLIC RELATIONS

CHICAGO	NEW YORK	LOS ANGELES	WASHINGTON, D.C.	HOUSTON
444 N. Michigan Ave.	300 E. 44th St.	3345 Wilshire Blvd.	1717 K Street, N.W.	836 Esperson Building
60611	10017	90010	20036	77002
(312) 644-8600	(212) 661-3400	(213) 385-5271	(202) 296-3049	(713) 237-9221

FROM: Carl M. Oldberg (Chicago Office)   FOR IMMEDIATE RELEASE
       John DeFrancesco (Chicago Office)

FOR: GLOBE-AMERADA GLASS CO., INC.
       2001 Greenleaf Ave.
       Elk Grove Village, Ill. 60007

GLOBE-AMERADA INTRODUCES GLASS THAT ACTS LIKE STEEL

Elk Grove Village, Ill., Sept. 29 -- Globe-Amerada Glass Co., Inc.
has introduced a new security glass strong enough to replace steel in many
applications, without sacrificing the "look" and versatility of traditional
float glass.

SECUR-LITE 3X and 4X are the latest additions to Globe-Amerada's
SECUR-LITE line of security glasses first introduced back in 1969. 3X and
4X are three and four-plys, respectively, of specially strengthened thin
float glass, laminated with layers of clear security vinyl. Together, they
make a security glass tough enough to resist penetration by bricks, hammers
and even baseball bats.

"We spent almost two years developing these products," says Richard
Miller, company vice president. "SECUR-LITE 3X and 4X are durable products
with the versatility to be used in any environment and application."

This product versatility means 3X and 4X are ideal for banks, retail
store fronts, mental health facilities, mass transportation vehicles,

(Subsequent pages of release not included)

MILWAUKEE SENTINEL

A Shatter-Proof Sentence

By WILLIAM JANZ

For centuries, prisoners have tried to remove steel bars from their cells, and Monday they were offered help by a window company.

Miller's the name, glass is the game.

In a booth filled with broken baseball bats and an unbroken window, Richard R. Miller wanted people to know that when you commit a crime, the world isn't made of Secur-lite 4-X laminated glass. But it should be.

A man wearing a suit full of muscles picked up a Little League bat in the booth at the American Correctional Association meeting in MECCA's Convention Hall. He puffed up his strength, took a deep breath, whacked one of Miller's windows three times and broke the bat.

"It won't break," Miller said. "A 200 pound man could run across his cell and throw himself at this window and it wouldn't break."

In case any prisoners read this, we should state right here high up in the story that the window also won't open. It will take curtains, though.

A Matter of Justice

"Windows won't make it a country club," Miller said. "They're just a matter of good criminal justice."

Without the fervor of an old time temperance meeting, Miller took up the slogan of 50 years ago and said, "We want to replace all the bars."

Judges should realize that Miller is as dangerous to their syntax as he is to steel bars. He wants to use an eraser at the end of their sentences.

If Miller's company prevails, a judge will have to sentence a particularly rotten defendant to spend the rest of his natural life behind a window.

And you'd be able to hear Circuit Judge Christ T. Seraphim, who has been called the hanging judge of Milwaukee County, shout at a bad man, "You belong behind a window."

Steel bars have been such an integral part of our punishment system, and with the help of the sun they make such interesting geometric patterns on prison walls, Miller was asked what exactly was wrong with bars?

"Nobody likes bars anymore," Miller said. "They're depressing. Even the federal government doesn't want them because a window doesn't give that restraining feeling night and day and it'll provide psychological therapy . . . ."

He tapped a Little League bat against the window, " . . . with clear vision to the out of doors."

Carries His Guarantee

A judge would then be able to show mercy by sentencing a defendant to a room with a view. And if there were a question whether someone should be imprisoned in a facility with glass or one without, the judge could inquire, "By the way, son, do you do windows?"

Miller guaranteed that prisoners carrying bricks, hammers, chisels or screwdrivers won't be able to crack his company's product. He said the glass is even burglar proof, although that raises the question why anyone would want to try to break in.

Miller is marketing vice president of Globe Amerada Glass Co., of Elk Grove, Ill., the manufacturer of Secur-lite 4-X, which, at this point in time, has not become a part of our English or whatever we call the words we use.

"A crowbar will crack it or a fire ax, but prisoners aren't generally permitted to have crowbars and axes," he said, smiling.

After listening to Miller, some people probably thought it'd be a good idea to have tinted windows and velvet drapes in all the cells in our system. But think of what windows would have done to a legendary old prisoner in California.

Without an opening to the world of his little friends, his hobby blocked by Secur-lite 4-X, that beautiful, old man would have suffered terribly all those years. Good grief, the Birdman of Alcatraz would have had to collect stamps.

Blink! It looked easy, but no one could break through the SECUR-LITE 4X invisible glass shield.

Broken bats, undamaged glass — these told the story at Convention's end.

The media found the Globe-Amerada exhibit the "hit" of the show.

Dick Miller explains the features of SECUR-LITE 4X glass to a correctional official.

SECTION TWO

A NEW, COMPLETE, PRACTICAL THEORY OF PUBLIC RELATIONS COMMUNICATION

LETTERS THAT
GET ACTION

"The first paragraph in a letter to a producer should immediately and succinctly give him an idea for his show," says Virginia Sheridan, ace travel publicist. "It shouldn't just say, 'I represent so-and-so.'"

The Chinese New Year letter in the previous chapter illustrates this basic principle. It immediately promises the readers (TV producers) a benefit (featuring the Chinese New Year) for their shows.

No matter what action is desired—a donation of cash, time, or things, or merely a request for more information—a letter must promise a benefit to be successful.

The Eisner's letter, for example, on the following page offers account executives at brokerage firms the benefit that their customers will appreciate their services more. This letter along with a reply card (also shown) was mailed to 4,000 account executives at brokerage firms in the Northeast. Over 300 replied. (The name of the stock and a few key facts have been changed.)

The benefit may be material or psychological, concrete or abstract, strongly stated or politely implied, but there must be a self-oriented reason for the person getting the letter to do what the writer wants. There is nothing anyone is so interested in, so concerned about, as him- or herself. To get along with others, we have

Benn & MacDonough, Inc.

111 BROADWAY · NEW YORK, N. Y. 10006 · TEL: (212) 267-6900

July 18, 1977

Dear Registered Representative:

Some of your shrewdest customers may be interested in the common stock of Eisner's, Inc., listed on the New York Stock Exchange. Particularly those who:

* are aware of studies which indicate that stocks with <u>low price-earnings ratios</u> tend to outperform those with higher multiples. (Eisner's has a <u>P-E of seven</u> based on a recent price of 6 3/4.)

* are interested in <u>total return.</u> (Eisner's board of directors has adopted a quarterly dividend policy, and paid 10¢ per share in June, 1977. Indicated yield: 5.9%).

* look for <u>intrinsic worth.</u> (Eisner's stock is selling not only for less than half book value but also <u>below working capital per share.</u>)

* <u>look beyond the immediate present.</u> (Earnings before an extraordinary credit for the last full fiscal year were up 24% from the previous year. Earnings for the most recent nine months, however, were below the year before period. Eisner's 16th store was opened in April, in Portchester, N.Y., and sales are exceeding expectations. Another store is scheduled for opening in Newark in late summer. And serious discussions are being held regarding the opening of Eisner's 18th store in Connecticut. Every year since Eisner's was founded, sales have been higher than the year before.)

If you'd like to know more about Eisner's, telephone me. We're the financial public relations agency for Eisner's. If you prefer, mail the enclosed card.

A direct line to me is (212) 267-6900.

Sincerely,

Alec Benn
President

I am interested in knowing more about a stock with an indicated yield of 5.9%, a low price-earnings ratio, selling below working capital per share, and in a company with expansion plans. Please send me the material checked on Eisner's.

( ) Fact Sheet
( ) Annual Report

Name_____
            (printed or typed)
Firm Name_____

Address_____

City_____State_____Zip_____

all learned in varying degrees to disguise our self-interest, but it is self-interest that motivates our actions.

For more than 50 years, advertising people have been placing advertisements suggesting people take action—direct response advertisements. The coupons and telephone calls resulting from different kinds of direct response advertisements have been counted, and there is no doubt that the more a communication concentrates on the self-interest of the reader, the more likely the reader will respond as desired.

Common Mistake #12: Not concentrating a communication sufficiently on the self-interest of the audience. This mistake is made so often because of our basic instincts. All writers, all executives who approve letters, are more interested in the needs and wants of themselves and their corporations than in those of their audiences. It's hard to put someone else's needs and wants first.

While the promise of a benefit should usually begin letters to producers, sometimes the promise belongs elsewhere when the audience, purpose, subject matter, and other conditions are different, but the promise is always there.

The promised benefit in the letter to residents of Harbor Point asking them to fill in the survey is this: The requested action may improve their living conditions. The Globe-Amerada letter to correctional officials offers the obvious benefit of better equipment for correctional institutions, but the implied benefit, which probably gets the action, is: Recipients had better know about this development if they are to be considered knowledgeable in their profession.

The promise of a benefit is one of the three essential elements of a letter designed to get action. The second most important element may seem obvious, but many letters that aim at action omit it. **Common Mistake #13: In a communication that aims to get action, not stating precisely the action desired.** Why do so many letter writers make this mistake? Sometimes because they have not thought out exactly what they want the readers to do. Sometimes because they think what they want is obvious. And sometimes because they're being overtactful. One of Murphy's laws applies here:

"If a message can be misunderstood, it will be misunderstood." If the recipient of a letter is not told precisely what to do, he or she is not likely to do it.

In the Harbor Point letter, the reader is asked to fill out and mail the survey. The Globe-Amerada and Eisner's letters both ask the recipients to send for more information and tell them exactly how to get it. The Chinese New Year letter asks the broadcaster to send for slides.

The third vital element in an action-getting letter relates the promised benefit to the action requested. These are the words necessary to convince the reader that the requested action will result in the promised benefit. Sometimes the conviction consists of a few words, sometimes pages. The length depends on what the reader is asked to do, the reader's attitude and prior knowledge, and the desirability of the benefit. More about length later in this chapter.

In a letter, there are no fixed positions for the three vital elements (benefit, action desired, conviction) needed to get action. In a direct response *advertisement*, however, the order of the elements is fixed: (1) benefit, (2) conviction, (3) action desired. This is because of the nature of the form in which the message appears. An advertisement is placed in a newspaper or magazine and thus must compete with other ads and with the editorial content for the reader's attention. While a number of devices may be used (attractive illustration, putting the promise of a benefit in the form of news, arousing the reader's curiosity), advertisements that don't promise a benefit in the headline or illustration seldom pull well. People usually don't respond to an advertisement that, for example, has a headline that entertains but promises no benefit, primarily because the readers who are drawn to the advertisement are interested in the entertainment, not in the benefit they'll get by taking the action desired. The wrong people are usually selected.

A letter is not under the same handicap as a direct response advertisement. The competition for the reader's attention is not nearly so strong. What is more, a letter by its very nature appeals to the reader's self-interest. An advertisement is obviously aimed at a group; the reader must determine whether he or she is part of that group. A letter ostensibly contains information meant for the individual to whom the letter is sent, even if it's addressed to the resident at such-and-such address. It is the nature of the form that makes the difference.

A letter may follow the same outline as a direct response advertisement—benefit, conviction, action desired—as the Eisner's letter does. Such a letter will seldom be ineffective, but sometimes the determinants make a different order preferable.

Consider the Harbor Point letter that accompanied the survey questionnaire. It begins with the action desired in order to avoid **Common Mistake #14: Causing the audience to think "Why are you telling me all this?"** When recipients opened the letter, their attitude was likely to be, "What am I supposed to do with this?" So the letter immediately answered that question.

Avoiding Mistake #14 may be the most important rule of all communication. A reader who doesn't know why he or she should listen or read turns off his or her attention. An irrelevant advertisement is not read. A letter from someone the recipient doesn't know is thrown away as soon as it no longer relates to the recipient personally. A speech filled with information that has no apparent application to the audience puts the audience to sleep. Grammar and high school classrooms are filled with bored, inattentive students because teachers don't tell students why they should learn what is being taught. Students are compelled to attend school, but the audiences for public relations communications must be attracted by information that is always relevant.

Mistake #14 is seldom made in news stories and direct response advertisements because their rigid outlines usually insure relevance, but this mistake is particularly easy to make in nonrigid forms, such as letters and speeches. Note how in all the letters included in this book—in fact, in all the communications examples of any nature in this book—no reader can ever say, "Why are you telling me all this?"

Because the form of the letter is so fluid, there are at least six effective ways to begin a letter designed to get action. Two have already been discussed: the promise of a benefit and a directive as to what to do. A third is a reference to a previous letter or other communication that is being answered.

A fourth effective way to begin an action-getting letter is with a promise of entertainment. People are eager to be amused. A letter that begins in a way that makes the reader feel he or she is about to be made happier will be read. An entertaining beginning works better for a letter than for a direct response advertisement because the reader of the letter has been selected by the address, not the appeal of the entertainment. (In an advertisement, the entertaining headline does the selecting.) There are drawbacks, however:

1. The reader is likely to stop reading when he or she realizes the entertainment is a ploy.
2. The amusement content may distract the reader from the purpose of the letter. The reader admires the letter and enjoys what it says, but doesn't do what the letter wants.

Note that in the Chinese New Year letter the amusement relates directly to the benefit.

A fifth, and very effective, way to begin a letter is with news. The Globe-Amerada Glass Co. letter is an example. In this instance, to begin with the promise of a benefit—better environment for prisoners—could be boring. By beginning with the news about unbreakable glass, the letter makes the subject exciting. Emotions are aroused. The reader pays attention and is consequently likely to do what the writer wants—send for more information.

Note that the beginning also fulfills the function of a news headline; the rest of the first paragraph tells who, when, where, and what; and the second paragraph tells why. At the same time, these paragraphs are dramatically convincing. They leave no doubt that the product will deliver the promised benefit: "ideal for high security industrial installations, . . . barless windows in all levels of correctional facilities."

A sixth effective way to begin a letter in some instances is with the technique known as "identification"—that is, causing the reader to want to be associated with the writer or feel that he or she is already associated with the writer. One obvious way of doing this is to state that both are members of the same organization or have the same interests or characteristics.

Another way of using identification is through praise. People are hungry for praise. The noted psychologist B. F. Skinner rates praise highly as a technique for conditioning human behavior. Soldiers are willing to risk death for the praise symbolized by a bit of colored ribbon they can wear on their chests. A letter that begins by praising the reader tends to make the reader like the writer and to want to be associated with that person. Praise makes the reader want to hear more, which is the function of the beginning of a letter.

None of these six beginnings is exclusive, of course. They can be combined and in fact often are to some degree. Most effective beginnings are newsy in that they communicate or promise to communicate something that the reader doesn't already know. A letter with a boring beginning seldom gets the attention necessary for the readers to take the action desired. A letter that promises a material benefit in a way that will make readers feel cheap or dishonorable will seldom, if ever, get the desired action.

Something that arouses curiosity is a vital element of all effective beginnings. The reader must be stimulated to read on. But arousing curiosity alone will be ineffective if it is not drawn from the substance of one or more of the three key elements of an action-getting letter: the material or psychological benefit being offered, the action desired, and the ideas and words that will convince the reader to take the desired action. The reader is likely to feel "so what?" The curiosity will lack relevance.

Despite the great flexibility of the letter as a form of communication, it is difficult to conceive of an effective action-getting letter ending in any but one way: by specifically stating what the reader is expected to do. Even a letter beginning with the action desired usually needs to state it again at or very near the end. All successful direct response letters aiming at sales do so.

There are differences between direct response letters—that is, sales letters sent to mass audiences—and some letters written for public relations purposes. Often a public relations letter is written to just one person, or just a few. And the expected percentage response is different. While the rule-of-thumb response for a successful direct response letter is 0.5 percent, a public relations letter may fail unless the response is 100 percent.

A competent professional public relations letter writer knows the rules of direct response letter writing and applies them—or does not apply them—as the conditions dictate. Some observations and rules follow that have been tested by thousands of successful direct response letters.

A P.S. is the most read part of a letter. Most readers look down at the signature to see who the letter is from before reading much of the letter. They are attracted by the nearby P.S. and so read it first. Then they read it again when they finish the letter. Results show that a letter with a strong P.S. pulls more responses than one without. Some direct response experts say they compose the P.S. first and work hardest on it, before writing the rest of the letter, because it is so important. However, a public relations writer usually will not use a P.S. because it implies that the information it contains is an afterthought.

The more personalized the letter, the better. Computer letters with the addressee's name in the salutation and sometimes also in the body of the letter pull better than letters with generalized salutations, even though readers today know that their names appear courtesy of a computer. As stated in the beginning of this chapter, there is nothing anyone is so interested in as much as himself or herself. The public relations letter writer often has an advantage over the direct response letter writer in being able to make the letter much more personal.

Handwritten notes added to a typed letter increase the responses. They make the letter more "person to person." But their apparent casualness and/or suggestion of lack of respect may make them inappropriate in a public relations letter.

Letters signed in colored ink pull better than letters signed in black. This rule is so important that direct response people go to the extra expense of printing in two colors just so that the signature will look more personal—even though careful inspection shows that it isn't.

Letters to business addresses pull better if they don't arrive on a Monday. Businesses receive so much mail on Monday, each letter receives less attention. There is more of a tendency to discard or ignore letters of marginal interest.

Two-page letters outpull one-page letters. While this rule is generally true for direct-mail letters, it should be viewed with particular skepticism by public relations letter writers. Here's why: A direct response letter usually asks readers to send money to someone they don't know, perhaps have never even heard of. As a rule, the only reason for readers to send the money is a narrow, selfish one; there is no feeling of contributing to society. This takes a great deal of persuasion.

Public relations letters encompass a much wider spectrum, and most do not face such difficult obstacles. Readers are asked to do something that will help them in their jobs (using a person on TV), to send for more information (as in the Globe-Amerada letter), to donate something of little or no value (worn-out tires—see case history in Chapter 16), or to do something else to which they have little resistance, such as filling in a survey form. A feeling of doing what is right often helps motivate the recipients, and often they know or have heard of the person or organization writing the letter. Consequently, a short letter is often more effective.

Some public relations letters face obstacles as difficult as those faced by direct response letters—fund raising letters, for example. In those instances, longer letters are necessary, or a short letter accompanied by a brochure.

The point for public relations letter writers is this: No flat rule can be made as to how long a letter should be. The length, as well as so much else, depends on the audience, the subject, the purpose, the writer, and their relationship to each other. What is the attitude of the audience toward what it is being asked to do? What is the audience's knowledge of the subject? Is what the audience is being asked to do easy or difficult? How does the audience regard the writer?

The easier it is for readers to respond, the more likely it is they will do so. The most obvious example is enclosing a postpaid, self-addressed card or envelope.

Giving the readers a reason to respond immediately will increase responses. Actions that are postponed are often not taken at all. In a public relations letter, however, care must be taken not to be so pushy as to be self-defeating.

Put a benefit on the envelope. Public relations people normally and correctly shrink from this, as it smacks of high pressure. However, it does indicate that the message begins, not with the first paragraph of the letter or even the letterhead, but with the envelope. Experienced public relations people consider the effect of the return address (the source) on the addressee. Sometimes the return address can be changed or modified so it doesn't seem self-serving.

To summarize, the standard outline for an action-getting communication is:

Source (return address, letterhead, possibly first paragraph).
Promise of a material benefit (first paragraph).
Conviction (body).
Action desired (near end).

One way, perhaps a foolproof way, to write a letter that will get action, if getting action is at all possible, is to tentatively consider the standard outline. If the source is attractive or at least not a negative, fine. Otherwise, consider whether the source can be modified. Then consider ways of beginning the message itself other than with the promise of a material benefit:

Reference to a previous communication.
News.
Action desired.
Psychological benefit.
Entertainment.

In deciding between different kinds of first paragraphs, consider the attitude and knowledge of the audience, particularly regarding the purpose (action desired), the subject, and the source. If an alternative first paragraph is used, be sure that some kind of benefit—psychological or material, tangible or intangible, real or fancied—is included somewhere in the letter.

Personalize as much as possible. Give a reason at the end for the reader to take immediate action. And keep everything relevant.

7

SPEECHES THAT
CHANGE ATTITUDES

Read this chapter even though you never intend to give or write a speech. It contains information pertinent to any communication that aims to persuade.

Picture a chief executive officer of one of the country's largest corporations speaking seriously to an audience of security analysts. It's difficult to conceive of the CEO's speech having much in common with an episode in a TV series like "The Rockford Files," but the fact of the matter is this: They both must follow the same standard outline if they are to be successful, even though the purpose of the TV drama is to amuse and that of the CEO's speech is to make the audience feel more favorably toward a corporation.

Every one of the hour-long episodes that make up "The Rockford Files" opens by establishing the central character (played by James Garner) as admirable and likable. In one episode, for example, his relationship with his father causes the audience to feel empathetic toward him—that is, to want to identify with him. He treats his father kindly, with understanding, while preserving his own independence and doing what he wants and needs to do. He behaves in a way that both fathers and sons, as well as mothers and daughters (which includes everyone who might watch the program), consider exemplary. In this episode, the CIA asks him for help. He gets into more and more trouble as the simple task he was supposed to carry out becomes more and more complicated. Finally he gets out of trouble and all ends happily.

The outline is:

Establish an empathetic hero.
Put him or her into a hole.
Get the hero out.

(Literary buffs will recognize this as also the traditional outline for a short story.)

Now let's look at a speech given by William H. McElnea, president of Caesars World, Inc., before the Los Angeles Society of Security Analysts. (The full text appears in the Appendix.)

The drama begins before McElnea gets up, with his introduction by the chairman of the meeting. This introduction, the substance of which has been prepared by a Caesars World public relations person, helps establish McElnea as empathetic. Besides the pertinent steps in his career, it includes the fact that he was a pilot in World War II, which has nothing to do with whether McElnea is a good president of Caesars World or not, or whether Caesars World common stock is a good investment.

McElnea himself begins in the same way as in a TV drama—by getting the audience on his side. He says, as so many speakers rightfully do, how flattered he is to be speaking before this group. This is not meaningless chitchat. It establishes that he recognizes the group as superior to himself. While McElnea may be superior to any individual in the audience, society (in this case the group he is addressing) is superior to any individual. Deference to the group erases the association we all have with charmless speakers with force on their side—drill sergeants and schoolteachers determined to make us better than we want to be. He then takes advantage of a happy circumstance in a masterly way. He says, "I personally feel very comfortable in this group. I think we speak the same language. I still maintain my membership in the New York Society of Security Analysts. I still send in my $50.00 a year. My name appears in the big book, so I feel as though I am not quite as out of place as I might have been if I had come out of the casino business in Steubenville, Ohio."

He then moves toward the substance of his remarks while slipping in another statement that helps the audience identify with him: "I'd like to talk today about several things. This is the last day of our fiscal year, it is also my twelfth wedding anniversary, and so I am very much up today, and . . . "

While some members of the audience may be single, and some unhappily married, most like to identify with a happily married man. Corny? Yes. Bad speech writing? No.

Unlike Jim Rockford, Bill McElnea doesn't need to be put into a hole. He's already in one. The audience knows, and he knows, that he is in the hole of needing to convince the audience that they should recommend Caesars World common stock. His speech is one long struggle against the ignorance of his intelligent audience. The villains are offstage—those people supplying the analysts with information designed to cause them to recommend other casino stocks or other kinds of stocks. When McElnea feels he has told them all he can to convince them, he gets out of the hole by summing up and stating as explicitly as is tactful under the circumstances that they should recommend Caesars World common stock. He begins his summing up, "In conclusion, I would like to be somewhat presumptuous and put on my security analyst hat for a moment and suggest those criteria that I think are important for analysts to consider when they look for an opportunity to invest in our business." (Note the deference to the audience plus the reminder that he is one of them and a fellow expert.)

McElnea's criteria, needless to say, point directly to Caesars World common stock as the best choice. He is out of the hole.

That McElnea's speech and "The Rockford Files" follow the same outline should not be surprising in light of the similar conditions under which they are communicated. Both feature live actors—two in McElnea's case (the chairman and McElnea). Both must hold the attention of the audience for an extended period of time. Centuries of experience going back as far as Euripides prove that the hero-in-a-hole outline succeeds in holding an audience better than any other. The hero needs to be somebody the audience enjoys being with. The audience must root for him to get out of his dilemma. In a drama, the audience wants its fear for the hero to be alleviated. In a speech, the suspense is necessarily more intellectual and is intensified by the audience's feeling that it may learn something to its advantage.

Without this outline, a TV drama would be a collection of skits, a form that requires considerable ingenuity by writers and actors and that has a record of limited success. "Laugh-In" depended only on the hope for more similar entertainment to hold the audience's attention. Similarly, a speech that does not follow this outline has only the audience's hope for more similar information as its attention holder. It's theoretically possible to succeed, as "Laugh-In" did, if the information is of intense interest to the audience and each fragment is presented in an emotion-arousing way, but at best it's difficult and risky.

Note that the hero-in-a-hole outline applies to speeches designed to change the audience's attitude—the usual purpose of a public relations speech. Speeches with other purposes may follow a different outline, or no outline at all. Many speeches are simply cheer-leading—that is, they are part of a ritual in which the speaker utters sentiments with which everyone in the audience already agrees. That's why they are so dull so often. The best are prose poems. In most cases, ceremonial speeches, like thank-you notes, don't need to be done well, they just need to be done—and to be short.

But changing people's attitude is another matter, and usually the speech must be of some length. Successfully changing people's attitude means causing them to revise their opinion so fundamentally that they will act and speak differently on a certain subject than they did before. Seldom will informing them of a single key fact or idea in a few words accomplish this. Generally they must be communicated with at some length—or repeatedly, as with advertising.

People's memories must be strongly affected. While we don't know too much about how memories function, many scientists believe everyone has two kinds: short term and long term. The short-term memory seems to serve as a barrier that prevents our thought processes from being overcluttered. People who can remember long lists of trivia for years seldom are good at creative thinking. A single fact or idea is held in the short-term memory for a while and then erased unless it is reinforced or is so powerful that it breaks through into the long-term memory. Since a speech that will change people's minds must be of some length to be successful, the audience must be psychologically prepared for extended listening. The message must pierce the short-term memory barrier.

All too often speakers or speech writers concentrate so hard on assembling the facts and organizing their import in a coherent manner that they neglect human nature. Or they may feel, as many people with training in science or other logical disciplines do, that an ad hominem approach sullies the purity of their arguments.

The fact is that people judge the validity of information by its source. It's a matter of common sense. In the real, everyday world, we don't have time to follow the twists and turns of every proposition we are exposed to. Often we know we don't have the expertise. And we always feel that whatever we are being told may not be the complete story. The teachings of Jesus, Buddha, and Gandhi would never have become so widely accepted if each did not exemplify his own precepts. People tend to disbelieve anyone they don't admire, like, or empathize with.

Business speakers generally know their subject. They follow the old, proven principle: "Tell 'em what you're going to tell 'em. Tell 'em. And then tell 'em what you told them." The middle of the speech follows some logical progression, giving it cohesion. But most speakers neglect to endow themselves with the qualities that will make them admirable, such as success, modesty, similarities to the audience, bravery, good family relations—all of which were readily attributed to McElnea.

Sometimes making the speaker empathetic is not easy, especially when the speech is being written by someone who will not give it. One device that fits all speakers is telling a joke, which is why it is used so often. Robert Orben, jokesmith to clients ranging from Red Skelton to President Gerald Ford, says a joke about inflation can be a great opening because it establishes a bond with the audience. "They feel," he says, "it's you and I against them." The "them" of course are people outside the group that is being addressed. Note that not any joke will do. It must have some pertinency to the subject and it must not ridicule anyone in the audience.

Here are some Orben jokes for speeches by businesspeople to businesspeople:

"If voluntary guidelines worked, Moses would have come down from Mount Sinai with the Ten Guidelines."

"I have the same reaction to inflation that I have to Howard Cosell: Will it never stop?"

"Years ago I used to be a stockbroker, and that's a fascinating business to be in. You'd be surprised how many people used to drive to our office in a *Mercedes* to get financial advice from people who came to work in a *bus*."

Great humor? No. But even a poor joke may serve to communicate to the audience that the speaker is trying to please, which is always flattering, and that the speaker is against what the audience is against.

Bernard Schoenfeld, vice president of Irving Trust Company, one of the few economists who is an accomplished speaker, opened a speech before a group of marketing executives with this joke:

"A man suffered such a severe heart attack that he needed a heart transplant. It so happened that at the time a young professional football quarterback and a middle-aged banker both died in an automobile accident and their hearts were available. He was offered his choice. The doctors were astounded when he chose the heart of the banker instead of that of the young quarterback. They asked him why. He said 'I want one that has never been used.'"

Note that the joke is on himself—a banker. Further note that the slam at bankers is so outrageous that the audience tends to side with the banker who is speaking to them, as we all do when someone is unjustly criticized.

Joke writing and joke telling, however, are special skills. Executives and writers without proven success in this field are best advised to use some other technique for establishing empathy.

There are usually better ways. In speaking before a group of

101

corporate executives, lawyers, accountants, and similar people at a club in New York City, Harold Williams, chairman of the Securities and Exchange Commission, prefaced his remarks with the fact that there would be a question-and-answer session following his speech. He dwelt on how the session would give him some feedback, which he and others in the federal government didn't get enough of from people in the corporate world. Note how this immediately made him a listener as much as a talker—put him on the same side as the audience, made him in fact an instrument of the audience's power.

A speech writer is most challenged when part of the audience is strongly antagonistic to the principal point the speaker wishes to make. Jenkin Lloyd Jones, editor of *The Tulsa Tribune*, in a speech made some years ago wanted to convince his fellow editors that they should upgrade the editorial quality of their papers. (The full text appears in the Appendix.) But he doesn't begin by revealing his intention. To do so would be to antagonize the very people he wants to convince. He begins by establishing that he is going to be factual—not argumentative—and that he is hardworking but not holier than thou:

"Last week in New York, instead of joining the high and pleasant wassail of the convening newspaper publishers, I spent some hours in the statistics section of the New York Public Library, and the research rooms of the Magazine Bureau and the ANPA Bureau of Advertising.

"Normally, I am neither this studious nor this holy. But I wanted to . . ."

(Note that if you're a big drinker at conventions, you think he is one of you. And if you're a nondrinking worker bee, you think he is one of you. Masterful!)

Jones then goes on to vigorously espouse the principal axiom on which his opponents build their attitude.

"Some of our schools are still wading around in the Dismal Swamp of 'progressive education.' Many of our children have never been handed an honestly objective report card. Many of them have played at 'keeping store' instead of learning abstract mathematical principles. Our high school graduating classes are thronged with ladies and gentlemen who move their lips as they read their comic books. Eccentricities in spelling have been looked upon with benign tolerance. And we are staggering into the space age leading a lot of normally smart and normally eager young people who never got closer to real science than raising pollywogs in the second grade window."

By espousing the fundamental argument used by the practitioners of yellow journalism, he causes them to agree with what he says. He gets his opponents on his side. He then goes on to show factually that, despite the miserable job our educational system is doing, newspapers will be better off following the examples of *Time*, *Newsweek*, and *U.S. News & World Report* instead of *True Story*, *True Confessions*, and *True Romance*.

He concludes with a rousing statement:

"As a medium for titillating citizens who seek only diversion, television has us backed against the wall. If we only do badly what TV does well we are headed for trouble. But why play the other man's game? Why not perfect our techniques for recording the swift march of history, for explaining the new world of science, for reducing complicated political issues to plain and clear dimensions. The public wouldn't understand? Baloney!"

If he had begun with his concluding statement, he would simply have stiffened the opposition, no matter how cogent and factual his arguments. By beginning with a strong statement with which his opponents will agree, he gets them on his side and makes them empathetic. People's emotions are always intertwined with their logical reasoning. "Cold" reasoning is a myth, as anyone knows who has seen how excited a scientist can get trying to communicate the beauty of a new theory. Between the speaker's establishment of an empathetic hero and the final message that shows he is out of the hole are the struggles of the hero. In a drama, what the hero does and what happens to him illustrate the message. Witty dialog there may be, but usually the ideas enunciated by the actors are secondary. In fact, if people in the audience believe they are being propagandized, they will resent it.

In a speech the reverse is true. The information and the ideas count most. That's what people come to hear, although they are always pleased when they are amused as well.

The rhetorical tools of persuasion are the same as those described in the previous chapter for getting the audience to take immediate action. There are only two: *identification* and *benefit*.

Sometimes a speech uses mostly identification, such as a speech for a candidate for public office. The speech may pretend to be about the issues, but every phrase by most politically competent candidates is designed to cause the audience to identify with the speaker.

Most speeches by executives, however, must rely on one or more material benefits to the audience. Identification techniques are used to get the audience on the speaker's side, but the burden of the convincing is on the selfish benefits to the audience. In McElnea's speech the benefit is unstated: Recommend Caesars World common stock and you'll be regarded as a better analyst. In Jones's speech the benefit is a gut, pocketbook benefit to newspaper publishers: "The newspaper that ignores this trend is headed for circulation malnutrition and, if we must be crass about it, advertising anemia." All the facts and ideas in McElnea's and Jones's speeches support a benefit to the audience.

Most speeches composed by executives fail because the executive does not have a clear concept of the benefit to the audience. Consequently, the thread of the talk becomes tangled, and the audience becomes bored and confused. Most speeches written by public relations people for executives fail because the writer puts pleasing the executive above pleasing the audience. What the executive wants to say takes precedence over what the audience wants to hear. A good public relations speech writer converts what the executive wants to say into what the audience wants to hear.

If possible, it is better to state the benefit explicitly as in Jones's speech than to leave it unstated as in McElnea's. It's not only better for the audience but also often better for the writer in the task of composition. The benefit serves as a guide for including or omitting any idea or fact. If the information doesn't support the benefit, it probably doesn't belong. There may be times when a digression is desirable, in which case the effective speaker states what the digression is relevant to, if the connection is not obvious.

In a speech, because of the length, the golden rule of communication—never allow the audience to think, "Why are you telling me all this?"—is particularly important. If the listeners know why they should pay attention—and the reason appeals either to their self-interests or their self-regard—they will pay attention.

If this rule is followed, it's easy to organize the body of a speech. Often there's more than one way, each equally or nearly equally good. McElnea simply took different parts of the Caesars World business and described them in turn. Jones wanted to prove that there was a growing thirst for information, so he began the body with the most fundamental argument—that potential readers are better educated than ever before. Then he showed how this increased education has affected magazines and books before he showed how it has affected newspapers.

The body of a speech can be in logical or chronological order; it can be organized like a trip to a foreign land, even if it is quite abstract, or like a chase. The weakest organization probably is the laundry list, in which the speaker lists the topics to be covered and then goes on to cover them; but even this is better than no organization at all. What counts is that the body have a pattern and that the audience know the relevance of everything the speaker says.

Here then, in a convenient form, is the standard outline for a speech that aims to change people's attitude and the parallel TV drama outline:

Story Outline	*Attitude-Changing Outline*
1. Establish an empathetic hero.	1. Establish the source (speaker) as empathetic.
2. Put the hero in a hole.	2. State the subject and why the audience should listen.
3. The hero struggles to get out.	3. Convince.
4. The hero gets out.	4. Succinctly state the message.

8

OTHER FORMS
OF PERSUASION

Not only speeches, but any communication that aims to change attitudes, can be based on the outline at the end of the previous chapter. It is appropriate for booklets, magazine articles, slide presentations, letters, whatever.

How can an empathetic source be established in a booklet? By naming and describing the sponsoring organization or author in empathetic terms. Remember the last time you, as a consumer, received a booklet in the mail advocating some position—say, that eggs are not harmful if eaten in moderation. Didn't you look for the sponsoring organization or author? And didn't you downgrade the contents of the booklet if the source was obviously self-serving, not on your side, not empathetic?

Common Mistake#15: Not making the source of a communication sufficiently empathetic.

Executives and public relations people make this mistake so often because more times than not no effort is required on their parts for the source to be considered empathetic. They supply information and ideas to intermediaries—newspapers, magazines, community leaders. These are the sources so far as the audience is concerned. In a magazine article or newspaper feature, the publication and/or a by-lined writer is the empathetic source. People subscribe to or regularly buy a certain magazine or newspaper because they have confidence in it, or at least are comfortable with it. It is on their side. News in an unfamiliar newspaper seldom carries the same impact as news appearing in one's regular paper.

The source in a slide presentation can be made empathetic, but often it is not—one reason such a presentation is often more boring than a live speaker. The empathetic source for a slide presentation may be established before the lights dim and the slides are shown, but the best presentations take advantage of the form and use the hero-in-a-hole outline. The pictorial nature of slides makes it possible to evoke the empathy of the audience. It's simply a matter of casting. The roles to be filled are those of the hero and the savior that gets the hero out, with a prototype of the audience assuming one of the roles. If the purpose of a presentation is to change the audience's attitude toward senior citizens, it can begin by making one or more senior citizens likable and admirable. The presentation can then go on to describe the difficulties older people face—the hole they're in. Or perhaps even better, the film can begin with a hero the same age as the audience and have him grow old.

A successful motion picture made to change the attitude of consumers toward independent insurance agents established an agent as empathetic, then put him in a series of holes—having to help a series of clients out of difficulties.

Just as the order of elements in an action-getting outline may be changed, so the elements in a communication that aims to change attitude may be put in a different order, depending on the conditions—some may even be left out if understood.

A booklet need not begin by establishing the source as empathetic—in fact, this is seldom desirable. In a speech before a live audience, it is possible to begin with the source because the audience will not get up and leave without giving the speaker a chance to say a few words. This is not true of a booklet sent through the mail. The reader's attention must be attracted immediately. Sometimes indicating who the communication is from will do this, but more often the benefit will be of more interest.

Precisely when the source is revealed and how it is described depends on the subject, audience, source, and form, plus their relationship to each other. One solution that fits booklets under a number of conditions is to put both the subject (title) and the source (name of corporation or organization) on the cover and a description of the source on the inside cover. Members of the audience are thus informed of the source and can read more about it if they want. Of course, if the source is an unavoidable, unmodifiable handicap, it should not be prominently displayed.

Familiar, empathetic faces have a great advantage on television because little if any time can be used to establish the source. TV audiences are impatient; their attention must be held immediately and continuously or they turn to another channel.

Besides affecting the order or inclusion of elements in the outline, the form and other conditions affect the choice of words and phrases in a communication that aims to persuade. Audiences will accept language in a speech that they won't in print. Words and phrases that aim obviously and directly at the audience's emotions may even be desirable. People like to have their emotions aroused. That's why they watch TV series. That's why Jones deliberately uses metaphors, "Dismal Swamp of 'progressive education,'" and draws dramatic word-pictures, "high school graduating classes . . . who move their lips as they read their comic books."

Speakers can be more subjective than communicators through the printed word. A speaker who shows emotion both in choice of words and in tone of voice will be more liked and more attentively listened to than one who is cold. A speaker who shows emotion is more likely to arouse that emotion in the audience. An ancient drama critic said, "If you would cause me to cry, you must first shed tears; if you would amuse me, you must first laugh." Emotion is contagious.

Speakers can use more emotion before live audiences than on TV, where they are seen so close-up that small changes in facial muscles will convey their attitudes. The emotion must be of an acceptable kind and expressed at an acceptable level. In a poorly written and directed TV drama, the actors show too much emotion in the opening scenes in an attempt to stimulate the audience.

In a successful speech or drama, the audience increasingly identifies with the speaker and the world created. So more emotion can be shown by the speakers or actors at the end than at the beginning. Winston Churchill always began his speeches quite matter of factly. It was toward the end of a speech that Churchill said, "Let us therefore brace ourselves to our duty and so bear ourselves that if the British Commonwealth and Empire lasts a thousand years, men will say, 'This was their finest hour.'"

Jones says "Baloney!" to his opponents' arguments toward the end. McElnea, however, is objective throughout, which is appropriate for his subject, audience, and purpose.

How emotionally subjective a communication can safely and effectively be depends on the subject, the audience, the source, the forms, and the professional. Subjectivity and obvious emotional appeals risk alienating the audience if any of the following is true:

1. The subject of the communication is scientific or technical (such as analysis of a stock).

2. The audience does not strongly identify with the source and cannot be made to. (The appeal must be Euclidean.)

3. Revealing emotion is contrary to the character of the source (for example, if the only source from the audience's viewpoint is a corporation).

4. The professional is not skilled in the use of emotion-arousing techniques. (Not everyone has Jenkin Lloyd Jones's creative abilities or Franklin Delano Roosevelt's delivery.)

5. The form is print only (no speaker to give the words personal emphasis; no pictures to arouse emotion; no combination of sight, sound, and motion to engage the audience).

The audience must feel that the source is sincere, which is not the same as the source really being sincere. In fact, there is a conflicting relationship. The outline and the language necessary to convince an audience is directly opposed to true sincerity. An emotionally sincere communicator begins by blurting out in egotistic terms how he feels about the subject. A successful persuader begins by appearing to be on the side of her opponents and brings them over to her side through the use of ideas, each of which the audience must agree with in turn. The language used may only coincidentally reflect the persuader's own emotions. It is chosen because it will heighten emotions the speaker wants the audience to feel.

9

HOW TO JUDGE, EDIT, OR WRITE ANY PUBLIC RELATIONS COMMUNICATION

The employees of an aircraft manufacturing company are anxiously waiting to hear if their company will get a certain government contract. Getting it will mean employment for all and advancement for some; not getting it will mean unemployment for many. The president is eating his lunch at his desk when he gets the word. He walks into the cafeteria to announce what he has learned. Does he use the persuasion outline? No, he follows the news story outline. He gets their attention with the significance: "I've just heard about the government contract." Then he goes into the lead, "We got it." And he continues with the tail: "This will mean . . ."

A Boy Scout leader is about to address a group of scouts just before they go out to collect tires. The most tires of the right sort will be collected if the speaker uses the action-getting outline, especially the essential elements: (1) a strong material and/or psychological benefit (be a better person, get a merit badge, help the community, get money for scouting activities); and (2) what precisely they are to do (where to go to collect tires, the kind to collect, and where to bring them). The persuasion outline is not specific enough.

It is the purpose not the form that determines which outline is best to follow. **Common Mistake #16: Assuming the form primarily governs the way a communication is best written.**

This mistake springs partly from the fact that certain communication forms are commonly used for certain purposes, but mostly because of a natural tendency to think in concrete terms: how to write a letter; how to write a press release; how to write a magazine article; and so on. It seems the obvious way to go about it, but this traditional way of classifying has made a sensible analysis of communication difficult. Like ancient astronomy, which was based on what seemed obvious—that the sun revolves around the earth—the present system of classifying communication techniques works to a degree for savants but even for them has serious limitations.

Suppose a letter needs to be written replying to a complaint to the CEO. The purpose of the letter is to change the attitude of the person lodging the complaint, so the persuasion outline, not the action-getting outline, is appropriate:

1. Show that the company is on the side of the complainer.
2. Give the complainer a benefit for not being antagonistic to the company.
3. State facts and ideas supporting the benefit.
4. Conclude with how the company wishes the complainer to feel.

Or suppose a public relations professional is assigned to get publicity for vitamins and there is no real news. The professional writes a self-help feature on nutrition. What is written may look like a press release, but it follows the principles of the action-getting outline, especially the essential elements: (1) the benefit—better health—and (2) the specific action—take vitamins.

Or suppose an executive has been corresponding with a magazine writer regarding an industrial process at one of the company's plants. There's a new development. The executive writes a letter using, not the action-getting outline, but the news story outline.

So far in this book, we have established three standard outlines, each suitable for a specific public relations purpose: the news story outline for informing, the action-getting outline for getting action, and the hero-in-a-hole outline for changing attitude and/or amusing. The persuasion outline is simply a more convenient formulation of the hero-in-a-hole outline. These are the only outlines an executive or writer concerned with public relations needs to know. Communications that don't aim at making or preventing a change don't need to follow an outline, they just need to be done with taste.

Every public relations plan has some change as its purpose—or the prevention of some change. A public relations communication may cause the change to take place (or not to take place) by enlightening people, by persuading them to act immediately or by making them feel differently. That's all. It can't force them, and it shouldn't deceive them.

Any of the standard outlines may, and in fact often should, be modified to fit the various conditions under which the communication is made.

Sometimes the form affects the outline radically. Consider the telephone call, for example. The ease with which this form can be used is deceptive. It's an audience of one, which is an advantage, but, unlike in a face-to-face meeting, the caller can't tell how the person at the other end of the line is reacting. The caller can't see how attentively the other person is listening—or whether the person is listening at all. It's easy for the listener to hang up, mentally or actually. Further, just listening without seeing is a strain for a protracted period. It's unnatural.

Salespeople have done the most testing of the best way to use the telephone. They want to get action immediately—to cause the unseen person at the other end of the line to buy. The action-getting outline is indicated, but experience has shown that the standard outline is often ineffective on the telephone. More often than not, the prospect stops paying attention before the salesperson gets through the conviction section and asks for the order. Therefore, an experienced salesperson gets in as early as possible the two essentials—the benefit and what the salesperson wants the prospect to do. The respondent almost always answers with an objection, because he or she has not been given the convincing information. The salesperson then counters the objection with convincing information, ending with the specific action the salesperson wants the prospect to take. Sometimes the salesperson repeats the benefit, such as "Send me a check today and you can own gold at today's prices."

An experienced public relations person uses the same pattern in selling a story to a reporter over the phone. The caller begins by identifying himself or herself and then tells the reporter why the idea or information will make a good story. The reporter almost always answers with a question (objection), and the public relations person counters with more information, sometimes also saying, depending upon personalities, "I really think this is a story that would especially appeal to your readers."

The form, in this case the telephone call, radically affects the way the communication is made, but the purpose determines the essentials of the outline. Calls with different purposes will follow entirely different courses. A telephone call to impart news gets the heart of the news across fast and then goes into detail.

At the other end of the spectrum of communication forms is the slide presentation. Because it is so flexible and because the audience is captive, the form has little effect upon the outline. If the purpose is to inform, the presentation can begin with the significance of what is to be communicated, communicate the news rapidly, and then go into detail. If the purpose is to get action, the source is usually obvious before the lights are dimmed, so the slides can begin with a benefit to the audience and end by telling the audience precisely what to do. If the purpose is to change attitude, the slides may establish an empathetic hero, possibly a prototype of the audience, and end with a statement or precisely the way the audience should feel.

Note that the purpose that determines the outline is the purpose sensed by the audience, which is rarely identical with the purpose of the corporation, executive, or public relations person. A corporate executive may view the purpose of a news story as to favorably influence opinion and/or to fulfill government regulations. Reporters may view the purpose of the same release as to help them do their jobs better. Only the readers of the publication in which it will appear see its purpose as being to inform them.

Usually the relationship between the source and the audience is

113

straightforward. The source is consciously informing, persuading, or amusing the audience, and the audience is conscious that an attempt is being made to inform, persuade, or amuse, but sometimes the conditions make it desirable or necessary to conceal or minimize the real purpose. For example, the purpose of a company newspaper from management's viewpoint may be to improve employee morale and thus reduce strikes and absenteeism, but the more conscious the audience is of this objective, the less effective the company newspaper will be.

The purpose as sensed by the audience determines the outline. The form may cause the outline to be modified severely, not at all, or to any degree in between. Other determinants—source, subject, audience, authorities, and the professional—affect the choice of ideas, words, and phrases.

What is credible for the source to say? What has been the source's previous position on the matter? How does the source usually communicate? (Putting Jenkin Lloyd Jones's metaphors into the mouth of a plain-talking executive would make him or her ridiculous.)

If the subject is highly technical, and the audience is technically trained, the writer better be expert enough—or become expert enough—to use technical terms and use them correctly. Plain talk is best most of the time, but technical terms can be valuable. To audiences aware of their meanings, technical terms can communicate much in a short time and communicate those thoughts more exactly. Sometimes only by using technical terms is it possible to communicate the more advanced ideas within a reasonable length of time.

In other words, the communication should be in the audience's language. If people speak only Spanish, put it in Spanish.

No sensible executive or public relations person ignores the authorities—that is, those who have the power to restrict or change what is written. Occasionally this is a government body, but more often the authorities are the writer's or executive's boss or clients. Even a chief executive officer, writing his or her own speech, may consider the attitudes of the chairman or other directors, or the views of principal stockholders.

The extent to which the writer or executive considers the authorities—and how to handle them—may depend on how much experience the public relations professional or executive acting in that capacity has.

A young, inexperienced professional may deem it wise to focus on what the boss or client wants in choosing words, sentence structure, facts, and ideas. An experienced professional with a reputation to uphold may feel duty-bound to write according to the other conditions—purpose, audience, form, subject, and source—and persuade the boss or client of the aptness of what has been written.

Every professional has limitations. Not everyone can create the metaphors of Jenkin Lloyd Jones or the sonorous sentences of Churchill. Fortunately, public relations seldom requires great writing of that kind. Almost always, clarity is more important than rhetorical devices. Further, subjective writing—that is, writing that revels in the emotions of the source—usually hampers rather than aids conviction.

The greatest struggles occur when a public relations communication has more than one purpose and/or is aimed at audiences with conflicting needs, different amounts of prior knowledge, and conflicting attitudes. These communications are difficult to write and get approved, not only because their lack of focus tends to make them inherently so but also because those in authority seldom realize what is involved. **Common Mistake #17: Underestimating the difficulties and overestimating the effectiveness of a multipurpose, multiaudience communication.**

The Japanese have a saying, "He who tries to kill two rabbits with one arrow often goes hungry." Executives as well as professional public relations people continue to make this mistake. They do so because all they have read and heard about how to communicate from grammar school on up has been in terms of form. They haven't been exposed to the overriding importance of the conditions under which the communication is made. They are not sufficiently aware that the more directly and concretely a communication focuses on the audience's specific needs and wants, the more effective it will be. Different audiences may have a different appreciation of the same event, need different benefits in order to act, and need different arguments for their attitudes to be changed. And even when the audiences' prior knowledge and attitudes, as well as their needs and wants, are the same, different language may be required for different audiences.

Ideally, a public relations plan is designed so that no communication is weakened by aiming at more than one audience or trying to accomplish more than one purpose. Press releases sent to trade journals are different from those sent to the mass media. Different letters are sent to appropriate audiences. Speeches, slide presentations, and magazine articles are modified as each purpose and audience requires.

Sometimes, however, a communication of great importance must have several objectives and several audiences. The corporation's annual report is a conspicuous example. The audiences range from unsophisticated investors to astute security analysts and include those who extend credit to the company, such as suppliers and bankers, prospective purchasers of the company's products or services, and perhaps possible merger or acquisition candidates.

Its ostensible purpose is to inform stockholders of what has occurred during the past year, why these events have occurred, the present status of the company, and the future plans of the management. But much of this information is not news. The most important news contained in the annual report—the earnings for the past year—has been reported many weeks previously. The purpose as perceived consciously or unconsciously by even the most unsophisticated audience is to convince the stockholders that the corporation is being efficiently and effectively managed.

The outline of an annual report may appear to be an amalgam of the news story and persuasion outlines. The cover gives the subject, usually includes an illustration, and sometimes carries an additional statement explaining why the report should be read. The year's earnings are usually given immediately, as part of or preceding the president's letter, along with their relationship to previous earnings.

The report begins with the earnings ostensibly because they are news. The fact is a report begins with the earnings because they are necessarily the focal point for indications of how well the management has performed. That is why the earnings are accompanied by a comparison with the previous year's earnings.

There is no easy way to write a multiobjective, multiaudience public relations communication such as an annual report, but here is a procedure that may make it less difficult:

1. Rank the audiences and objectives in order of importance. (For an annual report: Are we most interested in institutional or individual investors? Will the report be widely used to interest the prospective investors, or will its use be confined mostly to present stockholders?)

2. Try to establish an understanding among all those concerned with writing, editing, or judging the communication that this is the order of importance of the objectives.

3. Use ideas that will convince the audience most opposed, most reluctant to act. (If institutional investors are the number one audience of an annual report, include the amount of information institutional investors want and deal with concepts they are concerned with.)

4. Use sufficiently plain language and enough detail so that what is communicated will be understood by the least knowledgeable audience. (Even if institutional investors are the number one audience for an annual report, the language should be plain enough for the least sophisticated investor to understand.)

5. Ignore the standard outlines and create a new one.

This last suggestion requires some explanation—and the explanation supplies a key fundamental of all writing. As we have seen, the standard outlines time and again require modification because of one or more of the conditions. The truth is that the conditions are everything and the standard outlines are merely handy tools that work most of the time. The basis for all outlines is the emotional attitude of the reader.

All good writing, even the most factual news story, arouses emotion, even if it is only curiosity. The experienced writer begins in a way that takes into account how the audience feels before hearing or seeing the first word or picture. The writer continues with ideas, facts, words, and sometimes pictures that take into account the way the audience can be expected to react to what has previously been communicated and stops when the emotions of the audience are satiated: The audience has enough information, is ready to act, or feels the way the writer desires the audience to feel.

The perceptive reader will have noticed certain similarities between the standard outlines that reveal their common base—the emotional attitude of the audience. We have already seen how the persuasion outline is derived from the hero-in-a-hole outline. Now let's look at how the persuasion outline and the action-getting outline are similar.

They should be similar. The only difference between changing attitude and getting action is one of degree. In public relations, the only reason for changing attitude is to ultimately get action.

Let's look at the two outlines side by side:

Action-Getting Outline	*Persuasion Outline*
1. Source.	1. Establish the source as empathetic.
2. Benefit.	2. State the subject and why the audience should listen.
3. Conviction.	3. Convince.
4. Action desired.	4. Succinctly state the message.

Both begin with the source because anyone who receives a communication immediately wants to know who it's from. The persuasion outline, however, places more emphasis on the source because a successful change in the audience's attitude almost always requires a fundamental acceptance of the source. When at the end the audience leaves, or stops reading or viewing, its members are expected to *feel* as the source desires. How can they do so if they distrust, dislike, or despise the source? It's different with getting action. It's possible to buy a car from someone one doesn't like so long as the price is sufficiently attractive. Once a person takes the action, it is over and done with. A change in attitude, by definition, stays with one.

Because trying to change attitude is to attempt a higher hurdle, it usually takes longer. Consequently, the source needs to be tolerated for a considerable time.

Whatever the outline, the same techniques get attention and convince the audience. There are only two ways of getting people to act or to feel as the source desires: One is to appeal to their need or desire for a material benefit, such as more money or better health. The other is to appeal to their psychological needs and desires, most commonly to people's need and desire to be admired by other people, themselves, or both. In advertising, this second technique is called identification or attitudinal advertising. The advertising makes the reader, viewer, or listener want to be like the user of the product or service. Examples are the advertisements for Marlboro and Virginia Slims cigarettes.

Theoretically, both ways can be positive or negative. The audience may be promised a material benefit or may be threatened with the deprivation of a material benefit or even with direct harm. If identification is used, it may be suggested that the audience will be admired if the desired action is taken or that the audience will be despised or otherwise emotionally uncomfortable if the desired action is not taken.

In public relations, the positive is used most often, because of the possible harmful side effects of negative incentives. Only neurotics and psychotics—and few of those—like people who threaten them. However, a mild negative consequence, implied but not spelled out, can often enhance the effectiveness of a positive benefit or identification.

Both McElnea and Jones use identification at the beginning of their speeches to get the audience on their side, so the audience will listen attentively and be more easily persuaded.

Jones obviously uses both identification and material benefit even after he has established himself as empathetic with those most opposed to his view. Identification: People admire publishers who

119

appeal to the intelligence and taste of their readers and look down on those who appeal to an appetite for violence. Material benefit: Publishers who appeal to their readers' thirst for knowledge make more money.

McElnea cannot be so direct, partly because both he and his audience recognize other information must be considered before the analysts can recommend Caesar's World common stock. They will have to investigate Resorts International, for example. In addition, it would be tactless for McElnea to state the benefit—that by listening to him analysts will do a better job. This benefit is both psychological (they will be admired for being better) and material (possible higher salary).

Both speeches end with statements that tell audiences how they should feel and imply the action each listener should take. The endings differ only in degree from communications that aim to get action.

Experienced writers or editors of public relations communications therefore are not the slaves of any outline. They use the appropriate outline when it fits, because it makes their task easier and provides for a convenient check as to whether they are on the right track. But when faced with a multipurpose, multiaudience communication, skilled writers go back to the seven all-pervasive determinants from which the outlines are derived: purpose(s), form(s), audience(s), subject, source, authorities, and the public relations professional. They begin in a relevant way that will interest all their audiences. They use either or both of the only two ways by which audiences can be influenced (benefit and identification). They make sure that the audiences can understand and feel the relevance to their own self-interest of everything in the communication. And they leave their audiences satiated with information, and/or ready to act as desired, and/or with the target attitude.

That's all there is to it—but it's difficult, if not impossible, for an inexperienced writer. Or even for an experienced writer constitutionally incapable of feeling the emotional reactions of the audiences to the communication. That's why the outlines are so valuable. That's why it's wise, if at all possible, to plan so that multipurpose, multiaudience communications are not necessary.

SECTION THREE

HOW TO INFLUENCE
SPECIFIC PUBLICS

10

GETTING INVESTORS TO PROPERLY VALUE A CORPORATION

Despite the public relations revolution, some corporate managements still have this attitude: "We devote ourselves to running the company, to making it as profitable as we can over the long run. It's up to the financial community to decide how much our company's stock is worth. And anyway, nothing we do is going to make any difference."

Here's what is wrong with this attitude:

Consider first a corporation likely to need additional capital. An aggressive financial public relations program can save the corporation millions of dollars. It can cause the stock to sell at a higher price in relation to its earnings—that is, at a higher price–earnings ratio—as this chapter will show. Consequently, if additional stock is issued, fewer shares will need to be issued to raise a given amount of capital. To a lesser but still appreciable extent, an aggressive financial public relations program will reduce the interest the corporation need pay on bonds—and make convertible bonds with markedly lower interest rates attractive.

Many corporations are going to need additional financing if they are to survive. Inflation has pushed replacement costs of plants and equipment far above the amounts the government allows most corporations to set aside through depreciation reserves. Competition, domestic and foreign, forces many to buy more efficient, high-technology, high-initial-cost equipment. But even those corporations whose top executives believe they will never need to borrow or issue additional shares can benefit. Their companies are less likely to be the targets of unfriendly takeover attempts. Raiders look for companies that are low priced in relation to their worth, earnings, and prospects. A corporation that markets its shares—that is, actively improves the price–earnings ratio of its common stock through active public relations—will be a less attractive takeover target than one that does not.

Underpinning these economic benefits is a matter of moral responsibility. Stockholders have entrusted the directors and officers of the corporation with their money. Isn't it up to the directors and officers to take whatever steps they can, legally and ethically, to protect and enhance the value of the stockholders' investments?

Common Mistake #18: Not forthrightly making improvement in the stock's price–earnings ratio the objective of the financial public relations plan. Note: not improving the *price*, but the *price–earnings ratio*. There is much that can affect the price that is beyond the scope of public relations such as general stock market conditions. The proper objective for the financial public relations of most companies is to cause a higher value to be placed on the company's profits than otherwise.

There are exceptions, however. For example, a company's stock is selling at a price–earnings ratio that is much too high in relation to the corporation's possible future earnings. It might be wise to aim at convincing investors and their advisors to have a more realistic view of the company so that the inevitable drop in price will not be so severe. Another example: A company has an appropriate price–earnings ratio but has difficulty in obtaining bank loans. An objective of the financial public relations program might properly be to cause lenders to have more confidence in the company. A third example: A company's stock is concentrated in the hands of a few institutions and wealthy individuals. A proper objective might be to increase the number of individual stockholders. But under the economic conditions of the early 1980s most companies would be wise to aim at improving their stock's price–earnings ratio so as to reduce the cost of raising capital, to avoid being a takeover target, and/or to fulfill the trust put in the management by the stockholders.

Each of the nine determinants affects how this objective can be best carried out, but the most important determinant is the audience. Investors are necessarily the ultimate audience of a financial public relations plan that aims to improve a stock's price–earnings ratio. Other audiences are important only for the influence they have on investors.

From a corporation's viewpoint, investors are either stockholders or prospective stockholders. The fundamental objective of all communications to stockholders is to cause them to continue to hold their stock. Because the price of a stock is determined by supply and demand, causing a stockholder *not* to sell, say, 500 shares usually has the same effect as causing an investor to buy 500 shares.

In communicating to stockholders, the corporation has the advantage of communicating directly, without any intermediary, through the annual report, annual meetings, quarterly reports, dividend enclosures, and any other communications the corporation chooses to send. Unfortunately, because most of these communications are mandatory, they are often looked upon as time-consuming annoyances instead of opportunities to make stockholders more loyal to the corporation without third-party interpretation or possible misinterpretation.

Stockholders will mostly be motivated to hold their stock for economic reasons—satisfaction with the prospects for the stock's price and/or with the dividend and its prospects for continuing or increasing. But stockholders are not motivated solely by money. They are human. Many will continue to hold a stock long after its prospects have fallen far below those that caused them to purchase the stock originally. Some hold simply because they don't want to turn a paper loss into a money loss. Some may continue to hold because they like or admire the management; because the management has treated them fairly and communicated with them often and truthfully; because they see the officers of the company as decent people.

In other words, just communicating regularly and intelligently with stockholders can in itself improve a stock's price–earnings ratio, independent of the actual earnings and dividends.

But officers who limit the corporation's financial public relations to communicating with stockholders will usually find the stock of the corporation selling at a lower price–earnings ratio than it should. Some stockholders must sell from time to time for reasons independent of the company and its future. An individual investor may need cash for retirement, for a child's college education, or because he or she has been fired and has trouble finding a job. An institution may sell because interest rates make bonds more attractive than stocks, or special-interest groups bring pressure to bear, or, for one reason or another, the institution needs cash. In other words, there is always pressure on the supply side that must be balanced on the demand side. Some stimulus to buying is necessary to counter the ever present selling if a stock's price–earnings ratio is just to stay at its present level. It's not enough to do a good job defensively (like the United States in the Vietnam war); it's necessary to be successful offensively.

Further, for many stocks, there are advantages to simply increasing trading in the stock. The greater the amount of trading, the more comfortable security analysts feel about recommending the stock. They know that if they recommend the stock and it goes up, their customers will be able to sell. In a thinly traded stock, a recommendation may push the price up too far and, when those who bought try to sell, they will drive the price down too fast, so that few may profit.

Whether a financial public relations program is defensive or offensive, the true professional makes a conscious distinction between the needs of individual and of institutional investors. Individuals want brief information that is consistent with what they have heard before from their brokers or other sources. Institutions want more facts, answers to tough questions, and explanations for deviations from normal accounting practices.

Some corporations aim their financial public relations efforts principally at institutions, such as pension funds and bank trust departments. They reason that it is institutional buying and selling that normally makes the big differences in the prices of their stocks.

Institutions usually buy in blocks of stock—10,000 shares or more. Institutions are net buyers on the New York Stock Exchange, individuals net sellers. And institutions account for more than half of the volume of trading on the New York Stock Exchange. In the fourth quarter of 1980, 72 percent of the dollar volume of shares was accounted for by institutions and only 28 percent by individuals. This average, however, can be misleading for a specific company, particularly one with a low price. If, instead of *dollar* volume, the number of *shares* traded is examined, individual trades rise to 35 percent of the volume, institutional trades decline to 65 percent. The interest of individuals in lower-priced shares makes the percentage of trades by individuals lower when measured by *dollar* volume than when measured by *share* volume—28 percent versus 35 percent. But no matter how you measure it, institutions account for more than half the volume.

Institutional investors, however, tend to buy and sell in concert—a big drawback. One reason may be the human tendency to do what others do, but perhaps more important is the dependence of institutional investors on the recommendations of a relatively small number of brokerage firms. These recommendations tend to be similar because security analysts think similarly and generally have the same facts. What is more, some security analysts check with other security analysts before issuing a report or forecasting of earnings.

A corporation that depends heavily on institutional buying for the support of its price–earnings ratio runs the risk of big fluctuations. No company always has good news to report. Sooner or later a company's earnings drop below what is expected. When this happens, individuals are less likely to sell than institutions, partly because of the inertia described earlier and partly because individuals are less likely to get information that will cause them to sell. For example, a corporation's earnings may be higher than the year before, but the rise was made possible only by reducing research and development costs. Institutional investors may become aware of this as soon as the annual report is published because their own or brokerage firm analysts may make the year-to-year comparison. Most individual investors don't get this kind of information. It's publicly available for those who look hard enough, but most individual investors don't have the time or inclination to dig that deep or even listen that long to their brokers.

In addition, there are greater differences among individual investors than among institutional investors. Individual investors range from the complete novice to the highly sophisticated, from those who will hold onto their stocks forever, passing them along to their heirs, to in-and-out traders.

Consequently, unlike institutional investors, individual investors are less likely to all sell at once—and some won't sell at all—when a corporation's prospects dim.

Whether a corporation should concentrate on influencing individual or institutional investors depends on the corporation's situation and plans. A corporation, for example, with a low price–earnings ratio with plans to raise additional capital might be wise to concentrate on institutions. Receiving a slightly higher price for a new security issue could save the company millions. On the other hand, a corporation that already has sizable institutional holdings might be wise to concentrate on increasing its holdings among individuals, as a safety net. Some corporations, of course, have little or no choice. Some just don't have attributes attractive to institutions. They must aim at attracting individuals.

For most companies, the easiest and most efficient way to influence investors who are not stockholders is through security analysts at brokerage and advisory firms. There are nearly 15,000 analysts as measured by membership in the Financial Analysts Federation, to which virtually all analysts belong. Most specialize in one or more industries; about 20 percent classify themselves as generalists. Most are highly experienced, and many stay in their jobs their entire business lives. There are several reasons for this. Being a security analyst is enjoyable. They are courted by the most powerful corporations in the world. Their opinions are listened to attentively and acted upon by a large number of account executives and investors. Their ideas can result in the movement of millions of dollars. And they are well paid. The best earn well over $100,000 a year, the least about $30,000, with the majority earning $40,000–60,000.

And then there's the money analysts can make backing their own opinions, isn't there? Yes and no. Some analysts make money in the stock market, some don't. No creditable analyst has ever claimed, however, that an investor could get rich by backing all the analyst's recommendations. Most security analysts are employed by brokerage firms. Brokerage firms make money on the volume of trading that is done through them. The worth of a security analyst to a brokerage firm is how much business that analyst stimulates, not whether he or she makes money for investors. Of course, it is desirable that a good percentage of the recommendations turn out to be profitable, but that's not the principal raison d'etre for security analysts. It is more important for a security analyst to be plausible than to be right.

Not that security analysts don't try to make money for investors—of course they try. It is the uppermost thought in the minds of many, rather than stimulating commissions. But whether a security analyst continues to be a security analyst is primarily determined, not by the correctness of his or her recommendations as measured by the price movements of the stocks, but by how the recommendations are received at the time they are made. The plausible security analysts survive. Consequently, security analysts tend to favor companies that (1) give them enough information to form what they and their audiences believe is a sound opinion and (2) promptly inform them of any newsworthy developments. How can they recommend a company that gives them such sketchy information that investors cannot be convinced that the company's stock is a good investment? Wouldn't they be foolish to continue to recommend a company that continually leaves them out on a limb?

It is particularly important to keep analysts informed when their recommendations turn sour—the stock doesn't rise in price, earnings are not as high as anticipated, or a forecasted increase in dividends does not occur. What analysts want is a sensible explanation they can give registered representatives and investors. As a rule, this has happened to them before. They know how to handle it. All the company need do is give them the information they need.

SEC regulations forbid giving security analysts information before anyone else. But they do not forbid calling analysts as soon as a development is released so that they are sure to know what has happened as soon as anyone else—and any questions they may have can be answered immediately so they can volunteer opinions or answer any questions from investors.

Common Mistake #19: Not communicating promptly with security analysts when the news is bad. This mistake sometimes occurs because the corporation's executives feel defensive about the bad news. They think it might reflect poorly upon the ability of the chief executive officer.

It also occurs because some corporate executives think analysts are like reporters. Some reporters tend to be antagonistic; they look for the sensational and dramatic, and to play up bad news, because that's what their readers want. They treat good news in a ho-hum fashion except when they overdramatize a rise in profits to make corporations look greedy. Security analysts are nothing like that. They are on the company's side. They want to make the company look good. Their audiences are more interested in buy recommendations than in sell recommendations. They will present the explanation they are given as favorably as they can for the company and for themselves.

Does all the above also apply to security analysts not associated with brokerage firms? To those employed by banks and investment advisory services? Yes, for a number of reasons. In a bank the decision as to which securities the bank will recommend is usually made by a committee, so it's impossible to measure objectively how sound a bank security analyst's recommendations have been over a period of time. It's what the committee thinks about the analyst's recommendations that counts. Advisory services keep track of their own recommendations so that if they are profitable over a year's time this success can be used to get more subscriptions. (The SEC requires that at least a year be considered.) However, it is only occasionally that an investment advisory service achieves a profitable year when the gains and losses for all its recommendations are considered. Consequently, investors must base their decisions as to whether to subscribe on how profitable or otherwise advantageous the recommendations of the service sound. We're back to plausibility as the key to survival for most analysts.

Thus the stock of a company that keeps security analysts fully and promptly informed so that they can sound plausible will usually sell at a higher price–earnings ratio than the stock of a company that does not. (An exception is a company that is going steadily downhill. Then a lag in keeping the investment community informed may cause the downward movement of the company's stock to lag behind that of actual developments at the company.)

Security analysts are not the most important audience influencing possible investors for many smaller companies listed on the New York Stock Exchange and for most companies listed on the American Stock Exchange, other exchanges, or traded over the counter. Increasingly, companies whose managements want their stocks to sell at appropriate price–earnings ratios are communicating directly to account executives at brokerage firms. There are about 48,000 of them.

Account executives welcome getting information directly from companies for a number of reasons. First, many are not getting enough information from security analysts in their firms, simply because the analysts concentrate on the larger companies whose stocks are of interest to institutional advisors. Second, some are skeptical of the recommendations of their firms' analysts. Third—and for many aggressive account executives, the most important—because investing is competitive, there's the possibility of making big money for their clients if they can recognize the growth potential in a smaller company before analysts spot it and broadcast its virtues.

Account executives, however, will welcome this information only if they receive it in a form they can use. They are primarily telephone people. That's how they make their living, on the telephone. Most have more to read than they can manage. Written information on a stock should be on no more than a single sheet of paper. Why they should recommend the stock to their clients must be succinctly stated so they can communicate it easily and directly over the telephone and quickly answer any questions from investors. Account executives can be sent the annual report, but primarily as a backup, for credibility.

Like security analysts, account executives appreciate a prompt explanation of any bad news. Even more than security analysts, they need to be promptly informed of unexpected negative developments, because the bad news regarding a smaller company may not reach them through other channels. They want to know the bad news before their customers do and be ready with an explanation.

Besides being influenced by security analysts and account executives, investors are influenced principally by the press. The major publications that can have an effect on a stock's price–earnings ratio are: *The Wall Street Journal, Forbes, Fortune, Business Week, Barron's, The New York Times,* to a lesser extent newspapers in the other half dozen or so principal cities, and, of course, the mass newsmagazines, *Time, Newsweek,* and *U.S. News & World Report.* Most of the reporters, writers, and editors for these publications are highly knowledgeable, well educated, and alert. Many, particularly on *The New York Times,* have been on the same beats for many years and therefore thoroughly know the industries they cover.

Electronic media is less important for financial public relations, although it is becoming more so in the 1980s with the increased popularity of cable television carrying half-hour or longer financial news programs.

In setting up a financial public relations plan, a professional begins in the same way as setting up any other public relations plan: by asking questions about the subject. What is the corporation's record? What are its prospects for sales, earnings, profits, dividends? How does the company compare with others in the same industry? Why should the stock be bought in preference to other stocks? How has its price–earnings ratio changed in the past? Why? How actively is the stock traded?

This information is usually readily available. However, sometimes it's necessary to undertake special research, such as surveying stockholders, to get answers that may affect the public relations plan.

The answers to these questions enable the professional to:

1. Identify the kind of investors who are logical prospective buyers of the stock. (No stock is right for everyone.)

2. Formulate a sales story for the stock.

3. Determine the audiences to be emphasized and the forms of communication to be used.

For example, the professional who wrote the letter in Chapter 6 decided:

1. Individual investors were the logical prospective buyers for the stock.

2. Communicating directly to account executives should be emphasized through direct mail and telephone calls.

3. The stock's most attractive features were its total return (yield plus price appreciation), low price–earnings ratio, and high net asset value in relation to the stock's price.

A professional also asks questions about the corporation as a source. If, for example, the credibility of the corporation is low with one audience but undamaged with another, the professional may try to restore the corporation's credibility with the skeptical group or shift the emphasis of communication to the other audience, or, more likely, do both.

The source may be entirely credible but not very available. One company's chief executive officer was so busy running the company that he had little or no time for financial public relations. Yet the company had a great earnings record, a bright future, few negatives, and a very low price–earnings ratio. The professional recommended an advertising and direct mail campaign directly to the investing public, supplemented with communications to security analysts. Objective measures showed the campaign to have been successful.

Usually, however, the analysis of the corporation as subject and source indicates that the principal audiences to be influenced are the company's present stockholders and security analysts.

The stockholders are reached, at the minimum, through the annual reports, quarterly reports, and the annual meeting. These may be supplemented by special letters, a small newsmagazine for stockholders, and booklets of various kinds. (Examples include a reprint of a chief executive's speech, a sales brochure on the company's products, and an explanation of pending or just passed legislation.)

Security analysts are influenced through:

1. Telephone calls.

2. All the direct mail sent stockholders and all the releases sent the media plus some product material specifically tailored to their needs (for example, a one-page fact sheet summarizing key facts about the company, or a corporate data file detailing information about the company in a form convenient for security analysts).

3. Meetings of various kinds. (Examples include the chief executive officer appearing before the local society of security analysts, small meetings of a few analysts, and one-on-one meetings.)

Most security analysts' meetings consist of the chief executive officer giving a speech followed by questions and answers. Sometimes samples of the company's products are shown or given away. Sometimes a slide presentation is shown; occasionally, a motion picture.

In any communication, the professional must be careful to treat all investors and those who influence investors fairly and equally. The principal regulatory authority, the Securities and Exchange Commission, is particularly zealous in trying to make sure that no investor, analyst, reporter, or editor gets one iota of material information before anyone else.

Fulfilling this obligation is sometimes difficult when a knowledgeable, intelligent security analyst asks a question that no one else has the perception to ask. If the question is answered and new information that could materially affect the price of the stock is revealed, the company must as promptly as possible communicate the information to the mass of investors by whatever means available. The first routine way is by telephoning Dow Jones Newswire, Reuters Newswire, United Press, and Associated Press. Often it is advisable also to send the information out over the PR Newswire to insure national coverage. The PR Newswire and a similar service, the Business Newswire, charge for their services. The basic PR Newswire goes into over 150 publications, wire services, and electronic networks. Transmittal over the PR Newswire satisfies the obligation public companies have for prompt disclosure.

In every kind of public relations, the ideal professional is knowledgeable, skilled, and experienced, but these qualities are especially desirable in financial public relations. The professional should be able to talk as an equal with security analysts, account executives, sophisticated investors, and veteran financial writers. Yet they must also be able to translate technical terms into plain talk. Ideally, an annual report is easy reading for the least experienced stockholder while not boring to the most sophisticated security analyst.

Media releases must be written so that reporters and editors at broad-based or smaller publications can readily understand them, so that they can be used as is if an editor so desires. The professional needs to know enough to be able to make the task of reporters, editors, and writers easy. Many professionals, or executives acting in the capacity of public relations professionals, fall short of this ideal. Most conspicuously they make **Common Mistake #20: Failing to put the percentage change in a media release on earnings.** The principal news in an earnings press release is not the absolute amount of the earnings but the degree to which the earnings for the year, six months, or quarter exceeded or fell below the earnings for the previous like period. That's the significance. Absolute figures have little or no meaning to most readers of a publication.

When editors, writers, or reporters receive a release without the percentages, they must do the calculating. First, this annoys them unnecessarily, which may be reflected in their attitudes toward the corporation and how the release is rewritten or used. Second, they may calculate the percentages wrong. After all, they are human.

In financial public relations, there is usually plenty of time available for planning and execution. If meetings before the New York Society of Security Analysts or other local analysts' societies are desired, several weeks' notice is usually necessary. However, special meetings of small groups of appropriate analysts can be easily arranged. They just cost more.

The budget can affect the planning. Annual reports can be black and white, two color, or four color, 8 pages, 12 pages, 16 pages, or longer, include expensive photography and artwork or be just type. Quarterly reports can be elaborate or simple. Highly paid experts can be retained, or the work can be done mostly by the financial vice president. Direct mail to account executives may be used. Advertising can multiply the cost of financial public relations.

The decision as to how much money a company should spend on financial public relations depends on a number of factors: Will the company be raising additional capital in the future? Will the company be acquiring other companies? Is the company a likely take-over candidate with its present price–earnings ratio? How much can the company afford to spend on financial public relations? Can the company get its story across to a sufficient number of the right kinds of prospective investors solely through security analysts and the press? Are there large holdings of stock by institutions or wealthy individuals that may be offered for sale? Is the company's price–earnings ratio low compared to what it would be if the attributes of the stock were widely known? Are the less expensive avenues of communication closed to the company because of the company's small size, unglamorous business, or previously poor financial public relations?

It's not an easy decision to make. The best procedure is usually for a competent professional to devise a plan, stating how much it will cost and what it will accomplish. The chief executive officer need then answer only one question (if the CEO has confidence in the professional): Is it worth it?

To sum up: The fundamental purpose of financial public relations is usually to improve the price–earnings ratio. The ultimate audiences are individual and institutional investors. The intermediary audiences include security analysts, the press, and sometimes account executives. The most common forms of communication used are the telephone, press release, annual report, quarterly report, annual meeting, and security analyst meetings. A variety of other forms may be used. Which audiences to emphasize and which tools to use are determined primarily by the nature of the corporation (subject) and its credibility and ability to communicate (source). The principal authority, the SEC, insists that no investor or person who might influence an investor can be given information that is not widely available. The ideal public relations professional understands financial jargon but communicates in plain talk so that the significance of any information can be readily understood by all audiences. Time for planning and execution is seldom a problem, except in countering bad news and in fulfilling the SEC requirement for prompt disclosure. The budget can make a significant difference in what can be done. The amount a corporation should spend depends on the situation, size, and aims of the individual corporation.

HOW INTELLIGENT IDENTIFICATION CAUSED THE COMMON STOCK OF A DIVERSIFIED COMPANY TO BE PROPERLY APPRECIATED BY THE FINANCIAL COMMUNITY

(The name of the company is fictional and a few unessential facts have been changed, but otherwise this case history is true.)

In 1974, if a member of the financial community asked, "What kind of a company is Renwick Products, Inc.?" the answer was likely to be, "Oh you know us—we used to be the big coffee company."

The company had this backward-looking definition because it had only recently discontinued its coffee operations, in which it had been the world's leader, and begun to emphasize food-related products, without giving the financial community sufficient guidance. Its self-description was a jumble. Not that Renwick Products is easy to describe in a few words. It is in a number of businesses, including cocoa bean processing, lard, salad dressing, animal feeds, small loan, and trucking. Principally because of this lack of a clear identity, Renwick common stock was selling at a price–earnings ratio that was less than two-thirds the multiple of the Standard & Poor's industrial average. Management felt the stock price did not fairly represent the company's excellent earnings record and outlook, so an investor relations function was initiated to improve the situation.

The key to the solution devised by a former Wall Streeter now seems obvious—like Columbus' method of standing an egg on its end. It was to define the company as an Atlanta-based food company. This was accurate. The company was heavily concentrated in food and food-related businesses but in danger of being defined as a

137

conglomerate. Being defined as a food company meant that the stock was classified in an industry that had extensive coverage by securities analysts and a higher price–earnings ratio. And the food identification made it easier for security analysts, registered representatives, investment advisors, and investors to place the company. They knew where to begin.

The food identification was carried through all the company's financial communications. The annual report cover consisted of a foldout photograph featuring a broad variety of food products. Inside, the information was organized under the headings: Domestic Food Operations, International Food Operations, and Other Operations. Each press release included the following paragraph:

"Renwick Products, Inc. is an Atlanta-based food company whose major operations are in the United States, Brazil and Colombia. It processes and markets consumer and institutional foods, cocoa bean products, and feeds for poultry and other animals. The company's nonfood activities include Whittingham Insurance Companies, Martin Manufacturing and Atlanta Services, all headquartered in Atlanta.

As a consequence of this fundamental change in identification and the competent use of meetings with analysts, as well as a continued growth in earnings, the financial community paid more attention to Renwick Products. The stock's price–earnings ratio increased nearly 50 percent. The stock's price more than doubled in two years and then split two for one. A rose by any other name may not smell sweeter, but it sure is harder to find in the garden directory.

HOW A GROWING, UNDERRATED CAPITAL GOODS COMPANY LESSENED THE POSSIBILITY OF AN UNFRIENDLY TAKEOVER

In the seven years from 1971 through 1977, Midland-Ross had traced an enviable record of growth and diversification that was not being recognized by investors. Earnings had increased tenfold, to

$2.11 a share from 21 cents. Continuation of this growth was expected by management, but the company's common stock sold at a 4.4 percent discount from book value and at a below-average price–earnings ratio, making the company a potential takeover target. A few large New York banks owned 17 percent of the outstanding shares. These big blocks hung over the market, depressing the price and making a takeover easier.

A benchmark study conducted as the basis for planning disclosed that most investment professionals who knew the company at all considered it cyclical, "a rather mundane capital goods company selling mature products to mature markets." Standard & Poor's classified it "metal products—foundry." Research coverage by brokerage firms was extremely thin, with only five firms following the company and three of those in Cleveland. Even among investment professionals, few gave the company much chance of continuing its 13 percent annual growth in earnings per share. Awareness of the company's technological capabilities scarcely existed. Neither was there any awareness of the favorable dynamics of the company's markets. Opportunities for improving performance through better asset management were erroneously thought to be exhausted. Future performance was seen as depending more on general economic conditions and capital goods spending. Less than half the respondents rated the stock a "buy."

The fundamental objective of the company's financial public relations plan was to achieve a fair market evaluation for the common stock that would properly reflect both the record and prospects for the future, thereby diminishing the risk of an unwanted takeover at a bargain price, lowering the company's cost of capital, and enhancing its potential for favorable acquisitions and mergers.

The following strategies were recommended by the company's public relations agency, Carl Byoir & Associates, Inc.:

1. Increase awareness of the company among brokerage firm analysts, institutional analysts and portfolio managers, and registered representatives (brokers).
2. Increase research coverage by brokerage firms, particularly those serving individual investors.

3. Dilute the importance of a few large institutions by broadening the shareholder base.
4. Improve investor awareness of Midland-Ross's technological capabilities.
5. Demonstrate growth potential in existing and new markets.

Guiding principles in carrying out the program were simple in concept but demanding in execution: to establish an image of quality and efficiency for Midland-Ross in every element through which impressions would be formed, and to create and maintain a highly personalized style in establishing direct contact with the desired audiences. Meticulous planning and detailed follow-up were required. The following specific activities were undertaken:

• Twenty-four meetings with analysts, portfolio managers, brokers, and shareholders were held in several cities selected on the basis of investment demographics and location (St. Louis, Chicago, Los Angeles, San Francisco, Cincinnati, Columbus, Miami, New York, London, Cleveland, Boston, and Baltimore). Each event encompassed 12 distinct planning steps, from initial contacts in selected cities through engraved invitations to personalized mailing of transcripts. Analysts were selected on the basis of known stature; each meeting represented from 75 percent to 90 percent of funds managed in each city.

• A fact book was developed to meet the need of analysts and portfolio managers for in-depth information on the company not included in the annual report or SEC Form 10-K. This was given wide distribution to 7,500 analysts through computerized mailing lists; an additional 5,000 were requested by analysts and brokers.

• A corporate synopsis ("Highlights") was developed and mailed to 11,000 account executives at brokerage firms.

• A new corporate film was prepared, featuring Louis Rukeyser as narrator, along with an expanded and improved slide presentation covering operating and financial data, for use at investment presentations.

• A field trip to Midland-Ross's Technical Center drew 18 analysts and portfolio managers from six cities.

- A backgrounder was developed for use with the media to arouse interest in Midland-Ross and provide a handy reference source. It was distributed to 250 news outlets to increase media exposure. Media interviews were arranged in investment meeting cities and with Dow Jones for the first time.
- Annual and quarterly reports were improved, based in part on a survey of key analysts and money managers.
- A new corporate advertising program in which each ad was filled with facts about the company pulled 3,000 responses for more information (versus 200 for a previous campaign).

The results were as follows:

- Awareness of Midland-Ross's technological capabilities, as measured by before-and-after surveys, climbed dramatically. Before the campaign, only 13 percent of the target audience rated Midland-Ross as "superior" in research and development; afterward, 60 percent rated it this way.
- Coverage by research departments of brokerage firms also dramatically increased; 24 reports were written on the company compared to 8 in the preceding year.
- Retail buying put Midland-Ross common stock on the most actively traded list.
- Institutional holdings were diluted. Two New York City banks sold 674,000 shares, mostly to 14 other institutions that took new positions, as well as to individuals. Individual stockholders of record increased by 800, reversing a ten-year downtrend during which the number of individual stockholders had decreased 25 percent.

The stock's price climbed from a range of $14–16 in 1977 and $14–21 in 1978 to $27.625 at the end of 1979. This represented a premium of more than $6 per share over book value compared to a discount of $3 before the program was launched. During the year, the price–earnings ratio of the Standard & Poor's index declined, yet Midland-Ross's price–earnings ratio rose from 7.25 to 7.78—from 17 percent below the stock market's average, as measured by Standard & Poor's 500 Index, to 13 percent above.

11

IMPROVING
WORKER PRODUCTIVITY

In employee communications, the executive faces a different kind of central problem than in other kinds of public relations. All nine determinants need to be considered, but the emphasis is unique.

The fundamental purpose of employee public relations is primarily to reduce costs by improving worker productivity. This may be accomplished by improving worker morale, by making it easier for management to organize production efficiently, by making the company a better place to work and thereby more attractive to more productive employees, by reducing absenteeism, by helping to reduce the possibility of unionization, and by lessening the possibility of a strike.

There's no problem about identifying the audience. It's the company's employees.

The source of the communications is the management of the company.

The principal communication form is the company newspaper or magazine. Other widely used forms include meetings, letters, posters, bulletin board notices, booklets, handouts, and slide presentations. Less widely used are TV, motion pictures, telephone calls, and comic books.

Here we come close to the central problem of employee communications. Unlike other kinds of public relations, all the forms of communication and the subjects to be considered are under company control. Bad news need not be communicated or can be communicated precisely as the corporation wishes. There are no media to distort the news or decide what should or should not be communicated to the ultimate audience.

Just as the very flexibility of a letter makes it so difficult to write, so the freedom and control management enjoys in employee communications creates its own problems: What should be said? How should it be said?

The temptation is to talk only about what management would like to discuss and to communicate in the ways most convenient and comfortable to management. But it's dangerous to ignore news that is important to employees. They'll probably hear about it by word of mouth. And the rumors will probably be inaccurate and more damaging to morale than the truth.

Further, the subjects and forms that cause the least discomfort to management are probably not those that will best accomplish the purpose. The management of one utility, for example, decided to educate employees about the company's needs for lower taxes and permission to build more nuclear and coal-fired power plants. The management intended that the employees would then carry the message to their relatives, friends, neighbors, and acquaintances.

The form chosen was a video cassette shown to groups of employees by each local manager. One employee termed it "a slick, professional, typically unstirring industrial film." The result was the opposite of what the company had hoped. There were grunts, snorts, and derisory comments when the tape was on. One of the first comments after the end was, "This is bull." Answers to questions were greeted with laughter.

Management was talking about what it wanted to talk about in the way management wanted to. Management had ignored a vital requirement of persuasion—to make the audience empathize with the source or to so focus the attention of the audience on material and psychological benefits that the audience ignores or forgets the source.

In employee relations, the audience knows management controls the means of communication. It is therefore even more important than in other kinds of public relations that the communications deal with what interests the audience and be in the forms the audience prefers. As we shall see, audiovisual forms are not usually the most preferred forms of communication. And the most prevalent form—the company newspaper or magazine—has its limitations. *The New York Times* can heap praise on a company that would be unbelievable in the company's own newspaper.

What are the most effective forms? What are employees most interested in? Managements are becoming increasingly aware of the overwhelming importance of these questions. Some have surveyed their employees. Here is a case history with typical results.

HOW A LARGE CHEMICAL COMPANY DISCOVERED WHAT REALLY INTERESTS ITS EMPLOYEES

A less onerous than usual survey technique was recommended to a large chemical company by its employee relations consultant, Towers, Perrin, Forster & Crosby. Fifty-two subjects that might be discussed in company communications were printed on cards about the size of playing cards. Some of the subjects were:

- Company (or divisional) goals, problems, and financial results.
- New projects, ventures, and expansion programs.
- Organizational changes.
- How the work I do fits into the overall operations of the company (or my division/location).
- Various occupations throughout the company (or in my division/location).
- What the company is doing in export markets.
- The people who manage the company.
- Senior management responses to employee questions.
- Competition and how it affects our business.
- Where the company stands on important public issues (e.g., energy, bilingualism, consumerism).

- What the company is doing to protect our environment.
- Safety programs.
- Opportunities for promotion.
- Salary and wage policies.
- Employee benefits.
- Women in the company—jobs and opportunities.
- News of employee recreational activities.

A randomly selected sample of employees were asked to sort the cards under four different headings:

- I am *most interested* in getting more information about . . .
- I am *interested* in getting more information about . . .
- I am *not interested* in getting information about . . .
- I have *no interest at all* in the following subjects . . .

Before reading further, you may want to test your judgment of what really interests employees by answering these questions:

What one subject most interested a wide range of employees?

What single subject interested managerial employees most?

What subject did research and technical employees most often classify under "most interesting"?

The answers are given in the next paragraph. If you want hints, think back to previous chapters on motivation. What subject deals with a material benefit needed most by the kind of employees who necessarily identify with the company?

The answers:

"Salary and wage policies" was the only subject of overriding importance to a wide range of employees. Discussions with employees following the survey revealed that they were not unhappy about the amount of their pay but about the lack of information about how salaries and wages were arrived at. They wanted to know what the ranges were, how the pay of similar employees in different locations compared, and how their pay compared with that of similar employees in other companies.

Many employees wanted more information on promotional opportunities, job security, and employee benefits. College-educated employees, in particular, ranked promotional opportunities high, as well as company goals, problems, and financial results. Employees over 40, not surprisingly, showed a lower interest in opportunities for promotion and a higher interest in employee benefits than younger employees.

High-ranking subjects among all employees included "what the company is doing in other parts of the world" and "the end uses of our products and materials." Subjects in which employees were interested but felt they got enough information were safety programs and personal news, such as anniversaries, retirements, and promotions.

Managerial employees were most interested in "where the company stands on important public issues."

Research and technical employees ranked first the card with "company goals, problems, and financial results."

Among clerical employees, the subject "how the work I do fits into the overall operations of the company (or my division/location)" ranked very high.

To test the merits of various forms of communication, 16 different means of communication were put on cards. Here are some:

Group meetings.
A company publication.
Booklets and brochures.
Bulletin board notices.
Newsletters.
Union meetings.
Annual or periodic printed reports.

Employees were asked to classify the cards under two headings:

I *now* get information about the company from the following sources.
I would *prefer* to get information about the company from the following sources.

Employees ranked the existing sources of information in the following order:

1. A company publication.
2. Bulletin board notices.
3. Group meetings.
4. Newsletters.
5. Letters from management.
6. Booklets and brochures.

The order of the forms they preferred, however, differed significantly. The overwhelming preference was for group meetings. Other media ranking high on the preferred list were: letters from management, bulletin board notices, a company publication, newsletters, and annual or printed reports.

The results of this survey are consistent with similar surveys. AT&T, for example, asked employees in more than 20 of its subsidiary companies what articles in the company publication interested them most. The answer was articles on career advancement and personal benefits.

A company exists, so far as an employee is concerned, in order to pay the employee wages or salary. That is its primary purpose. That's what employees want to know about. They are not stupid. They know that some employees get paid more than others. They know that some companies pay more than others. They want their company to be fair to them. It may be easier to explain salary and wage policies in a capital-intensive company, because salaries and wages will be above average, but lucid explanations may be more necessary and more productive in a labor-intensive company. That's where employee public relations can make the biggest difference.

Moreover, practically every employee in the United States wants something more from his or her company than simply fair pay. Most want an opportunity to get ahead, a company they can be proud of, and a decent pension when they retire. They want both material and psychological benefits. "Where the company stands on important public issues" ranked highest among managerial employees in the chemical company survey because the managers' leadership positions cause them to identify with the company more. But other employees also want to work for a company that is socially constructive. They want to feel they are part of something worthwhile, bigger than themselves. That's why "what the company is doing in other parts of the world" and "the end uses of our products and materials" ranked high. It's why clerical employees wanted to know "how the work I do fits into the overall operations of the company (or my division/location)."

Employee communications can accomplish their purpose only if they fulfill the material and psychological needs of the employees. Contrast the following case history with the example of the utility that used the video cassette to try to educate its employees about its need for lower taxes and less restrictions on nuclear power development.

HOW AN EMPLOYEE COMMUNICATIONS PROGRAM HELPED COUNTER CONTINUING NEGATIVE PUBLICITY IN THE PRESS

TV, radio, newspapers, and magazines were continually attacking Standard Oil of California. The company recognized that answering the charges through press releases and company statements would be committing Common Mistake #1 (giving further publicity to bad news in an attempt to rebut it), but communicating rebuttals to employees would not. Employees read and remember every criticism of their company that appears in the press, on radio, or on TV. If they fail to see it on their own, family and friends tell them about it.

Communicating directly to employees would minimize the effect of the negative publicity on worker morale and would, in addition, favorably affect other audiences. Some employees are also investors. All 35,000 employees are citizens who influence legislation, and all 35,000 have relations, friends, and acquaintances with whom they can be vocal in the company's defense or silently assent to criticism of it.

The professional public relations people at Standard Oil of California recognized the need for rapid rebuttal to each specific charge. The longer a charge goes unanswered, the more effective it is. They aimed at responding to each charge within 48 hours, within 24 if possible. They decided on a form consisting of a one-page printed sheet that began with the heading "Charge" and followed with a brief summary of the accusation along with its source. Below that was a heading, "Response," followed by four paragraphs of objective facts (not mere arguments and opinions) that could easily be quoted.

The sheets were handed to employees in the company's corporate headquarters at noon and at quitting time at the exits to the seven buildings where they work. Each rebuttal was wired to two dozen field headquarters in North America and Europe, where it was immediately posted on the bulletin board. Some field locations also printed and handed out copies to employees. Similar communications were sent to all retired employees. Additional copies were given to any employee who asked for them. One asked for three full sets so he could "get my teenage kids off my back."

A poll of employees conducted several months after the campaign showed that about 80 percent felt the rebuttals were credible and of value in discussions with families and friends.

Note the difference in subject matter between the utility's effort and that of the oil company. The oil company's employees didn't like what their families, friends, and neighbors were saying or might be thinking about the company they work for. The communications program filled an emotional need of the employees. In contrast, the utility's communication filled no such felt need. Employees don't see how a company's taxes affect them. And they don't like the company going against what may be the public good.

Note the difference in the forms. The oil company's communication was direct, so apparently unslick the audience was unconscious of the form, only conscious of the content. ("The art that conceals art.") The utility's video cassette was indirect, mechanical, inhuman; the form drew attention to itself and detracted from the message.

Employees don't want information that seems canned. (Audiovisual communications ranked low in the chemical company survey.) They want direct communications as personal as possible, preferably with opportunities for them to communicate to management and for management to respond.

Of course, the time and therefore money involved in meetings must be carefully weighed, but if not overdone, meetings can be highly cost-effective. Pitney Bowes, for example, has been holding two-hour jobholder meetings every year during April and May for over 20 years. At these meetings, management reports to the employees on wages, benefits, profit sharing, the condition of the company, and the outlook. Employees ask questions of the management from the floor or submit them in writing. The questions need not be signed. When management cannot answer a question immediately, the employee is told, "We'll look into it." And management does, reporting back to employees.

As a consequence, morale is high at Pitney Bowes. Employee turnover and absenteeism are below industry averages. Productivity is better than in other factories. Employees are willing to pitch in with extra effort during crises.

There is, however, no substitute for a company publication. Pitney Bowes reinstated its company newsletter, while continuing the meetings. Mississippi Management, Inc., found that a company publication could make a big difference. Here are the facts:

Mississippi Management supervises 11 Holiday Inns in the states of Mississippi, Louisiana, and Florida and in the Cayman Islands. In 1974 employee morale was low and turnover high. The company had no publication for its 900 employees, so management decided to start one. The company's public relations counselor acted as the publisher; the secretaries at each of the inns were the correspondents. Training sessions were held for the secretaries at headquarters. Each received a manual describing the kinds of stories and photographs desired and how to present the facts.

Some stories in the eight-page tabloid newspaper dealt with material benefits and company policy, but perhaps more important in this instance were the stories that appealed to each employee's need to identify with an admirable organization—with something bigger than himself or herself. For example, a story about a successful opening or expansion of a hotel interested employees of other hotels and caused the employees of the hotel being discussed to feel pride in their accomplishments. The newspaper also included a gripe column that allowed for two-way communication.

As a direct consequence of the newspaper, morale improved and employee turnover was reduced.

The attitude of management is all-important in employee communications. Blessed is the employee communications professional working for a company in which the chief executive officer realizes the need to communicate to employees about topics that interest them in the ways they prefer. Cursed is the professional who is given no straw to make bricks, who is expected to flimflam employees.

Professionals who can carry out the mandate of an enlightened management are not in short supply. Usually only straight newspaper-style writing is needed: factual, objective, clear. Short sentences, words in common use, concrete personal nouns, and action verbs will make what is communicated easy to understand and interesting to read.

Of course, if employee relations have degenerated so far that unionization threatens—or in any already unionized company, a strike threatens—then more specialized communicators are needed. In particular, communications in these circumstances must be carefully tailored so as not to violate the rules of the authorities, principally the National Labor Relations Board.

No new common mistakes are introduced in this chapter because most of those made in employee communications are the same as those made in other kinds of communications, principally: #12—not concentrating a communication sufficiently on the self-interest of the audience; #14—causing the audience to think "Why are you telling me all this?"; #15—not making the source of a communication sufficiently empathetic.

All three result from the unique fact that in employee communications there is no intermediary audience between the source and the ultimate audience. In publicity and financial public relations, the media, investment firms, banks, and advisory organizations screen out the nonrelevant and are themselves empathetic sources.

151

12

MINIMIZING
HARMFUL LEGISLATION
AND REGULATION

Successful lobbying is one reason some reporters and some of the general public distrust business.

Put yourself in the place of a citizen who, along with others, is opposing a change in zoning regulations that would allow a factory to be erected near your home. Suppose the change is effected without your knowing why. Wouldn't you feel some chicanery was going on? Wouldn't you feel antagonistic toward the company? Wouldn't you discourage your relatives and friends from working there? Wouldn't it be difficult to persuade you that the company was right on another issue at a later date?

Proper public relations can minimize or even eliminate the resentment you and others may feel when the proposed regulation is passed. Public relations can do even more. It can help, even be the chief ingredient, in getting a bill or regulation passed or defeated.

Influencing legislation and regulations differs in an important respect from a corporation's other public relations efforts: The ultimate audience is limited. In most public relations, it is the knowledge, attitude, or actions of a mass audience that count: customers, investors, or employees. In contrast, the ultimate key audience for most public relations that aims to influence legislation or regulations usually is a small group: members of Congress (sometimes only key members), the president of the United States and his advisors, members of certain regulatory bodies, or state and city legislators and officials. The mass audience, the voters, is usually influenced only because voters in turn will influence those in government positions. Exceptions are public relations efforts to block or enact initiatives and referenda.

Since the shortest distance between two points is a straight line, the tendency is to by-pass the voters and deal one-on-one with those who control legislation and regulations. Lobbying is so much simpler. Contributions to a campaign fund by a corporation's political action committee can make the politician receptive to hearing the corporation's viewpoint. The corporate representative can explain, say, how a proposed bill will hamper the corporation's productivity or sales and may therefore result in layoffs at the company's plants. Politicians don't need to be told that increased unemployment in their districts will reflect badly on them and may make their reelection more difficult.

Lobbying is not only an attractive way to influence legislation and regulation, it is essential for practically every sizable corporation in the United States, either through its own representatives, an industry association, or both. Every year hundreds of thousands of laws and countless regulations are proposed, any one of which could seriously affect the sales, costs, profits, or survival of an individual company. Lobbying is part of the cost of doing business successfully today. Continual watch needs to be maintained over national, state, city, and other government and regulatory bodies. What they do needs to be monitored so that laws and regulations that will damage a company or industry without a commensurate benefit to people generally can be prevented or modified.

Most of the time this is easy to do so long as the company or industry devotes the necessary number of people with appropriate expertise to the task and establishes a working relationship with legislators whose districts contain plant facilities and a sizable workforce. Often just bringing a politician's attention to a pertinent fact, or even the mere statement of opposition, will be enough. Many proposals are poorly thought out or have weak support.

153

However, the material and position presented to a legislator or regulator must be factual and related to the public interest. A corporate government affairs representative needs to retain credibility in order to be effective.

Nowadays an experienced lobbyist keeps in mind that legislators have many demands on their time. The lobbyist is concise and to the point. The modern lobbyist is thoroughly familiar, even expert, in all aspects of the matter under discussion. Questions are answered quickly, firmly, and easily when at all possible. No longer does being an old buddy of the legislator or regulator suffice.

There are several degrees of pressure a lobbyist can bring to bear. The following case history shows what can be done directly, without influencing the mass of voters. The name of the company is fictitious, but the events and other organizations named are real. It is written by Andrew R. Paul, who has been practicing government relations for multinational corporations in Washington, D.C., for over ten years.

HOW A PROLABOR BILL THAT WOULD HAVE RAISED PRODUCTION COSTS WAS DEFEATED

The Maxi-Universal Corporation is a large manufacturer of construction equipment, machine tools, aircraft parts, and other industrial products with an annual revenue of over $2.5 billion.

Earnings had increased in 1977 and 1978, but the company's administrative costs have been increasing disproportionately. The primary reasons are increased regulation of industry by government in the areas of environment, energy, and workplace safety, and increases in costs imposed by government, such as higher social security taxes and a higher minimum wage.

The company was also under government pressure to reduce its consumption of fuel oil at its major fuel-burning installations and to switch to a less scarce fuel such as coal. Such a conversion would entail substantial capital investment.

Finally, new union settlements for machinists and other skilled workers, coupled with increases in the cost of material, had forced

Maxi-Universal to raise its prices to its customers in order to maintain its profit margin, already in danger of being further eroded by inflation.

Concurrent with the increase in labor and overhead costs, legislative activity by the unions was stepped up. In March 1977, for example, the House of Representatives defeated by a margin of only 12 votes the Common Situs Picketing Bill, which many companies feared would result in numerous secondary boycotts at their facilities. Another bill creating an Agency for Consumer Protection was narrowly defeated only through concerted action by industry government affairs executives, such as Maxi-Univeral's Washington vice president.

In May 1978, more labor-oriented legislation, the Labor Law Reform Bill, arrived on the Senate floor for vote, having already passed the House. This bill would have speeded up the union election process at plants, given unions the right to equal access to plant sites in addressing employees, and forced employers to pay back wages and benefits under a "make whole" provision where there had been a delay in contract disputes. The management of Maxi-Universal considered the bill highly inflationary and viewed it as an attempt by labor to bolster an already decreasing membership.

Because of industry-wide opposition to the Labor Law Reform Bill, Maxi's Washington vice president elected to work hand in glove with the National Action Group of the National Association of Manufacturers and the U.S. Chamber of Commerce, acting as a clearinghouse for information and guidelines for opposing the bill.

It appeared that there were sufficient votes in the Senate to pass the bill. Realizing this, a large antilabor bloc of senators elected to organize a filibuster on the Senate floor as a strategy to defeat the bill. They chose this legislative tactic knowing that many of the senators who would vote for the bill because of pressure from their labor constituents would *not* vote to invoke cloture (limit debate) during the filibuster.

Industry now went to work to support the filibuster. The real effort lay in persuading other senators to vote against cloture each time a vote is called (normally three).

It was now up to Maxi-Universal's Washington office to generate a flow of communication from the plants in the field to their respective senators. Maxi's Washington VP immediately prepared a memorandum to all the plant managers outlining the objectionable aspects of the bill and requesting them to write their senators. Even though the memo included a sample letter, the Washington VP insisted that the managers discuss in their own words the impact of the bill on their operations in order to make the approach as personalized as possible. Because Maxi maintained plants and major offices in seven states, a total of 14 senators were contacted from the field.

In addition, Maxi's VP personally visited these senators, as well as others, in order to convey the company's opposition to the bill. As an integral part of his job as corporate public affairs VP, he had taken the time to cultivate working relationships, and often friendships, with the senators and their respective staffs. These relationships, coupled with the company's economic importance in each of the states, gave him access to the legislators when it was needed.

As the filibuster continued, a first then a second attempt to invoked cloture failed. With prospects for a third vote coming up, the industry rallied to keep those senators who appeared marginal and whose position became less clear.

In the meantime, with the help of the National Action Group, Maxi identified three key senators from states where the company maintained plants and whose votes against cloture were essential. The plant managers from the three states were flown to Washington and, together with the Washington VP, paid personal visits to the senators to reemphasize the importance of defeating the legislation.

As history shows, after six unsuccessful votes to invoke cloture, the Senate referred the Labor Law Reform Bill back to committee where, for all intents and purposes, it will remain until perhaps it is revived in another session of Congress in a more palatable form.

The efforts of Maxi-Universal alone did not prevent the vote for cloture from being successful. The efforts of 500 companies and industry associations utilizing the same public affairs techniques to inform their senators won the day. The actions of Maxi-Universal illustrate the avenues available to companies to make their views on national issues known.

Even though the salary or fees of a lobbyist may seem high, the cost of lobbying is small compared to the cost of influencing voters who will in turn influence government officials. But sometimes going the long way round is necessary.

And when lobbying is successful, giving publicity to the company's point of view along the way can reduce the backlash from disappointed opponents. The media will feel the public has been informed. Less rabid opponents will grant that the company's position has some merit. Undecided people won't be easily swayed to be against the company.

Ideally, therefore, a public relations plan that aims to influence legislation or regulation includes both lobbying and public relations. The mixture depends primarily on (1) the degree of interest among voters and the media; (2) how important the outcome is to the corporation or industry; and (3) how strong the opposition is. Sometimes only a simple release to trade media is necessary; sometimes a full range of communications devices is warranted, including holding press conferences, arranging meetings, advertising, setting up a speakers bureau and writing speeches, arranging for proponents to appear on radio and TV, sparking a letter-writing campaign, conducting a direct mail campaign to raise funds and/or influence voters, and monitoring the opposition's appearances on radio and TV so as to appeal for equal time.

Meetings are often the heart of any political public relations plan that goes beyond lobbying. A successful meeting does more than convince the people at the meeting of the views desired by the source. The people at the meeting become themselves vocal expositors of the desired view. And the meeting is covered by the press, giving additional exposure to views that may no longer be news.

Setting up a series of meetings requires organizing talent plus abundant energy. As a rule, the functions can be divided into two categories: (1) establishing when and where the meetings are to

157

take place; and (2) providing the information and communication aids for each meeting. Here's an example.

HOW A SERIES OF MEETINGS HELPED CHANGE
THE GOVERNMENT OF YONKERS

In the 1930s, the city of Yonkers had the traditional mayor–council system of government. A local committee of the League of Women Voters decided that the city manager system was superior and decided to change the city's form of government. This small committee, chaired by a woman we'll call Mrs. B., decided on a series of teas. Operating completely outside any political party, the committee held its first tea for a group of women friends and enlisted the aid of Edith P. Welty, a former schoolteacher who was active in community affairs. Mrs. Welty spoke at the meeting and convinced those attending not only that the city manager plan of government was superior but that each of those attending should hold a tea inviting none of those present but all new people who would in turn hold teas inviting new people, and so on. It was the pyramid plan applied to politics. When a woman decided to have a tea, she called Mrs. B., who arranged for Mrs. Welty or some other speaker to attend. Each meeting was reported to the city's only newspaper, *The Yonkers Herald Statesman*. Men interested in community affairs, although not previously in politics, became involved, followed by some who had been active in the Republican party but who were dissatisfied with the party's local leadership. *The Yonkers Herald Statesman* ran supporting editorials. Enough signatures were obtained to put a referendum on the ballot in 1936.

The referendum was defeated, but the effort was not. The pyramiding teas continued. Again the referendum appeared on the ballot. Again it was defeated. More stories and editorials appeared in *The Yonkers Herald Statesman*. Again in 1939 the referendum to change the form of government was put on the ballot, and this time it passed.

When the city government was reorganized, Mrs. Welty became the mayor, now a nominal post. She chaired the commission that enacted the laws and appointed the city manager. A new district attorney conducted investigations that resulted in the imprisonment of a former councilman and in the chief of police shooting himself.

While the support of the local newspaper was essential, this support only came about because of the efficient organizing of the meetings.

However the meetings are organized, the responsibility for each meeting needs to be lodged in a single person, even though he or she may be assisted by others. The success of a meeting, like the success of any other form of communication, depends upon how well the nine determinants are fulfilled.

CHECKLIST FOR SETTING UP MEETINGS FOR A POLITICAL PURPOSE

Purpose: What is the audience expected to do? Vote as desired? Organize or attend another meeting? Get people to attend another meeting? Write to a legislator or official? Contribute? Volunteer for committee work?

Subject: Is there widespread interest in the subject? What is the attitude of the audience toward the subject? Who are the recognized experts on the subject?

Audiences: How will the audience be attracted to the meeting? Will most of the audience feel the same way toward the subject and the speaker—that is, will the audience be cohesive? Or will varying degrees of knowledge and attitude be represented? How will these meetings be used to influence other audiences? Should reporters be invited? Will they come? Will the reporters want to talk to the speaker afterward? Or before? Where should this take place?

Source: Who will speak? Who will introduce the speaker? Is having several speakers or a panel of speakers a good idea? How will the speaker get to the meeting? Might the speaker cancel at the last minute? What then?

Forms: How many people can the meeting room hold? (In politics, it's better to have too small a room than one that's too large, so as to engender a feeling of excitement and overwhelming interest.) Where is it located? How will people get there? How will they know how to get there? Are any visual aids or props to be used? Who will make sure the aids or props are there in plenty of time? How soon can anyone get into the meeting room? Is food or beverages to be served? When? Will there be questions afterward? Is it desirable to have some questions planted in the audience to stimulate discussion? What should the press release say? Is an advance text of the principal speech available? A biography of the principal speaker?

Professionals: What is the public relations professional's experience in conducting meetings? What is specifically required of the professional?

Time available: When does the meeting need to be over? What is the best length of time for the meeting? Does the speaker know how long he or she should speak?

Cost: How much will it cost? Is the expected result worth the cost?

Authorities: Who must approve the meeting place, the cost, the speech, the speakers, and so on? How detailed an explanation needs to be made to the authority or authorities?

In the following case history, note how meetings and publicity were combined to achieve a favorable result.

HOW VOTERS IN THE STATE OF WASHINGTON WERE CONVINCED THEY SHOULD CONTINUE TO PAY HIGHER TAXES

Washington State voters went to the polls in November 1977 to settle a controversial tax issue embodied in Initiative 348. Initiative 348 called for the repeal of a variable tax on gasoline sales that had gone into effect the previous July. (This was before the country became seriously concerned about the energy crisis.)

The new tax—the first of its kind in the nation—meant that revenues for transit and road programs could rise or fall depending on the price and consumption of gasoline. All other states had flat, cents-per-gallon taxes that remained static despite a doubling of gasoline prices and construction costs in the preceding five years.

Washington's variable tax set a floor of 9 cents a gallon (the existing rate prior to the new tax) and a ceiling of 12 cents. The actual price would fluctuate between those two figures. As it went into effect July 1, 1977, the tax was 11 cents a gallon.

Opponents of the tax immediately filed a repeal petition. Their ability to gather 200,000 signatures one week after the tax went into effect indicated vast voter antagonism to the levy.

Projects earmarked for the proceeds of the tax included road and bridge repairs, subsidies for local bus operations and the ferry system, construction of parking lots for bus riders, and construction of bicycle and pedestrian paths.

Public officials and leaders of business and labor knew that repeal would damage the state's economy, which was dependent on road and waterborne transportation; would require an increase in ferry charges; and would endanger the lives of motorists and pedestrians.

In late July, assistance was requested from The Road Information Program (TRIP) and its public relations counsel, Carl Byoir & Associates. TRIP, located in Washington, D.C., is a research and information agency supported by the roadbuilding industry in several states, including Washington.

Byoir had a little more than three months to plan, develop, and execute a program for TRIP that would turn voter sentiment in favor of the new tax so that repeal could be defeated. The problem was clear: How do you convince people that it is worth their while to pay higher taxes in order to get better roads?

The philosophy the agency developed for the TRIP program held that in order to get people concerned about their roads and to want them improved, people had to be convinced that they would derive some strong benefit from road repair. It did little good to tell people that their roads were in bad shape. Most already knew that. They had to be convinced that repairing the roads was worth the added cost to them personally.

Agency researchers immediately got busy checking Washington's road and bridge system to learn how it affected auto operating costs. If the annual extra cost to drivers of bad roads could be shown to be significantly higher than the annual cost of the tax, Stop 348 would have a strong pocketbook issue with which to kick off the campaign.

Using data from state and federal agencies, the research team found that Washington's motorists paid an average of $129 extra each year to drive over bad roads. This compared with the estimated $13 per year extra that each auto owner was being asked to pay under the tax to fix the roads. The difference was so significant the agency recommended that the cost comparison become a major theme of the campaign. The comparison was, in fact, used extensively in discussions with editors, press releases, backgrounders, brochures, and advertising.

The research staff spent two months putting together its data, and a report containing its conclusions was released to the media September 27 in Olympia, the state capital, and in Seattle and Spokane, the two largest cities in Washington. (See the press release on the following pages.)

Media response was immediate and thorough. The papers in Spokane and Seattle carried multicolumn stories (shown on the following pages), AP and UPI carried long summaries, and there were two television and five radio news reports in Seattle and Spokane. In all, 28 of 29 daily papers and 84 weeklies carried stories on the agency's findings and 14 papers followed with editorials opposing repeal of the tax using Byoir's figures to buttress their position.

An agency staffer then embarked on a six-day swing around the state for meetings with editors and columnists to explain the need for the tax, all the while emphasizing the cost differential between the tax and the extra amount motorists were forced to pay because of bad road conditions. These contacts resulted in numerous columns and editorials supporting the tax.

Back in Seattle, another agency representative helped organize a citizen's committee to defeat the initiative. He handled the public relations functions of developing campaign strategies, writing releases, organizing press conferences, and setting up media interviews for the committee members. He also researched and wrote releases on how each of the state's 36 counties would benefit from proceeds of the tax in terms of road and bridge repairs and mass transit and other transportation improvements.

The last major effort of the public relations campaign involved the planning and organizing of public forums on the tax issue. These were called "Local Government Days," and they provided an opportunity for city and county officials to meet with the public to tell constituents how the tax would benefit their communities. The forums were held in 54 cities and towns on November 1, a week before the election.

The vote on Initiative 348 was about as close as an election can get. More than 900,000 votes were cast. The initiative was defeated by only 834 votes, but because of the closeness of the tally, a recount was required by state law. As repeal opponents held their collective breath, the recount was completed on December 8. The final figure increased their margin of victory to 884 votes.

Whether to go beyond lobbying into meetings or other methods is usually decided by the lobbyist or other person in charge of government affairs, often not a public relations person. The lobbyist may handle most items without bringing in a public relations person at all. But when publicity is required, the recommendations of a public relations professional are often not just valuable but essential. As we have seen in Chapter 1 particularly, the principles that make for success in one-on-one and adversary situations are sometimes in conflict with the principles of mass persuasion.

From: Chad Hill   For release Tuesday, Sept. 27, 1977
        Western States Representative
        The Road Information Program
        100 Bush St. (415) 362-6971
        San Francisco, CA 94104

For: THE ROAD INFORMATION PROGRAM
        1750 Pennsylvania Avenue, N.W.
        Washington, D.C. 20006
        (202) 783-7010

BAD ROADS HIKE

DRIVING COSTS

OLYMPIA -- Rough roads add $280 million a year to Washington drivers'
costs because of wasted fuel, excessive tire wear and extra vehicle repairs,
said a study released today.

The typical Washington motorist drives an average of 5,000 miles a
year on bumpy, broken pavement that inflates annual vehicle operating costs
by an average of $129 per driver, according to The Road Information Program
(TRIP) of Washington, D.C.

Fuel savings alone would amount to 154 gallons per driver, worth
more than $97 a year, TRIP reported. The projected statewide fuel savings
of 335 million gallons is 17.8 percent of the state's average annual
motor-fuel consumption.

The research and information agency found:

-- Drivers use up to one-third more fuel when stopping or slowing to
   pass safely over rough, broken pavement before resuming normal
   speed.

-- Thirty-seven percent of Washington's 23,003 miles of paved main
   roads are deficient. This includes 5,226 miles rated "fair" and
   3,317 miles considered "poor" by inspection standards adhered to
   by all the states.

-- It costs an average of 45 percent more to drive on the 8,583 miles
   of "fair" and "poor" roads in Washington than on "very good"
   roads--8.4 cents-per-mile versus 5.8 cents-per-mile.

-- In King County alone, substandard roads added $52.7 million to
   drivers' costs in 1976--one-third more than it would have cost to
   drive on the same roads if they had been in good condition.

-- In Spokane County, substandard roads added $23.5 million to
   drivers' costs in 1976. This is 26 percent more than it would
   have cost to drive on the same roads if they had been in good
   condition.

TRIP reported that the state's drivers traveled 10.7 billion vehicle
miles in 1975, the latest year of record, on "poor" and "fair" main roads
at a cost of $897.8 million. Had these roads been in "very good" condition,
the travel would have cost only $617.7 million--a saving of $280.1 million,
or $129 per driver, the agency estimated.

(more)

TRIP's study included only the paved arterial and collector systems, which account for 40.4 percent of Washington's 56,879-mile total road system, but handle 96 percent of all traffic. Included were roads under state, county and municipal jurisdiction.

"Washington motorists are paying a premium to drive on uncomfortable, hazardous roads," said TRIP spokesman Jay Grant of Spokane, who announced the study findings.

"The state, counties and cities have fallen behind in road renewal because of a lack of funds," Grant said. "Washington needs to preserve and protect its roads to minimize highway maintenance costs and to reduce the number of accidents where poor pavement is a factor."

TRIP estimated it would cost $1.08 billion to rebuild the 3,317 miles of roads in "poor" condition and $381.3 million to resurface the 5,266 miles of roads considered "fair." Much of the mileage involved is eligible for federal-aid funds covering between 70 and 90 percent of the total cost.

An adequate road renewal program is essential to keep pace with an estimated 28 percent increase in traffic volume in Washington within the next 10 years, the study said. Three-fourths of the state's roads were built before 1940 and were not designed for today's traffic volume, maximum speed limits or vehicle weight.

TRIP's findings were based on scientific road tests that measured fuel consumption along with tire and vehicle wear relative to the physical condition of the pavement in use. Road tests were conducted by Paul J. Claffey and Associates of Potsdam, New York.

The tests showed that drivers used up to one-third more fuel when stopping or slowing to pass safely over rough, broken pavement before resuming normal speed.

Driving on substandard pavement also increased tire wear an average of 156 percent a year and accelerated brake, steering and suspension system wear by an average of 72 percent, according to the tests.

Study cites cost of rough roads

Rough roads cost Washington motorists an extra $280 million a year in wasted fuel, excessive tire wear and vehicle repairs, according to a highway-industry-sponsored study released yesterday.

The study was conducted by the Road Information Program of Washington, D.C., an organization which does research and distributes economic and technical data on transportation issues. It is sponsored by road builders, construction-equipment manufacturers and suppliers and others involved in highway engineering construction and financing.

The organization, known as TRIP, said it became interested in Washington when a national survey showed that poor roads are costing state motorists an additional $129 a year—compared with a national average of $91.

In King County, the study said, substandard roads added $52.7 million to drivers' costs in 1976—one third more than if the same roads had been in good condition.

State motorists drove 10.7 billion miles in 1975 on roads rated as poor and fair at a cost of $897 million, the report said. Had those roads been in very good condition the travel cost would have been only $617 million, the report said.

The report said 37 per cent of the state's arterial and collector roads are rated "poor" or "very poor" under standards of the American Association of State Highway and Transportation Officials. The major problems are rutted and broken pavement, worn shoulders and narrow lanes.

"In addition to the deterioration of arterial and collector roads, some sections of the interstate system in Washington are now 20 years old and need to be resurfaced or rebuilt," TRIP said.

The cost of rebuilding the state's 3,317 miles of poor roads and streets would be $1.08 billion, the organization said. Repair of roads described as fair would cost $381.3 million.

Over a five-year period, however, the savings to motorists would total $1.4 billion, the report said.

Poor roads add to drivers' costs

Rough roads in Spokane County add at least $23.5 million a year to drivers' costs because of wasted fuel, excessive tire wear and extra vehicle repairs, a private study has disclosed.

The study, prepared as part of a nationwide project by The Road Information Program (TRIP) of Washington, D.C., and released Monday, claims Spokane drivers' costs are only part of a $280 million bill rough roads provide statewide.

TRIP researches, evaluates and distributes economic and technical data on transportation issues. It is sponsored by road builders, construction equipment manufacturers and suppliers and other businesses involved in highway engineering, construction and financing.

The typical Washington motorist drives an average of 5,000 miles a year on bumpy, broken pavement that inflates annual vehicle operating costs by an averge of $129 per driver, according to TRIP.

Fuel savings statewide would amount to 154 gallons per driver, worth more than $97 a year, the report said, with an annual combined savings of 335 million gallons or 17.8 per cent of the state's average annual motor-fuel consumption.

W. Jay Grant, E1120 Twentieth, TRIP representative in the Spokane area, said agency research shows that drivers use up to one-third more fuel stopping or slowing for rough, broken pavement before resuming normal speed.

"For example, a standardized sedan traveling at a speed of 40 miles per hour used 16 percent more fuel when required to slow twice per mile, compared with not having to slow at all.

"Furthermore, the same vehicle at the same speed used 32 percent more fuel when it had to slow and then also stop twice per mile because of deteriorated pavement, compared with not having to slow or stop at all," he said. Grant noted that these stops were in addition to those required by traffic conditions.

He added that test vehicles operating on rough, bumpy and broken pavement also used extra fuel because of loss of traction on the uneven road surface and because of uneven power flow through the drive train as a result of excessive vibration.

The problem of rough roads applies to about 37 per cent of Washington's 23,003 miles of paved main roads, Grant said. This includes 5,228 miles of road rated "fair" and 3,317 miles considered "poor."

According to TRIP, driving on the 8,583 miles of "fair" and "poor" roads in Washington cost an average of 45 per cent more than driving on the "very good" roads.

"Washington motorists are paying a premium to drive on uncomfortable, hazardous roads," said Grant.

"The state, counties and cities have fallen behind in road renewal because of a lack of funds," he said. "But Washington needs to preserve and protect its roads to minimize highway maintenance costs and to reduce the number of accidents where poor pavement is a factor."

TRIP estimates it will cost $1.08 billion to rebuid the 3,317 miles of roads in "poor" condition and $381.3 million to resurface the 5,286 miles of roads considered "fair."

Much of that mileage, said Grant, is eligible for federal aid funds covering 70 to 90 percent of the total costs of the repair projects.

CHECKLIST FOR FORMULATING A PUBLIC RELATIONS PLAN TO INFLUENCE LEGISLATION OR REGULATION

Purpose: Is the aim to block a specific bill or proposed regulation or to enact it? What is the company or industry's specific position? (Establishing the specific purpose is not always easy, particularly in an association effort.)

Subject: What is the specific bill or proposed legislation involved?

Audience: Who can be most influential in blocking or helping to enact the legislation or regulations? What is his, her or their position? How much wider an audience needs to be influenced, if any? What is this audience's knowledge and attitude?

Form: What is the best way to influence the audiences?

Source: Who can best do the influencing of the audiences? What is their knowledge, attitude, and capability?

Professional: Can the lawyer or lobbyist accomplish the purpose alone? What other experts are available or needed?

Time available: When will the next step in the legislative or regulatory process occur? Is it desirable to take action at that time or before or later?

Cost: How much effort will be required for success? What are the chances for success? Is the attempt worth the cost not only in cash outlay and time of professionals and corporate officers but also in terms of using up goodwill? That is, what will be the reaction and/or side effects of an effort to block or enact the legislation or regulation?

Authorities: Who needs to approve the plan and objective?

In the following legislative case history, it was obvious that a full range of lobbying, public relations, and advertising techniques would be necessary for success.

HOW THE U.S. SENATE WAS INFLUENCED TO RATIFY THE PANAMA CANAL TREATIES

Before the signing of the Panama Canal Treaties by President Jimmy Carter and General Omar Torrijos on September 7, 1977, a concerted, well-orchestrated effort was launched against such treaties. There was, however, no coalition supporting them.

At a White House breakfast on September 7, some 70 prominent government, corporate, academic, religious, and labor officials were briefed on the treaties. Father Theodore Hesburgh, president of the University of Notre Dame, suggested that a citizens' committee be formed, outside the White House, to conduct an effective educational program supporting ratification. The proposal drew support from others, including S. Lee Kling, chairman of the board of Landmark Bancshares, Inc., of St. Louis, and former finance chairman of the Democratic National Committee.

A few days later, another attendee at the White House breakfast, John O. Marsh, Jr., was contacted by former President Gerald R. Ford, whom Marsh had served as counselor. President Ford explained the reasons for his own support of the new treaties and encouraged Marsh to help in the formation of a citizens' committee. Marsh agreed and said he would like to bring in Milton Mitler, also an alumnus of the Ford White House and now executive vice president of the public relations firm of Fraser/Associates, to assist with the formation of the committee and with all follow-up public relations activities.

From that small beginning, the Committee of Americans for the Canal Treaties (COACT) was developed. The committee enlisted additional members, especially on a grass-roots level, raised funds, and conducted a nationwide information program based on the importance of the Panama Canal Treaties to America's future.

OBJECTIVE: To encourage and win United States Senate ratification of the two Panama Canal Treaties by:
- Communicating to the American public, in an objective and unemotional manner, the existing military, political, and economic need for new Panama Canal Treaties.
- Communicating the fact that support for the new treaties was completely bipartisan historically, as well as within COACT.
- Encouraging local community grass-roots participation and personal involvement in the formation of protreaty coalitions on the state level.

• Utilizing the endorsements of supportive, nationally prominent individuals and organizations.

METHODS:

Organizational Meetings—On November 2 and November 18, meetings were held to broaden COACT's financial base and generate grass-roots activity in behalf of the treaties. Over 1,200 invitees attended the November 18 event. People from every state but Nevada heard briefings by Vice President Walter Mondale and Henry Kissinger and participated in workshops to assist the campaign back in their respective states. After the meeting, the 1,200 attendees were transported to a White House reception hosted by President Carter.

News Conferences—On December 18, for example, former President Ford, a COACT member, held a news conference at the residence of former Governor W. Averell Harriman, in which he outlined his reasons for supporting the treaties. Coverage by *The New York Times*, UPI, and national press, radio, and TV resulted. The event heightened public awareness of the existence and role of COACT as a leading advocate for ratification.

National Advertising—At the outset of the campaign, three-quarter-page ads were run in *The New York Times*, *The Los Angeles Times*, *The Washington Post*, and *The Washington Star*. The ads featured pictures of Presidents Truman, Eisenhower, Ford, and Carter in an appeal to bipartisanship, noting that the administrations of each had participated in negotiating the treaties and emphasizing the importance of ratification to the nation's long-term economic and security interests. The ads included the names of committee members. Advertising space was later purchased in *Publisher's Auxiliary* and short fact sheets were prepared for the North American Precis Service.

Direct Mail Operations—The focus was to inform the public why the treaties were in the best interest of the United States, to solicit contributions, to counteract misconceptions about the treaties, and to generate supportive mail to the Senate. An average of 90 percent of the respondents indicated support for the treaties, and 60 percent indicated they would write their Senators. Forty thousand informational brochures were requested by those contacted.

Radio Spots—COACT prepared six tapes for broadcast on "In the Public Interest," which supplies some 325 commercial and public radio stations in the United States with recorded opinion statements three to four minutes long. The committee arranged for taped statements on the treaties by President Ford, Ambassador Sol M. Linowitz, Senator Stuart Symington, Former Secretary of State Dean Rusk, General Maxwell Taylor, and Theodore Roosevelt IV. Each reached at least 10 million listeners and represented air time worth over $200,000 according to "In the Public Interest." Later, three radio spots targeted for key states were done by actor Kirk Douglas, Mrs. Margaret Truman Daniel, and General William Westmoreland at COACT expense.

Field Operations—To complement the work of the national committee, a network of local committees was formed to provide the substructure for the entire COACT effort. By the time of the first Senate vote, COACT had worked with groups in 24 states, including 14 fully active state committees representing 1,500 active members.

Speakers Bureau—The bureau's function was to make as many speakers as possible available to respond to the demand for information on the treaties, especially from the Rotary and Kiwanis clubs, whose practice is to devote regularly scheduled meetings to consideration of current public issues. In all, 64 major requests in 27 states were filled by the speakers bureau.

Liaison with National Organizations—In order to use existing national organizations as a means of disseminating information on the treaties, a campaign was conducted to seek out established groups that would be supportive. Briefings were held for representatives of farm, women's, youth, veterans', foreign policy, professional, religious, and senior citizens' organizations—some 60 groups in all.

Committee Publications and Research—(1) *COACTION*, a monthly newsletter of current committee activities, recapped Senate deliberation on the treaties, relevant congressional hearings, Senate floor debates, and organizational endorsements. (2) COACT

171

Handbook, an easy-to-follow how-to guide, provided the grass-roots supporter with sample op-ed columns, letters to the editor, TV and radio announcements, speeches, and Senate addresses and phone numbers. (3) Several question-and-answer brochures analyzed the treaties' basic provisions.

RESULT: United States Senate ratification of the final Panama Canal Treaties on April 18, 1978, by a 68–32 vote.

SECTION FOUR

SPECIAL CONSIDERATIONS

13

CORPORATE ADVERTISING—
WHEN AND HOW IT CAN
BE COST-EFFECTIVE

"More companies are using corporate advertising than ever before, and they're using it more effectively," says Harry L. Darling, vice president of the Association of National Advertisers (ANA). "There's less ego-tripping by chief executive officers (although there's still some of that), more continuity, and more objective testing to measure readership and effectiveness."

From 1975 to 1980, the ANA estimates, the number of very large companies placing corporate advertising increased nearly 40 percent. This growth reflects the growing concern of corporate managements with how their companies are regarded by people generally and by specific groups.

Corporate advertising has also spread rapidly because it is easier psychologically for top managments to adopt than other public relations measures. An executive who decides to reform his or her company's media relations faces many obstacles. Loyal employees may need to be fired and replaced by strangers. Executives must be persuaded to justify their actions publicly and to take time away from other responsibilities to do so. The results are gradual. And the compliments, if any, are few. Good media relations are often taken for granted.

Corporate advertising, in contrast, can be virtually painless, if sufficient mony is available. The problem is handed to the advertising agency. The agency creates enchanting messages that portray the company in a favorable, even heroic light. The advertisements appear in prestigious publications or on TV. And the management receives compliments on the ads' appearance.

Have corporations been lured into spending many millions of dollars, some estimate as much as a billion dollars a year, on corporate advertising when the same or superior results could be obtained for much smaller sums?

There is no question that corporate advertising can be very effective. Before-and-after surveys of individual campaigns have shown significant changes in audience attitudes. And a few studies have shown that corporate advertising in general can significantly change attitudes and actions. Studies by Yankelovich, Skelly and White, Inc., sponsored by Time, Inc., for example, have shown that corporate advertising in general improves the attitude of upper-income familes toward the companies doing the advertising.

One Yankelovich study compared the reputations of companies spending modest sums or no money on corporate advertising with the reputations of companies that spend over half a million dollars a year. All the companies in both groups were sizable; sales ranged from $60 million to $1.5 billion annually. Consequently, even those companies with low or no corporate advertising were relatively well known and well regarded. Twenty-seven percent of the audience surveyed had a highly favorable overall impression of the average corporation with little or no corporate advertising. However, 35 percent of the audience had a highly favorable impression of the average corporation with a corporate advertising budget of half a million dollars or more. The survey showed that spending a sizable sum on corporate advertising improved the average company's reputation by 8 percentage points (35 less 27). If this percentage is applied to the total universe the sample represented—people with four or more years of college living in households with incomes of $30,000 or more—half a million people were influenced to favor the big corporate advertisers. (The universe as of 1976 was 6,515,000.)

Note that the 8 percent figure is an average. Some corporations in the survey obviously did much better. An example follows.

176

HOW AN ALUMINUM COMPANY TURNED A NEGATIVE INTO A POSITIVE, REVERSING PUBLIC ATTITUDE

The general attitude toward the aluminum industry declined from 65 percent favorable in 1968 to only 39 percent favorable in 1973.

Top executives at Reynolds Aluminum decided to reverse this decline as far as their own company was concerned and asked their longtime advertising agency, Clinton E. Frank, Inc., to create and place a corporate advertising campaign. The budget ranged from $2 million to $4 million a year. Both TV and print were used, a combination that has generally proven to be more effective than either alone, when the budget is big enough.

The campaign was based on the premise that all businesses had shared in the decline in favorable attitude but the reasons were different for different industries. For the aluminum industry, one reason—perhaps the chief reason—was that the manufacture of aluminum necessarily requires large amounts of electricity.

The campaign met energy glutton criticism head-on by showing that aluminum from Reynolds saves energy instead of wasting it. Of course, the criticism was never mentioned so that no additional negative exposure occurred.

The energy-saving theme was of interest to viewers and readers because of the tenor of the times. One ad (shown on the following page) had the headline, "Reynolds Aluminum. Helping the cars we love get mileage we can live with." Another featured aluminum cans and noted that aluminum's lighter weight saves energy when beer and other drinks are shipped in aluminum, that aluminum doesn't break, and that aluminum can be recycled. A TV commercial dramatized how much less an aluminum truck weighs than a steel truck and explained, "The reduced weight saves enough fuel in its lifetime to run this truck for six years." Other commercials showed how aluminum pipe, siding for homes, and use in passenger cars saves energy.

The favorable attitude toward Reynolds Aluminum climbed from 39 percent in 1973 to 74 percent in 1978, above the average for the industry before the decline in attitude began.

Other advertisers in the Yankelovich survey also scored much

177

Reynolds Aluminum.
Helping the cars we love get mileage we can live with.

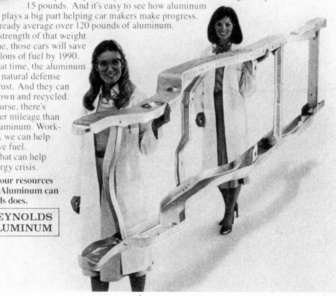

Fuel shortage or not, most Americans don't want to end their love affair with the car. So at Reynolds Aluminum, we're helping to engineer a reconciliation.

In 1973, Reynolds helped develop a new alloy and forming process for making aluminum bumper face bars and most recently a developmental aluminum truck frame. Those lightweight aluminum parts weigh less than half as much as steel ones. Every pound that aluminum trims, saves over a gallon of gasoline in a car's average lifespan.

Consider the cumulative economies of aluminum deck lids saving 25 pounds. Hoods saving 30 pounds. Wheels cutting up to 50 pounds per car. And intake manifolds lighter by 15 pounds. And it's easy to see how aluminum plays a big part helping car makers make progress. 1980 cars already average over 120 pounds of aluminum. And on the strength of that weight savings alone, those cars will save 3 billion gallons of fuel by 1990.

All that time, the aluminum parts have a natural defense against red rust. And they can be melted down and recycled.

Of course, there's more to better mileage than just more aluminum. Working together, we can help America save fuel.

And that can help ease the energy crisis.

Conserving our resources and energy. Aluminum can and Reynolds does.

REYNOLDS ALUMINUM

better than the average. Consequently, as a matter of arithmetic, some of the big spenders did much worse than average. Some, it is logical to presume, spent millions of dollars to no effect at all—which is not surprising when we consider this fact: Most of the corporate advertising done by companies in the Yankelovich survey was multipurpose and multiaudience.

As we know from Chapter 9, it is very difficult to successfully conceive, write, and design messages of this nature. It can be particularly difficult for an advertising agency skilled in consumer advertising. Copywriters are accustomed to zeroing in on the emotional needs of specific groups—homemakers, for example. They often have difficulty finding a benefit for a diverse audience. The people at Clinton E. Frank are to be complimented for finding such a benefit for Reynolds Aluminum, but for some companies, a pertinent benefit that appeals to all may not exist. Creating effective corporate advertising for a conglomerate is particularly difficult, but it can be done, as the following case history shows.

HOW A BIG, BUT LITTLE-KNOWN CONGLOMERATE MADE ITSELF BETTER KNOWN AND MORE HIGHLY REGARDED

"In 1973," said Stephen N. Bowen, director of corporate advertising for TRW Inc., "we discovered the identity void. Not in space, but right here on earth. And we were lost in it. The identity void is a research euphemism for . . . nobody wants you . . . nobody loves you . . . nobody knows you."

In that year, the company spent $1.5 million on corporate advertising and increased the amount over the years to $5 million in 1978. Most was spent on TV, some on radio, and some on print.

In making itself better known, TRW Inc. was handicapped by its name and its diversity. Initials are hard to remember. That's why ancient scriveners invented vowels and why initials that form words, such as WACS for Women's Army Corps, are used so often for organizations when feasible.

TRW's corporate advertising agency, Sapin & Tolle, created a

"Deep Water"
60-seconds

More television impact
from a company called *TRW*

ANNCR: In many places of the world the good earth has become the bad land

because there's only so much water

on our planet and it isn't always where

we want it, when we want it anymore.

But...when the water table

goes deeper

so does a pump from a company called TRW

a submergible electric pump that goes deep into the ground, making its way

around curves and bends into places and depths other kinds of pumps can't go...to where the water is.

All over the world, TRW pumps are working to keep the good earth

green and growing.

TRW MUSIC LOGO

a company called
TRW

SAPIN & TOLLE ADVERTISING

slogan for the company that, among other benefits, helped counteract the initials problem: "TOMORROW is taking shape at a company called TRW." On TV the appropriate letters in TOMORROW moved and dropped out to form TRW.

The nature of TRW's business is hard to describe—not unusual with conglomerates. One description, admittedly inadequate, states: "TRW is the full name of a multinational corporation which is a major industrial supplier of high-technology products and services for electronics and space systems, car and truck, and industrial and energy markets."

The creative solution was not to write selling copy, but to tell stories about how things the company makes or does benefit everyday life. Again, this approach highlighted material benefits that appeal to all.

A typical commercial is shown on the opposite page. Since it tells a story, the hero-in-a-hole outline is used. Mankind is the hero, and the hole is a shortage of water. Mankind is symbolized by a small boy. The savior, of course, is a TRW product—a water pump. Note that the commercial doesn't sell TRW pumps competitively but shows how they benefit people. What skill the writer had to write so poetically about a water pump!

Another commercial featured the rack and pinion steering equipment TRW makes for automobiles. Most featured TRW electronics. In every instance, how TRW products help people live better was dramatized.

A modest print campaign was placed in national publications. Spot radio commercials were also aired in selected markets, generally the same ones where TRW ads were shown on television. The bulk of the budget went for TV in specific key markets.

One survey of the audience was made after the campaign had been running for a while, in September 1974—another three years and eight months later, in May 1978. Between surveys, national awareness of TRW climbed from 43 percent to 50 percent, but in the key markets (where television was used), awareness climbed from 55 percent to 85 percent.

If a corporation has the money and the advertising agency the

181

ingenuity, corporate advertising can make a significant difference in how people feel about the corporation. But what is a corporation that needs corporate advertising to do when $2 million or $1 million or even half a million dollars is out of the question?

The solution for some corporations is easy, for others more difficult, and for some with champagne tastes and beer pocketbooks, impossible. In any case, the solution, if there is one, can be arrived at by using our standard technique of analyzing the conditions, particularly the target audiences and the purpose for which they are to be influenced. What is most important? To improve the stock's price–earnings ratio? To minimize or stop certain legislation? To improve employee morale? To increase sales? Or what?

By narrowing the audience and the purpose down to what is most important, it may be possible to achieve the objective at a sensible cost. Suppose, for example, the objective is to improve the stock's price–earnings ratio and to increase holdings by individual investors. The primary audience to be influenced might be defined as the 1.4 million investors with individual incomes of $35,000 a year or more who own common or preferred stock in a company other than the one they work for. The secondary audiences are security analysts at brokerage firms, advisory organizations, and banks plus account executives at brokerage firms.

Suppose ten quarter-page advertisements were placed in *The Wall Street Journal* during the year. Virtually every analyst and account executive reads the *Journal* regularly, so these two audiences would be exposed to practically every ad. Some individual investors don't read the *Journal* at all, and some read it irregularly. Consequently, some individual investors will be exposed to only one ad, some to all ten, and most to a number in between. Research shows that more than half the target audience of 1.26 million individual investors would be exposed to an average of five advertisements during the year—a sufficient number to achieve the objective. The cost is not several million dollars, not even half a million, but only $100,000 a year.

Just placing advertising, however, does not insure that a stock's price–earnings ratio will rise. There are two caveats:

1. The advertising must not only attract readership but also convince a number of readers to buy or recommend the stock, or to send for more information and then to buy or recommend it. This requires a copywriter who can analyze a stock like a security analyst and be able to communicate the facts about the stock dramatically yet clearly and apparently objectively.

2. The stock must be truly undervalued, according to criteria viewed as important by some investors.

An example of such an ad is shown on the following page. Every week this advertisement appeared in *The Wall Street Journal*, OKC stock rose in price and the volume of trading usually increased. Prospective investors who wrote asking for more information were sent material prepared by the agency that created the campaign, Benn & MacDonough, Inc. The number of stockholders significantly increased.

Finance is not the only category in which a small budget for corporate advertising can be made effective by focusing on a single purpose and a specific cohesive audience. If advertising to employees in public media is desirable, the cost is usually much lower than advertising to a mass audience. Most factories are located in relatively small towns, and the local media generally have low rates.

If the proposed objective is to influence legislation or regulation, the use of corporate advertising faces two obstacles. One is a peculiar regulation of the Internal Revenue Service. Corporate advertising is not deductible as a business expense if it aims to defeat or help passage of specific legislation. Here is the regulation:

A deduction will ordinarily be allowed for the cost of advertising which keeps the taxpayer's name before the public in connection with encouraging contributions to such organizations as the Red Cross, the purchase of U.S. Savings Bonds, or participating in similar causes. In like fashion, expenditures for advertising which presents views on economic, financial, social, or other subjects of a general nature, but which does not involve any of the activities specified in paragraphs (b) or (c) of this section for which a deduction is not available, are deductible if they other-

Compare the best dividend-paying growth stock you own with OKC common stock

	OKC CORP. COMMON	YOUR BEST STOCK
Indicated Yield (Approx.)	7½%	
Dividend Record	Increased cash dividend 3 times in 4 years.	
Earnings Record 1974 1973 1972	$7.01 per share 4.06 per share 1.42 per share	
Principal Business(es)	Oil Refining, Cement Making	
Prospects for Higher Earnings	1. Lower interest rates. (Construction would be stimulated, increasing the demand for cement) 2. Finding oil in Ecuador and/or the North Sea.	
What About Labor Costs?	Capital intensive, so increases in wage rates have little effect upon earnings.	
What About Competition?	Inflation and pollution control regulations make it costly to build refineries and cement plants similar to OKC's.	
Sales Record 1974 1973 1972	$110,097,000 53,290,000 48,709,000	
Price-Earnings Ratio	About 3	
Listed	American Stock Exchange	

How did your best stock make out?

If this preliminary examination indicates that OKC Corp. might possibly be a superior investment, shouldn't you get more facts about OKC? For more information, write

D. J. Fajack, vice president-finance, OKC Corp., 1949 North Stemmons Freeway, Dallas, Texas 75207.

wise meet the requirements of the regulations under Section 162.

Paragraphs (b) and (c) are as follows:

[E]xpenditures for lobbying purposes, for the promotion or defeat of legislation, for political campaign purposes (including the support of or opposition to any candidate for public office), or for carrying on propaganda (including advertising) related to any of the foregoing purposes are not deductible from gross income.

For example, the cost of advertising to promote or defeat legislation or to influence the public with respect to the desirability or undesirability of proposed legislation is not deductible as a business expense, even though the legislation may directly affect the taxpayer's business.

Consequently, corporate executives who want to use advertising to influence voters must make a choice. One alternative is to place advertising of a general nature that will cause some voters to side with the company *before* a bill or candidate inimical to the company is proposed. This kind of advertising is tax deductible. To be effective, it must be continuous. However, it is usually difficult to get money appropriated for this purpose because the need often is not imperative or obvious.

The other alternative is simply to place the kind of advertising the company needs and pay the cost completely out of profits without any tax deduction.

Only a few companies—Mobil Oil, for example—have chosen to do this nationally, taking the cost of advertising entirely out of profits. The total amount of so-called advocacy advertising has not increased in recent years. It may seem like more to some observers because the issues are more critical than ever before, the opponents to business are more vocal and the issue of free speech is involved.

Besides the IRS, cost is an obstacle to corporate advertising that aims to influence legislation or regulation. Voters are necessarily a mass audience, and the rates for advertising in mass publications and on TV are high. The purpose may be to influence legislators, but the advertising affects them primarily because they can see the arguments are being communicated to voters. A company can't dodge the higher costs. Of course, it makes a big difference if the legislation or regulation to be opposed is not national. Opposing state or local legislation or regulations by advertising can obviously be much less costly.

Corporate advertising that aims to influence customers also faces the obstacle of cost, as customers are a mass audience for most companies. The big question, however, regarding customer-oriented corporate advertising is this: "Why not product advertising?" Some of the biggest product advertisers, such as Procter & Gamble, General Mills, and General Foods, do little if any corporate advertising of any kind.

The most common reason—and a good one—for corporate advertising to customers and prospective customers is simply this: Sales of the company's products are made, not by a homemaker shopping in a supermarket, but by a salesperson calling on potential customers. Corporate advertising makes it easier for the salesperson to obtain appointments and gives whatever the salesperson says more credibility.

Corporate advertising is also warranted when the company's name has been besmirched. Advertising can restore a company's name fast; good publicity takes longer. Here's an example.

In a front-page article, *The Wall Street Journal* revealed the alleged deception a major investment firm had used in merging with another firm. The firm ran a full-page advertisement (created by Benn & MacDonough, Inc.) in the *Journal* a few days later with no mention of the accusation, just an unusually dramatic ad on what the firm had done for its customers (thus avoiding Common Mistake #1). A number of institutional investors said that only the advertisement made them decide not to take their accounts away from the firm.

Whether corporate advertising is aimed at customers or some other audience, the more specific the purpose and the audience, the more effective the advertising is likely to be. Advertising that aims at multiple audiences cannot pinpoint the needs, desires, attitudes, and motivations of its audiences. Investors want profits and dividends; consumers want lower prices and better quality; employees want higher wages and benefits; legislators, regulators, and voters want what is best for the country or other political unit. Even when the vital needs of each group are not actually in conflict, they may well appear to be.

Corporate advertising that tries to influence diverse groups must necessarily be based on some general benefit to all. Yet experience with all kinds of communications shows that usually the more specific the benefit, the greater the effect of the message. Investors and potential investors in TRW, for example, would be more motivated to buy the stock by hearing about the earnings, dividends, and future growth of the company than about how water pumps are vital to life on this planet.

Besides being more effective, the cost of single-purpose, single-audience corporate advertising is likely to be less—much less. Advertising agencies have a bias toward generalized corporate advertising. The more a client spends, the more an agency gets from its 15 percent rebate from the media. Generalized corporate ads necessarily appear in mass media—TV, newspapers, magazines such as *Time* and *U.S. News & World Report*—where the rates are high. It costs the agency no more to write and place a 30-second commercial or a full-page ad in *Time* than it does to write and place a quarter-page ad in *The Wall Street Journal*. Yet in 1982 a single 30-second commercial on "60 Minutes" costs over $150,000, a full-color page in *Time* costs about $60,000, but a quarter-page in *The Wall Street Journal* costs only about $14,000.

Agencies are motivated toward generalized advertising not only by profits. The more objectives an advertising campaign can be described as achieving, the easier it is to sell. Management may not be willing to spend much money to improve the company's price–earnings ratio, but if told that the corporate advertising will also make employees happier, voters and government officials more agreeable, and consumers more eager to buy—all probably true—the recommendation may be impossible to resist.

Finally, the more general the advertising, the more likely it will be approved by the company's lawyers.

As we have shown, corporate advertising can be very effective when properly used. Whether a company should use corporate advertising or not, how much it should spend, and whether the advertising should be aimed at a specific audience or at multiple audiences will vary from company to company. Analysis according to the nine determinants will give the answers. Here are some questions to ask:

CHECKLIST FOR DECIDING WHAT KIND OF ADVERTISING TO USE

Purposes: What are the purposes? What is the relative importance of each?

Audiences: What audiences need to be influenced? What is the relative importance of each?

Forms: What alternative public relations methods might accomplish each of the purposes and influence each of the audiences?

Source: Will the source of the alternative methods increase or decrease their effectiveness and how much?

Subjects: What would the corporate advertising say? What would the alternative methods say?

Professionals: Are the people with the necessary competence readily available? Who are they?

Authorities: How will what can be said by various methods be affected by government regulations?

Time available: How soon do the purposes need to be accomplished?

Cost: How does the cost of the corporate advertising compare with that of alternate methods?

14

AVOIDING
AUDIOVISUAL TRAPS

Since the general public is continually watching TV, doesn't it make sense to communicate audiovisually as much as possible when communicating to specific audiences? Yes and no.

Here are some arguments in favor of "yes":

1. *Conciseness:* A picture is worth ten thousand words. A graph can communicate the relative import of numbers fast.

2. *Conviction:* A photograph, filmstrip, or videotape conveys a feeling of truthfulness and accuracy as no descriptive words can.

3. *Assured professionalism:* The success of the communication does not depend on the ability of the speaker. As a corollary, the same communication can be made many different times, even by different people, with assurance that the presentation will be at or above a certain minimum standard.

4. *Memorability:* Dramatic photographs may be remembered better than a comparable description. Words are remembered better when they are both seen and heard at the same time.

These are powerful reasons for using a slide presentation or other audiovisual tool instead of a speech. However, audiovisual methods are often chosen not for these but for other, wrong reasons. Sometimes just so an executive, department, or agency can appear more modern. Sometimes because of a fascination with gadgetry. Sometimes just to make it easier on the speaker. Sometimes because corporate officers are reluctant to give speeches and recommending a slide presentation avoids the awkwardness of convincing them. Sometimes in the mistaken belief that a fancy form will make up for weak content.

Often overlooked are these three deficiencies of audiovisual forms:

1. *Loss of source:* In a slide presentation, or voice-over motion picture or videotape, the source is disembodied. Gone is the potential for building the kind of empathy possible with a live speech. Even though empathy may be established before the presentation begins, it's difficult to exploit that identification with a film or tape.

Marshall McLuhan coined the phrase "The medium is the message," overstating, but dramatizing, that the nature of the form has a strong effect on the audience. Substituting a mechanical means of communication for a live person implies that the source does not regard the audience as worthy of being communicated to personally.

2. *More difficult to produce:* The loss of source can be compensated for by skillful writing. Empathy may even be aroused. But it's not easy. Writing a slide presentation or other audiovisual communication takes more skill than writing a speech. The pictures and the words must be conceived together. All too often a slide presentation, for example, is just an illustrated speech. We've all attended presentations in which a single slide stays on the screen interminably while the speaker drones on. In a well-written presentation the ratio of slides to words is high. The audience quickly comprehends the meaning and significance of a picture or of the words shown on the screen. In an interest-holding presentation the slides move along quickly, taking maximum advantage of the form. The message can almost be understood simply by looking at the slides. (In a slide presentation written in connection with the Tire Retread Program discussed in Chapter 16, a slide appeared every eight words or so.) The writer of a slide presentation must know how to communicate, not only by words, not only by pictures, but by both together.

Ideally, the slides show pictures, not words. Among the worst-written presentations are those in which each slide consists of a list of topics that the speaker then covers. Better that each topic be a single slide. Even better, usually but not always, that each topic be pictorially illustrated. Possible exceptions occur when the audience is heavily motivated to learn or when remembering key words is paramount.

A motion picture or videotape can be even harder to write than a slide presentation. The audience subconsciously, even consciously perhaps, compares what it is seeing with the regular television fare, yet the subject of a public relations film or tape usually has less intrinsic interest.

The people with the authority to approve a script further complicate the production of a slide presentation, motion picture, or videotape. When reading a script they almost always place more emphasis on the spoken words than on the descriptions of the pictures. It's difficult for them—in fact, it's difficult for anybody—to visualize the impact of the pictures simply from the script. Even skilled readers of scripts have this difficulty. That's one reason so many TV pilots don't make prime time and why so many movies and plays fail.

3. *More risks:* I was in the audience once when a speaker rose, was so overcome by stage fright that he suffered a heart attack, and was carried off to the hospital. That's about all that can prevent a well-chosen speaker from delivering a well-written speech effectively. Not so with audiovisual presentations. That's where Murphy's First Law originated: "If anything can go wrong, it will." Here is a by no means exhaustive list for slide presentations:

- The bulb burns out, and a replacement can't be found.
- The cord is not long enough to reach the outlet.
- It's not possible to get into the room early enough to set up.
- The slides get out of order.
- The room can't be made dark enough.
- The flashlight can't be found, so the speaker has difficulty reading the script.

Everyone concerned with audiovisual presentations has his or her own horror story, each so peculiar as to seem unlikely of repetition. But the point is: There are so many of them. At a meeting before a group of public relations professionals, the speaker, before beginning a slide presentation, drew an intended, empathetic laugh simply by saying, "Nothing can go wrong." Everyone there knew the dangers.

Common Mistake #21: Not recognizing the handicaps of slide presentations and other audiovisual forms.

Faced with a decision as to whether or not to recommend an audiovisual form, the wise executive analyzes the situation according to the nine determinants. Here are some questions to ask:

CHECKLIST FOR DECIDING BETWEEN A SPEECH AND A SLIDE PRESENTATION

Purpose: Is the purpose to inform? Or to get action? Or to change attitude? (Both forms may be excellent for all three. It's the relationships of the purpose to other conditions that count.)

Source: Who would be the source for a speech? How good a speaker would he or she be? Is it important that there be an empathetic source to lend authority if the purpose is to inform, or to promote identification if the purpose is to get action or change attitudes? Or is it preferable to use cold logic—that is, material benefits only?

Subject: Does the subject lend itself to pictorial representation? For example, would diagrams help?

Audiences: Is the same communication to be given to several audiences? By several different people? What is the attitude of the audience or audiences toward a possible source? How big is the audience?

Forms: Are individual slides to be used or a film strip? How elaborate a presentation is desirable? Shall more than one projector be used? Could the same or better results be obtained by a live speaker holding up exhibits or placing them on an easel?

Professionals: Is someone available who is skilled in writing slide presentations? Who will design the slides? Who will be the producer? Who will show the slides or slide film?

Time available: Can a slide presentation be produced in time?

Authorities: Who must approve the script? Does that person understand that the pictures in a slide presentation are as important as the words, if not more so? Is the authority likely to butcher the script—that is, is a speech safer?

Budget: How much will a slide presentation cost? If producing the script as originally written costs too much, can the cost be cut and the objective still be obtained? Is the cost justified in terms of the objective and possible results?

By similar analysis, a competent executive can make a sensible decision as to whether to produce a motion picture or videotape, or whether to install an in-house TV system. A couple of words of caution follow.

Producing a slide presentation can often be done competently either in house or by the public relations or advertising agency, but a motion picture requires special expertise. Once it is decided that a motion picture is needed, most company or agency executives interview representatives of several motion picture production companies and retain one to produce the film in its entirety. Logical, administratively simple, but there is a better way—that is, to have a script satisfactory to all written before choosing a production company. This avoids the possibility that the producer will scrimp on what the writer is allocated and consequently be unable to retain a writer with sufficient skill and experience. The script is all important. A poor movie may be made from a great script, but no great movie has ever been made from a poor script.

Further, presenting each competing production house with an approved script makes it easier for the producers to determine accurately what the film will cost. A company or agency executive experienced with motion picture production will, however, set aside (preferably unknown to the production company) a sum for above-production expenses. A motion picture is a work of art, not an assembly-line product. Unforeseen costs often arise. Sometimes after the first cut is made, it is obvious that shooting additional scenes, or reshooting, would significantly improve the film. You've read about Hollywood films going over budget. It's difficult to escape.

Regarding installing in-house video equipment: The best warning may have been uttered by Bruce Pennington, communications consultant with Hay Associates, in the August 20, 1980, issue of *Jack O'Dwyer's Newsletter:* "Over $20 million worth of videotape equipment has been bought by corporations and is no longer used. The production quality turns out to be both poor and inappropriate. Employees ignore the medium, and the equipment is soon shoved into a back room somewhere."

Properly used, audiovisual equipment can greatly improve a corporation's public relations efforts, sometimes obtaining objectives impossible to achieve by older ways. Improper use can be a waste of money and time; it can even do more harm than good. Executives who carefully analyze the proposed use of audiovisual equipment according to the nine determinants can enhance rather than damage their own reputations.

15

WHAT CAN A PUBLIC RELATIONS AGENCY DO THAT A CORPORATION CAN'T DO FOR ITSELF— AND CHEAPER?

William G. Kuhns, chairman of General Public Utilities Corporation, owner and operator of the nuclear power plants at Three Mile Island, was asked, "What advice would you give other chief executives confronted with a similar accident?"

"Get out of town," he replied facetiously, and then seriously: "Be sure you have a sufficient number of knowledgeable, competent public relations people immediately available. You will be deluged with reporters, many of whom have no knowledge of nuclear power, no knowledge of economics, and no sympathy with business."

Meeting these requirements is one of the several services an agency can offer a corporation. *An agency can handle intermittent workloads economically.* Public relations normally consists of heavy workloads at certain times (annual report time, in particular) and light loads at others. For a company to hire sufficient staff of the right caliber to handle the peak loads is usually uneconomical. In making a cost comparison, the salaries of the in-house public relations executives need to be at least doubled or tripled to cover the

costs of support people (such as secretaries) as well as other overhead.

Other advantages offered by an agency include:

Objectivity. Corporate executives often have an exaggerated
opinion of the worthiness of their corporation and certain accomplishments—as well as an exaggerated opinion of the unworthiness
of certain defects. An outsider may have a better sense of propor-
tion.

Specialized talents. A large agency may have experts in such
areas as financial public relations, government relations, or speech
writing. A small agency may be chosen for the specific expertise it
has. It is difficult to conceive of in-house people developing the
Harbor Point public relations program, for example (see case history in Chapter 5).

Wider and more frequent media contacts. An agency is communicating with the media not for a single company but for several.
Consequently, the agency may have clearer and more current
knowledge of what the media is interested in.

Greater freedom to counsel management frankly. It is usually
more difficult for executives employed by a company to oppose a
misguided directive than it is for an outside consultant. Company
executives may lose their jobs and have difficulty finding comparable ones. The agency only risks losing an account. Further, the
agency has its own reputation to think of and therefore may be
compelled to argue against an incorrect course. Lastly, rightly or
wrongly, the counsel of an agency may be more highly regarded
than the counsel of a company executive simply because the agency
is an outsider. In actual practice, the advice of an in-house executive
combined with that of the agency can be most effective.

Acts as a buffer. Sometimes it is desirable for there to be consul-
tation within the company before replying to a media question. An
agency may be better able to defer replying.

Can be fired more easily. If the volume of public relations work
decreases, a company need have little compunction in firing an
agency but certainly has a responsibility toward a conscientious
employee or employees. If the volume and type of public relations

work increases or changes in character (more government relations, for example), one agency can easily be replaced by another; an employee is less easily replaced.

All the above, of course, presumes that a competent experienced agency of the right kind is chosen. Public relations agencies vary widely in their capabilities and in their sense of responsibility. Ten or twenty are giants offering practically any service a client might ask for. Most—several thousand—are small. Some consist only of an executive-writer and a secretary, yet each may perform excellently in its specialty: travel, entertainment, finance, or whatever. A couple of hundred agencies are medium sized, offering a spectrum of services but limited in one way or another.

Sad to relate, some agencies have a poor sense of responsibility. They expend great efforts to get clients but spend little time servicing them. That brings us to **Common Mistake #22: Basing the choice of a public relations agency too much on the promises the agency makes.**

Experienced executives emphasize different criteria in choosing a public relations agency than an advertising agency. In advertising, the agency can properly be judged largely by a speculative advertising campaign. An advertiser who chooses that agency knows what the advertising will be like. Certainly the advertiser will check on other aspects of the agency, but the presentation can count the most.

Not so in public relations. There are too many imponderables, and too much depends on the qualities of the company itself, its products, or its people. No agency can get a corporation president on the cover of *Time*. Or, if one agency can, *any* agency can. It is the newsworthiness of the president, not the ability of the agency, that makes the achievement possible.

A responsible agency may have difficulty knowing specifically what it can achieve for a client until after it has worked with the client for a while. Making the chief executive officer an industry leader may be a great idea, but unworkable. Facts about the company's future plans, not yet communicated to the general public and therefore not known by the agency, may make an otherwise sensible financial public relations recommendation out of the question.

But within a short period, a responsible agency will know enough about the corporation, its products, and its people to achieve what public relations can achieve—enough, in fact, so that media people would just as soon talk to the agency as to an in-house public relations persons.

In public relations, an agency is better chosen by the quality of its people and what the agency has done for others—in other words, by standards similar to those the company uses in hiring executives. These include the abilities and personalities of the people working on the account and of the agency's principals, the nature of the agency's clients, and what the agency's clients and others say about its work.

An agency can do much for a corporation that the corporation can't do for itself. And the cost, when intermittent loads and overhead are considered, may be less. But the agency must have the appropriate expertise and character.

HOW CONTEST PUBLICITY DOUBLED THE EFFECTIVENESS OF ADVERTISING FOR A DOG FOOD

The Wayne Pet Foods Division of Allied Mills had for many years produced dog food for sale through veterinarians, breeders, and kennels. Although the division enjoyed a strong position in this specialty segment of the market, Wayne was not participating in the tremendous growth that occurred in the high-volume consumer pet food business during the early 1970s. In order to take advantage of this growth opportunity, the company made a commitment to enter the consumer market in 1975 with Solo dry dog food.

Problem: A number of dominant manufacturers—Ralston Purina, General Foods, Quaker Oats, and Carnation—had well-established entries in the dry dog food area, all of which were heavily advertised and promoted. As a result, the overall noise level in this product category was among the highest of all consumer packaged goods at that time. The problem was to gain consumer attention for Solo in this extremely competitive environment.

Solution: With the need to generate consumer awareness as a primary objective, the agency, Burson-Marsteller, focused its creative efforts on development of a publicity device that would:

1. Deliver broad reach in consumer media.
2. Provide strong support for the advertising message.
3. Be newsworthy and memorable.

A creative publicity peg that would meet these criteria was found in the product's introductory advertising. The commercials featured solo-singing dogs that, after tasting the product, would sing "O Solo Mio." The agency's research indicated that this advertsing provided very effective brand name registration in an amusing and memorable way.

From this advertising concept, a publicity event was developed that was expected to generate strong add-on awareness of the product name.

The event was the Solo-Singing Dog Contest.

Implementation:

1. The contest was announced via small-space newspaper ads and publicity directed in advance to local columnists. The event was held in a major midcity hotel and was conducted by Burson-Marsteller staff. A key attraction was Candy, winner of the Johnny Carson singing dog contest, and her owner, Ed Bolton, a nightclub entertainer. Television and radio stations were alerted the week prior to the event and follow-up calls were made one day in advance.

2. A supplementary TV tour was also booked on talk shows to augment the Singing Dog Contest news coverage. A staff spokesperson, trained as an animal communications expert, was booked along with Candy and Ed on all available broadcast shows.

3. Complete press kits were developed and distributed to all print media the week prior to the contest.

Results: The program was first implemented in Solo's Wichita test market. A control market—one that included all advertising and promotion elements but no publicity—was set up in Albany. Publicity in Wichita was timed to coincide with the start of advertising.

Six weeks after the start of advertising, a 250-respondent post-advertising awareness study was conducted by the research firm Market Facts in both cities. The expected awareness objective was 34 percent.

In Albany, where no publicity was conducted, the awareness level was 30 percent. In Wichita postadvertising awareness was 60 percent. Market Facts and client attributed this difference in consumer awareness of Solo to the publicity program, which was the only variable between the two test markets.

On the basis of these results, the client approved expansion of the introductory publicity program into 12 additional markets. Broadcast and print results in each instance were outstanding, totaling 50 million impressions on a local market basis. An additional 75–100 million impressions resulted from national coverage of the Solo Singing Dog Contest on NBC-TV, ABC-TV, and TVN syndicated news as well as a front-page feature in all editions of *The Wall Street Journal*.

16

THE MORALITY OF
PUBLIC RELATIONS

Some people—even some public relations people—feel that public relations is immoral. Some say "public relations is a bunch of lies" or at best distorts the facts in favor of big business. Some resent the fact that public relations often manipulates people without their knowing it. Some believe the American business system itself is immoral and consequently that public relations, as the vocal prop of that system, is immoral.

Let us begin with this last criticism, since it is fundamental.

The American business system is based on capitalism—and capitalism in its raw form is not an easy faith to be enthusiastic about. A capitalist organization—corporation, partnership, or private proprietorship—theoretically charges its customers as much as will yield the highest profit, pays as low wages as will result in efficient production, and employs the fewest number of suitable people possible. Unrestrained, capitalism results in higher prices when products are scarce, low wages when suitable labor is plentiful, and unemployment when demand for products is low. The capable are rewarded, the less capable and the incapable suffer.

The innate pitiless selfishness of uncontrolled capitalism seems to contradict much of the morality that we are all taught by parents, schoolteachers, ministers, and priests—and that is reinforced by political speeches, TV series, and other popular communications—to be kind, to consider the welfare of others, and to work for the common good. Yet capitalism is morally sound for a number of reasons. A full explanation would require a book of its own, but here are three reasons sufficient for our purpose.

Most important, the manager of a successful corporation, partnership, or proprietorship merely carries out the inexorable laws of economics. These laws may be distasteful, as the concept that the earth is not the center of the universe was to some leaders in the Catholic church in the time of Galileo, but the laws of economics are as unchangeable as the laws of physics. Not that we know them all. In fact, economic knowledge may well be where knowledge of the physical world was 300 years ago. Many economists seem more like astrologers than astronomers. Political obfuscation and the infeasibility of laboratory experiments make accurate definition of economic laws difficult, but just as the tide wetted King Canute despite his commands, so those who defy the laws of economics suffer and those who adapt—whether by instinct, knowledge, or trial and error—prosper.

The second reason capitalism is morally right springs from the first. It is more efficient than an economy not stimulated by the profit motive. History has shown that capitalism provides a higher standard of living for all. A business in a capitalist society that fails to produce what people want at a price people can pay will not long exist. The laws of economics sentence it to death and allow businesses that produce more of what people want at lower prices to flourish. The managers of a business may strive to charge as much as they can, but the laws of economics in a free, competitive society make it impossible for them to charge more than is economically justified for any length of time.

A third reason supporting capitalism as moral is this: The conditions under which capitalism operates can be modified so as to ameliorate its unfortunate side effects. Antitrust laws can be passed and enforced to prevent the natural trend in most industries toward monopoly. Being out of work can be made bearable with unemployment and old age benefits. Welfare payments can help those in need.

Safety regulations can reduce accidents. Environmental regulations can prevent businesses from prospering at the expense of general living conditions. Income taxes can handicap the more capable and the more fortunate to the benefit of the less capable and the unfortunate.

Capitalism is morally sound because no other system can possibly produce so much for so many and because its deleterious side effects can be cured or assuaged. The American business system—and similar governmentally modified capitalistic systems, such as those of Japan and countries in Western Europe—are morally sound because they harness capitalism to the benefit of all citizens.

The conflict between business and government is inevitable—and healthy. Businesses should be striving for profitability and bigger profits. Governments—national, state, and local—should be passing laws and regulations that (1) reduce the harmful effects of the drive toward profits and (2) spread the benefits among the less capable and less fortunate.

Many people don't, or won't, recognize the inevitability and necessity of this conflict. They feel that business should voluntarily behave in a noncapitalist way. Instead of admiring the managers of a corporation that makes big profits, they criticize the managers for "greed."

The media foster this image of business as a villain. In our modified capitalistic system, the media should and do act as an umpire between business and government, but because of the nature of capitalism, a writer, editor, or commentator can feel and appear more virtuous calling fouls against business. Many reporters, particularly those called away from their regular beats in a business crisis, don't really understand how our economic system works, so they are automatically antibusiness without realizing it. And, anyway, it's hard to explain economic phenomena such as why price controls don't work, and the result usually makes for dull, difficult reading. It's more fun and better copy to berate the businessman.

Much of the blame lies with business itself. Only recently have corporate managements begun to recognize the importance of public relations. And American business still has a long way to go in explaining itself to the American people.

Few serious attempts, for example, have been made to inform voters of how low profits really are. The average manufacturing corporation makes about a 5 percent profit on sales in most years. Surveys show that most consumers believe profits not only are but should be several times higher than this.

Further, corporations with sound public relations policies don't—and shouldn't—stress their adversary relationship to government. Quite the contrary. Many not only stress their eagerness to cooperate but truly cooperate. Many intentionally behave in ways that they hope will make increased government regulations unnecessary.

Is it any wonder the general public doesn't appreciate the necessary opposition between business and government?

The public relations person is in the middle of this traffic jam of conflict and misunderstanding. The audiences to whom he or she must communicate don't understand how the American business system works, partly because even the experts are shaky and express contradictory views about its functioning. Many in the audiences are anticapitalist, many in the media antibusiness. Many people don't appreciate that under our system business and government must both work together and be in conflict. Further, the various publics to whom the public relations person communicates sometimes have conflicting interests. Analysts and investors like higher profits, consumers and consumer demagogues don't. Employees like higher wages, which may mean higher prices for consumers. Reducing the degree to which a company pollutes the air may please voters, but displease investors by reducing profits.

Some public relations people themselves suffer moral pangs because they don't recognize the inevitable conflict between business and government, or they don't understand the principles and morality of advocacy communication. (This is one reason many chief executives put lawyers in charge of public relations.) Many public relations people were previously reporters. As such, they believe they stated the facts as objectively as they could. No one ever told them that one person's objectivity is another person's distortion. If two people seated side by side at a tennis match can disagree about whether a ball is in or out, how much more difficult it must be for an observer of more complex phenomena to perceive the truth!

Further, few people comprehend how difficult it is to communicate the "truth" in words, presuming the truth is perceived. Events occur in three dimensions, in innumerable shades of color, and over a period of time. Words are merely colorless symbols, linearly strung out, and static. The writer or speaker, as we have seen, has a wide choice of how to begin, and that beginning can have a tremendous effect on readers' perception of the event—whether they will be interested and so continue on and get closer to the truth, and whether they will feel favorably or unfavorably toward the participants in an event.

Even when pictures are the principal communication tools, distortion is inevitable. The selection of pictures makes a difference, as well as their order of presentation.

The writer's or speaker's or producer's skill or lack of skill make a difference. The popular trust in sincerity is misguided. An unskilled but sincere writer or speaker may distort so much in his own favor that he loses credibility or concentrate so much on himself rather than on the audience that he antagonizes rather than persuades.

All communication distorts the truth to some extent. That's why we have the adversary system in our law courts. Each side is expected to communicate the truth as it sees it; consequently, what is communicated (except when confusion is intended) is pertinent and can stray only a limited distance from the truth.

Does this mean a public relations person should abandon all hope or intention of communicating the truth—be completely amoral? No, for a number of reasons, both moral and practical.

There is considerable difference between presenting the facts as favorably as possible and outright misrepresentation. It is morally wrong to lie to the media or any other audience, because each lie damages society by weakening the confidence that people have in communication. The efficient functioning of our society depends on a certain degree of trust in the relative accuracy of what people read and hear.

There is no question that some public relations people lie to the media and other audiences. This does not make public relations immoral—only those who lie.

Outright lying to the media is also the mark of inept public relations. A lie always runs the danger of being found out. If the principles in this book are followed, a company spokesperson will seldom be tempted to lie. The media will be on the company's side to the extent circumstances make that possible. The company's position on any matter will usually be communicated in as favorable a way as possible, or in the least unfavorable way. And the media will be inclined to write and edit the story in a way that company management may deem close to fair.

Granting all the preceding: Is the practice of sound public relations itself immoral? Some people might say so because good media relations results in readers, listeners, and viewers being affected favorably—or less unfavorably—without their being aware of the company's influence.

First, it's no secret that corporations and their agencies try to favorably influence the media. It's not only revealed in books like this one but shown on TV and in the movies.

Second, a competent public relations person does not change the facts or cause the media to communicate false information. Only the treatment, inclusion, or omission of facts is influenced.

Third, public relations often works backward; that is, it causes a corporation or business association to take actions benefiting society that would not otherwise be taken. The public relations activities that sold condominiums for Harbor Point also raised money for a museum and made people who already lived there much happier. In fact, every time the public relations activity known as "making news" is used, the sponsor benefits society. It's fundamental to the technique. That's what public relations people search for in trying to figure out what to do. They ask themselves, "What is there that needs doing for society that is not being done, and how can we make it happen so as to accomplish our public relations objective?"

Public relations also works beneficially backward when the public relations person is treated as a consultant and not a high-grade stenographer. Top management becomes more aware that whatever decisions are made must be justified to one or more publics, and therefore the decisions themselves are sometimes modified.

Fourth, the public would be much less well informed if it were not for public relations. The media are greatly understaffed in relation to their responsibilities. Most of the real work in collecting news is done by public relations people. Over 90 percent of the business news is public relations assisted, as is a high percentage of news in many other categories, including politics, sports, entertainment, fashion, and food. If the media had to do all that public relations people do, the cost of newspapers and magazines would be prohibitive, and there would be far fewer TV talk shows like "Meet the Press" or of any other kind.

The functioning of a free, highly civilized society depends on public relations. There is no public relations as we know it in the Soviet Union, only government propaganda. In a Communist society, consumers have little choice about what to buy, workers little choice about where to work and what they will be paid. Investors do not exist. Voting is a meaningless ritual. Government and party officials are in virtually complete control.

In a non-Communist society, consumers, workers, investors, voters, and government officials need and demand copious amounts of information regularly in order to make their decisions. Only with the aid of public relations can enough information be supplied.

Further, man and woman do not live by bread alone. How facts are perceived can make a difference between happiness and sadness, between boredom and stimulation. The aura that public relations gives a product can make using that product more enjoyable. Eating Chinese food on Chinese New Year is more fun than just eating Chinese food. Employees in a company that communicates to them as if they were people, not cattle, feel like people, not cattle. Something extra is added to the lives of investors when they feel the company in which they are stockholders not only pays good dividends and has good growth prospects but also behaves and contributes in ways benefiting society that go beyond the profit motive.

Which brings us to our final common mistake in public relations. It is made by people both in and outside the public relations industry. **Common Mistake #23: Not appreciating how much public relations contributes to the functioning and well-being of our society.**

HOW AN INDUSTRY SUPPLY PROBLEM WAS SOLVED TO THE BENEFIT OF THE NATION, LOCAL COMMUNITIES, AND MEMBERS OF THE INDUSTRY

Sometimes the solution of one problem creates another.

In 1973 sales of retread tires had reached an all-time low. A communications program was undertaken to create a better understanding of the value of retread tires, and sales steadily increased.

By 1976 the demand for retread tires had outstripped the supply of casings with worn-out treads. The following year was even worse, since the supply shortage brought sales to a five-year low. Many small businessmen were forced to close simply because their sales volumes were insufficient to cover rising overhead costs.

A new program was therefore developed by Burson-Marsteller, public relations agency for the Tire Retread Information Bureau. The program had three objectives:

1. To increase awareness among consumers of the casing shortage and the benefits of recycling, and to get them to help provide a regular supply of casings.

2. To obtain the active participation of members of the retread industry in solving the problem.

3. To continue to get widespread exposure for the quality of retread tires and the value of tire recycling in saving energy and improving the environment.

A pilot program was undertaken in Denver. It was kicked off with a press conference to which all the print and electronic media in Denver and the surrounding areas were invited. A press kit was handed out that outlined the casing shortage, described the benefits of tire recycling, and gave an overview of the program. Not only did local Denver television and radio shows, Denver newspapers, and 14 Colorado weekly newspapers carry the story, it was also carried, with photos, by Associated Press and National Enterprise Association, as well as a number of trade publications.

The help of the Boy Scouts was enlisted. The Boy Scout organization in Denver cosponsored a tire recycling project aimed at (1) demonstrating the environmental and energy-saving benefits of recycled tires and (2) making money for the Boy Scouts by paying troops for collecting tire casings. The mayor of Denver officially commended the Boy Scouts and the retread industry in a formal resolution and declared City Recycling Month.

The Denver Boy Scouts earned $2,500, and Denver retreaders received 5,000 tire casings (ten times more than in a normal month). Both the Boy Scouts and the tire retread industry considered the pilot project highly successful. A national campaign was therefore begun, with the Boy Scouts of America agreeing to cosponsor tire recycling nationally.

Russell Train, former head of the Federal Environmental Protection Agency, agreed to serve as honorary national tire recycling chairman. He also agreed to appear in a series of television and radio public service announcements and news spots. A 43-page how-to manual on conducting tire recycling drives was distributed to Boy Scout leaders and to 200 tire retreading companies and tire dealers. A slide presentation was produced and shown at the National Boy Scout Jamboree and at a number of trade shows and conventions. A radio disc, "Retreads, the Overlooked Resource," and a TV public service announcement, "The Recycling Tradition," were sent to stations all over the country. A brochure was written, printed, and distributed to all audiences. A continuous flow of informative hard news and feature articles about tire recycling benefits and the casing shortage was maintained to influential trade and consumer magazines, newspapers, wire services, and news syndicates.

The results: Articles appeared in numerous publications, including *Grit, The Star, Truck Market Merchandiser, Midnight, The New York Times, Motor, Mechanix Illustrated, Road and Track, Popular Science, Enquirer, Automotive News, Common Cents,*

Modern Tire Dealer, Tire Review, Enforcement Journal, National Sheriff, The Police Chief, Law & Order, Dealer News, National Observer, Rubber & Plastic News, Government Product News, and *National Star.* Russell Train's radio disc was used by 107 stations, reaching an audience of 20 million. His five-part radio public service announcement was used by even more stations, reaching an audience of 27.5 million. And his TV spot was used by 159 stations, reaching an estimated audience of 225.8 million. The public service announcement, "The Recycling Tradition," was used by 164 TV stations, taking up 74 hours of air time and reaching 232.6 million people.

SECTION FIVE

SUMMARY AND CONCLUSIONS

17

THE 23 MOST COMMON
MISTAKES IN
PUBLIC RELATIONS
AND HOW TO AVOID THEM:
A REVIEW

Mistake #1. Giving additional publicity to bad news by attempting to rebut it.

To avoid it: Establish a reputation of accessibility with reporters so they will check with the corporate officers or public relations professionals before publishing bad news about your corporation. Then respond promptly so that your corporation's view will be in the same story as the bad news, and at best the story may not appear at all. If this fails, take some rectifying, positive action that will not communicate the bad news to people who never heard it. (For example, see the Rockefeller anecdote and the Holland House and New York State Lottery case histories in Chapter 1.) If this is not possible, do nothing except build up relations with members of the press so they will check with the corporation's officers or public relations professionals the next time.

Mistake #2. Establishing an unrealistic public relations objective.

To avoid it: Do not confuse public relations with paid advertising. Remember that the press must be persuaded, cannot be forced, and should not be deceived. Remember mass communications differ from one-to-one communications. Prepare a carefully considered plan based on a knowledge of the realities of public relations and the nine determinants: purpose, audience, subject, source, media, authorities, professional, time available, and budget.

Mistake #3. Treating reporters as adversaries, not as people with a job to do.

To avoid it: Remember that how reporters feel about you and your corporation will make a difference in the way your company is written about. Help reporters and editors with information even when your company will not be mentioned. If at all possible, don't say, "No comment"; instead try to find some way to give each reporter a story.

Mistake #4. Not getting back to a reporter promptly.

To avoid it: Organize the communications function so that information and internal clearance can be obtained without delay.

Mistake #5. Organizing a corporation's communications function by techniques instead of by purposes and audiences.

To avoid it: Establish separate responsibilities and budgets for marketing, employee, legislative, and financial communications plus formal liaison between the people concerned.

Mistake #6. Not putting a headline on a news release.

To avoid it: Remember reporters and editors get piles of releases every day. If they don't gather the import of a release immediately, they are likely to ignore it. And the easier you make their job, the more they will cooperate with you.

Mistake #7. Failing to put the news in the headline and lead.

To avoid it: Remember the Civil War telegraph lines are a metaphor for human attention. If you don't get the news across immediately, the communication between your release and the mind of the reader may be cut before he or she gets to the news.

Mistake #8. Not tailoring a communication to the specific interests of its audience.

Remember that the closer your press release, speech, slide presentation, or other communication deals with the specific needs and wants of an audience and arouses specific feelings of identification, the more attention people will pay to it and the more likely they will be to respond in the way you desire.

Mistake #9. Failing to follow up a news release with a telephone call.

To avoid it: Remember messenger and mail services are increasingly unreliable. Remember your release may have been put aside by the reporter and forgotten. Remember reporters and editors don't mind being called about a press release so long as the item is newsworthy.

Mistake #10. Continually sending reporters, writers, editors, and producers information in which they have no interest.

Put yourself in the place of the reporter, writer, editor, or producer. Look at the subject from his or her viewpoint. And remember that continually bothering members of the press or producers with information they don't want diminishes your chances of success when you do have something they should be interested in.

Mistake #11. Cancelling advertising in a major publication because of negative publicity.

To avoid it: Remember it won't do any good. In fact, the absence of your advertising will leave the negative story unchallenged by your advertising messages. Anyway, where you advertise should be based on whether the publication efficiently and economically reaches and influences the audiences you want. If a publication does and you eliminate the advertising, you're cutting off your nose to spite your face.

Mistake #12. Not concentrating a communication sufficiently on the self-interest of the audience.

To avoid it: Analyze your audience and remember that there is nothing—no, nothing—that interests anyone so much as himself or herself.

Mistake #13. In a communication that aims to get action, not stating precisely the action desired.

To avoid it: Remember this variant of Murphy's Law: "If a message *can* be misunderstood, it *will* be understood."

Mistake #14. Causing the audience to think "Why are you telling me all this?"

To avoid it: Not only make every word and picture relevant to the interests of the audience, but also make sure the audience is conscious of the relevance. If necessary, tell the audience directly why they should listen, read, or watch.

Mistake #15: Not making the source of a communication sufficiently empathetic.

To avoid it: Identify the source as likable, admirable, socially responsible, and/or otherwise on the side of the audience.

Mistake #16: Assuming the form primarily governs the way a communication is best written.

To avoid it: Remember that a communication's purpose usually makes the biggest difference in how the communication should begin and end and that the other determinants may significantly affect what ideas are used, the order in which they're presented, the sentence structure, and the choice of words.

Mistake #17. Underestimating the difficulties and overestimating the effectiveness of a multipurpose, multiaudience communication.

To avoid it: Remember the Japanese proverb: "He who tries to kill two rabbits with one arrow often goes hungry."

Mistake #18. Not forthrightly making improvement in the stock's price–earnings ratio the objective of the financial public relations plan.

To avoid it: Remember that the higher the price–earnings ratio, the less funds for expansion will cost, the less likely a corporation will be taken over, and the more highly management will be regarded.

Mistake #19. Not communicating promptly with security analysts when the news is bad.

To avoid it: Call as soon as you know all the facts. Remember-that, more than anything, an analyst wants to be knowledgeable and plausible—to be able to tell account executives and investors why something happened—and that security analysts are on your side.

Mistake #20. Failing to put the percentage change in a media release on earnings.

To avoid it: Remember the percentage change in earnings is usually the significance of the news. Remember, too, that the easier you make the jobs of reporters and editors, the more likely they are to cooperate with you.

Mistake #21. Not recognizing the handicaps of slide presentations and other audiovisual forms.

To avoid it: Consider the risks when deciding whether or not to use an audiovisual form. If an audiovisual form is used, be extra thorough in writing, producing, and particularly in presentation, keeping Murphy's First Law in mind: "If anything can go wrong, it will."

Mistake #22. Basing the choice of a public relations agency too much on the promises the agency makes.

To avoid it: Check what the agency has done for others.

Mistake #23. Not appreciating how much public relations contributes to the functioning and well-being of our society.

To avoid it: Remember that over 90 percent of all news is public relations assisted and that there is no public relations as we know it in the Soviet Union.

18

HOW TO MAKE YOUR PUBLIC RELATIONS SUCCEED

Nearly all chief executive officers recognize that today they have no choice—they and their corporations must actively engage in public relations. Many, however, don't realize what this implies. Often they do little more than employ some public relations people, which is a good first step, but not nearly enough.

In a corporation with public relations sufficient for today's world, the chief executive officer personally devotes considerable time to public relations, perhaps a third of his or her working time. Other executives and the board of directors have a positive, cooperative attitude toward public relations. When a public relations crisis occurs or an objective is established, the chief executive officer charges public relations professionals with the planning or at least significantly involves them in it. He or she retains a sufficient number of skilled public relations professionals on staff and/or in the public relations agency not only to do all that needs to be done from day to day to successfully influence the corporation's several publics but to meet any crisis. The chief executive organizes the communications function for efficiency and prompt action, which means by purpose and audiences with budgets and authority corresponding to responsibilities. Executives who communicate with any of the corporation's publics, or whose subordinates do, know what successful public relations requires and how to communicate effectively in the forms they use.

More than anything else, this last means that executives know how to deal with the media and cooperate with those who do. Media relations remains the cornerstone of public relations, because the media influence so many other audiences and because people in those audiences regard the media as unbiased.

In fact, the media are biased against corporations. Even if an individual reporter is not intellectually or emotionally antibusiness, a sense of what makes a good story tends to make the reporter act antibusiness from time to time. The discreditable titillates readers, viewers, and listeners more than the praiseworthy.

In a corporation with sound public relations, this bias is countered by turning the other cheek—that is, with cooperation, thoughtfulness, and professionalism. Executives answer questions from the media promptly. When executives cannot answer directly, they make every effort to be helpful, supplying the reporter with story material whenever possible. Every executive and every communication avoids repeating negative information about the company as much as possible, yet every effort is made not to mislead reporters, even by what is left unsaid. News releases and other communications measure up to the highest professional standards. Whenever time, the budget, and other conditions allow, news releases and other communications are tailored to meet the needs and desires of each recipient.

These actions and policies avoid unfavorably affecting the attitudes of reporters, writers, and editors and therefore the *quality* of what the media print, show, and say. A corporation that needs to increase the *quantity* of its publicity needs to do much more. What can be done to gain additional publicity depends on the nine determinants, particularly the interest inherent in the subject, the media habits of the ultimate audience, the cooperation of the source, the budget, and the ingenuity of the public relations professionals.

Quantity and quality, however, are interrelated. Reporters tend to be friendlier toward publicity-seeking companies and executives simply because those companies and executives often help them do

219

their jobs better. Interestingly, some executives who have always aggressively sought publicity and some public relations professionals who concentrate on product publicity scoff at the notion that the media are antibusiness. The media have never been so in their experience.

The media are central to a corporation's public relations effort, but deliberately influencing other audiences often is more effective and always necessary today. Among these other audiences, chief executive officers worry most about government officials. Instead of deploring the mindlessness of our rulers, the modern chief executive minimizes the harm they can do. Proposed laws and regulations are monitored by a lobbyist, either the corporation's or an association's. Access to appropriate lawmakers and regulators is gained and maintained through political contributions; by cooperating wholeheartedly, even taking the initiative from time to time in helping officials; and by retaining a lobbyist who is well regarded by officials. People who present the company's position know the facts and respond promptly and accurately. They are experts on the subject under discussion. The arguments made to officials on the company's behalf are related to what is good for the country and particularly, but not blatantly, to what is good for those who vote for or otherwise influence the officials.

Company officers and other executives minimize ill feeling by treating even the most outrageous and illogical opponents courteously and reasonably. Most government problems are solved quietly, but when the public has been aroused by the media, the company's position is made plain, even though media exposure is not necessary for success, so as to reduce resentment. When public opinion needs to be mobilized behind the company's position, a comprehensive plan is set up and the appropriate communications forms, such as meetings, are used according to the nine determinants.

Because good community relations takes years to build, today every company needs a community relations program of some kind. There's no telling when a company may need friends in the local government or want voter support in a local community. In addition, a good community relations program improves the morale of present employees, facilitates recruiting, improves investor relations, and may increase sales.

Therefore, in a truly modern company, not only the chief executive officer but other executives and employees as well regularly participate in local governments and charities. And the company makes direct donations to worthy causes in the states, cities, towns, and villages in which it has offices or factories. The extent and budget for these activities usually depend on the gut feelings of the chief executive officer and perhaps those of the board of directors. Better yardsticks are the company's needs and level of profits. A company with continuing community problems, such as pollution, needs a more extensive program than one with no serious problems. A company with high profits not only can afford to donate more money and time—and has more to protect—but also is more likely to become a target for antibusiness and regulatory groups. In fact, high profits virtually guarantee that the company will be attacked sooner or later.

Inextricably intertwined with government and community relations is employee relations. Not only are employees voters, but each can influence a number of other voters. Employees with high morale and who have been informed of the rightness of the company's position speak up; those with poor morale or who are uninformed remain silent.

Company management can specifically urge employees to communicate the company's position to outsiders, but many will do so automatically if employee communications are achieving their fundamental purpose: to improve productivity.

Articles in the company publication and other communications to employees discuss what concerns employees the most: wages, benefits, working conditions, and opportunities for advancement. Employees are not insincerely exhorted to identify with the company; they do so because they get factual information showing that what the company does is socially worthwhile and how each of their jobs contributes. Employees don't get partial information from the public media about the developments that affect them. They are kept fully informed through the forms that communicate the information most effectively as determined by the nine determinants, particularly the source. Because management is inherently nonobjective, editors of employee communications bend over backwards to present information fairly and objectively.

For some company managements, successfully influencing another audience—investors—may be more important than influencing government officials, voters, or employees. A company that fails to devote sufficient attention to investors will pay more than it needs to when raising capital, runs the risk of being taken over by another company, and makes it likely that stockholders will receive less than they should when they sell their shares.

Every corporation willy-nilly must communicate with its stockholders. If this is done well, some stockholders who would otherwise sell will retain their shares. But the stock of a company that limits its financial relations to stockholders will sell at a lower price–earnings ratio than the stock of a company that attracts new investors. Some stockholders always need to sell for noninvestment reasons, and stock prices respond to demand and supply.

Corporations with successful financial relations programs aim their efforts, not just at attracting investors, but when feasible at attracting the kind of investors they need most. Attracting institutional investors moves a stock's price up rapidly. An overload of institutional investors carries the risk of a rapid decline. A goodly number of individual investors acts as a safety net.

Often, however, even the most skilled financial relations professional can make the stock of a corporation attractive only to individual investors; but when corporation management has a choice, annual reports, quarterly reports, and other communications are aimed at the kind of investor desired most, while adequately informing the other kind, as well as security analysts, the media, account executives, creditors, and other persons interested in the corporation's financial condition.

Just as the media are the cornerstone of public relations, so security analysts are the cornerstone of financial relations. Security analysts differ from the media in that they are on the company's side. Companies with sound financial relations keep security analysts fully and continually informed. A financial relations person calls promptly when there is unexpected bad news, such as a drop in earnings. The chief executive officer meets personally at least once a year with security analysts who specialize in the company's industry. When a company's stock cannot be made interesting to security analysts because of inactive trading, a small float, or any other reason, the company's financial relations people use other channels to attract investors: directly to account executives with direct mail, telephone calls and/or meetings; directly to investors with advertising and/or direct mail. In any case, public relations professionals and other executives produce communications that meet the highest professional standards. They tailor each to meet the needs and desires of each audience as well as the other eight conditions.

Fundamental to successfully influencing all these audiences is proper planning and communication. Every public relations program is different—radically, moderately, or slightly, but still different. Every communication is different. Executives can benefit by examining past successes, but each new objective or problem requires a newly created plan and one or more newly created communications. The nine conditions establish the parameters while stimulating intuition. So here is a planning checklist for chief executive officers, public relations professionals, and other executives.

CHECKLIST FOR FORMULATING A PUBLIC RELATIONS PLAN

Purpose: What is the objective of the specific plan or communication? What is the benefit to the company in terms of sales, lower costs, higher profits, survival of the company and its management, and/or gain or minimization of loss by stockholders? Will the objective be gained simply by informing the audience or audiences? Or is it necessary to change the attitude of the audience(s)? Or to entice or incite the audience(s) to act in a specific way?

Audience(s): Who needs to be influenced? What are their demographic, geographic, and psychological characteristics?

Subject: What does the audience(s) already know about the subject? What is their attitude toward it? Is the subject difficult or easy to explain? Which members of senior management are expert on the subject?

Source: What is the attitude of each audience toward the chief executive officer, the corporation, or other possible source? What does the audience already know about the source or possible source? How capable is the executive under consideration as a source in communicating to the audience(s)? In using the form under consideration? How much time can or will the chief executive or other source devote to being the source?

Forms: What forms are usually used for this purpose to this audience from this source? What other forms might be used? What are their advantages and disadvantages considering all nine conditions, particularly cost, time, experience of the present public relations staff in their use, and suitability of the available source?

Professionals: What is the experience of each of the available professionals in writing or otherwise communicating or preparing communications to each audience? For these purposes? In the proposed form or forms? What does each know about the subject? How well does each work with the member(s) of senior management who will be involved? What should be done in house? What by the public relations agency, advertising agency, or other outside supplier?

Authorities: What are their guidelines? What are they adamant about? Can they be persuaded to be less strict in this particular instance? How long do they usually take to give approval?

Budget: How much is it worth to the company to achieve the objective? Will a proposed method cause the budget to be exceeded? What other method can accomplish the objective within the budget? What is the likelihood of exceeding the budget? What will happen if the budget is exceeded?

Time available: Can the objective be accomplished in the time available? What will happen if the objective is not accomplished in time? Is a bigger budget needed to accomplish the objective within the time limit?

The writer of any public communication and the executives who approve it need to know the answers not only to the above questions but to many more. The fundamental question for any writer is: What facts and/or ideas will cause the target audience to know, feel, or act as defined by the purpose? The initial answer to this question, based on the audience and the purpose, may need to be modified because of other conditions. Coming from one source, certain ideas may be believable; coming from another, they may not be. Some facts and ideas may be communicated easily by certain forms, but with difficulty by others. Authorities, such as the SEC, may rule out the use of certain ideas or even facts. The form (such as a slide presentation) required to communicate certain ideas or facts adequately may be too costly, or there may not be enough time to put the ideas or facts into the form (such as a graph) that will communicate them clearly.

Often, deciding what to say is not too difficult. It's deciding *how* to say it that slows down the writing and production, particularly deciding how to organize the ideas and facts. So here's an organizational checklist for writers and producers, and for executives who review communications written by others.

CHECKLIST FOR ORGANIZING
A PUBLIC RELATIONS COMMUNICATION

Outline: Is the information organized in the best way to carry out the purpose—that is, the news outline to inform, the action-getting outline to get action, and the persuasion outline to change attitude? If not, is the organization justified by the multipurpose, multiaudience nature of the communication or by other determinants? In any case, is everything in the communication relevant to the purpose and the audience? Overridingly, will the emotions of the audience be successfully carried from the state before the communication begins to the desired state?

Beginning: Does the form allow the audience to easily ignore the communication (as in an advertisement), making it necessary to open in an irresistible way? Or is the audience captive (as in a speech), making it possible to begin more leisurely? Or is the situation somewhere in between? Is the source already well known and highly regarded by the audience, making it less necessary to create empathy than otherwise? Above all, will the beginning cause the target audience to pay close attention to the rest of the message with a receptive attitude?

Ending: If the purpose is to change attitude or get action, does the ending include a statement or at least an implication that would not be understood or well received by the audience at the beginning because of its succinctness, emotional content, and/or preemption? Whatever the purpose, does the ending leave the audience knowing, feeling, or acting as desired?

Besides determining the public relations plan, and the content and organization of each communication under the plan, the nine conditions also determine the best choice of words or pictures in each communication as well as the kinds of sentences to use or the manner in which the pictures are arranged.

It is more important today than ever before that most public relations communications be written in an objective, easily understood style, using short, usually Anglo-Saxon derived words that are familiar to the audience being addressed, and omitting emotionally loaded adjectives and adverbs. Metaphors and similes are best used only for clarity, not for arousing emotion. Short sentences and the active voice are generally preferable.

But there are exceptions, all determined by the conditions. If the purpose is to get action or to change attitude—and particularly if the technique of identification is to be used—emotional techniques, subtle or blatant, may be warranted and allowable: adjectives, adverbs, metaphors, and similes that bind the audience to the source or cause the audience to consider themselves the kind of people who will take the desired action or feel the desired way. Long sentences may be used for emotional effect or to communicate complicated subjects precisely to experts. Short sentences may make some audiences feel the source is being condescending.

The passive voice is usually less clear and interesting than the active voice, but the passive voice is sometimes essential for making the relevance of a key word, phrase, clause, or sentence obvious to the audience. When the audience is diverse, eliminating the doer of the action from the sentence, as can be done with the passive voice, may let all members of the audience presume the statement applies to them without categorizing each.

Parallel rules and exceptions apply to visual communications. Photographs, like objective words, are generally preferable to art-work because they are more believable, but artwork may be prefer-able when subjective emotion is useful and acceptable to the audience. When a communication consists of a series of communica-tion bits such as a slide presentation, a number of pictures each depicting a single fact or idea will usually hold interest better than a single complicated picture that is on the screen for a long time. Yet a single comprehensive picture may be preferable or necessary when the precise relationship of the parts is important. Pictures of people doing something, like the active voice, are usually more in-teresting than pictures of stationary people or objects alone, but when the person or object itself is of intense concern, including action or people in the picture may distract from the subject. An idealized picture of a typical member of the audience can help identification, but if the audience is diverse, including people may be counterproductive.

As can be seen, successful public relations today requires compe-tence up and down the entire corporate chain of command, from the actions of the chief executive officer to the selection of a picture by a production assistant. The audiences cannot be sufficiently in-fluenced by the chief executive alone, by professionals alone, or by other executives alone. A blunder, even by omission, can cause the corporation to be perceived unfavorably.

There's hope, however. Public relations people are becoming more professional and assertive as our economic system forces sound public relations on corporations. Out of necessity, the oil companies have been the leaders in some ways, and stories in the media about the oil industry are less unfavorable and more under-standing today than they were several years ago, although many stories are still far from ideal.

The conflicts between the media and business, and between government and business, will continue, but those corporations with the better public relations will be reported on more favorably by the media, besides gaining more support and encountering less opposition from other publics. These corporations will tend to make bigger profits, and fewer of them will be taken over by other companies. In fact, many will be the taker-overs. Companies and their managements that raise their public relations standards to the level required by today's world will survive because they are the fittest.

APPENDIX

The full text of two speeches discussed in Chapters 7, 8, and 9 follow. They are of contrasting styles. McElnea's is objective, or ostensibly objective, throughout—it uses plain, direct talk except for a few technical expressions that are part of his audience's everyday vocabulary. Jones's speech is subjective, even flamboyant, and makes much use of picturesque metaphors. Both are excellent speeches, however. The style of each is appropriate to the conditions under which each was made. McElnea's speech aims to convince security analysts that they should recommend Caesars World common stock. Anything that smacks of nonobjectivity would be counterproductive. Analysts conceive of themselves as acting on pure reason. Jones's speech aims to convince editors that they should upgrade the quality of their publications. A newspaper or magazine necessarily reflects the ideals of the time, hence editors are not adverse to an appeal to their idealism, so long as their pocketbooks benefit as well.

WILLIAM H. McELNEA, JR.
President, Caesars World, Inc.
Speech to the Los Angeles Society of Financial Analysts

Our speaker is Mr. William H. McElnea, Jr. He was born in Orange, New Jersey, and grew up in the environment of New York and came west. Mr. McElnea earned his Bachelor of Arts at Dartmouth and an MBA at Amos Tuck School of Business Administration. During World War II, he was a pilot with the United States Naval Air Services serving in the Atlantic and the South Pacific and in the Aleutians. He came to Caesars World through the investment business. He was a partner in Van Alstyne, Noel and Company from 1956 to 1972. While there he served as a Director of the predecessor company of Caesars World from 1966 to 1968 and then returned to the Board of Directors in March of 1969. He was elected President of Caesars World in November of 1972 and became President and a Director of Caesars New Jersey Incorporated upon incorporation in 1978.

Well, Bill, it may be that this Society is a little slow on the pickup because this is the first time that we have had a representative of your industry to appear before us. We are looking forward greatly to your presentation. Ladies and Gentlemen, Mr. William H. McElnea, Jr.

Thank You, Ted. Ladies and gentlemen, on behalf of all of us from Caesars World, we are very pleased and very flattered that we are here today and especially that we do represent the first casino company that has been invited to speak before your Society. I personally feel very comfortable in this group. I think we speak the same language. I still maintain my membership in the New York Society of Security Analysts. I still send in my $50.00 a year. My name appears in the big book, so I feel as though I am not quite as out of place as I might have been if I had come out of the casino business in Steubenville, Ohio.

I'd like to talk today about several things. This is the last day of our fiscal year, it is also my twelfth wedding anniversary, and so I am very much up today, and I'd like to talk a little about the gaming industry and about Caesars World and divide my remarks pretty much between the two.

The gaming industry, I think, has been recognized in the last few years as America's newest growth industry. It has achieved that distinction because of its demonstrated ability to produce earnings. I think the sociological and political changes that have occurred in our society in the last ten years have created large new markets and potentially very large profits for the industry. Another criterion of the growth industry is the professionalism of its management. I believe that we can say today that, in our company and other leading companies in this field, for the first time professional management is involved in the leading companies. Institutional lenders and investment bankers are backing our industry, and there is a growing support and public awareness of investment in our business. This will lead, I believe, to a new perception of gaming, a new acceptance in our society because gaming has become not only legalized, but has become legitimized.

I think Atlantic City has triggered this new awareness. I suppose because it's near the media capital of the United States and also it is in the middle of about 25% of the United States population.

If Atlantic City triggered it, I think that Las Vegas has supplied all of us who are analysts and students of the industry with a myriad of statistical information supporting the thesis that under our very noses for many, many years the gaming industry has in fact been growing and has been producing results which had Atlantic City not come along, might not even be recognized today. Just the fact that visitors going to Las Vegas since 1970 are up some 64%—in other words, 5 million new visitors on top of the 6 million who were there before. The fact that Las Vegas occupancy is running about 22% ahead of the national average, the fact that conventions have been increasing at a very, very large rate, are facts that we cannot dispute, and the Tourist Bureau, the Nevada Gaming and Control Board, and a number of other Las Vegas and Nevada organizations have produced very complete statistical evidence of what I am saying.

There is no slow season in Las Vegas. It's the only city in the

231

country that has been built and devoted entirely to visitors. I think in spite of the spectacular success of the casino gambling industry in Atlantic City, however, I don't see any threat posed to a continuation of Las Vegas's growth.

I think that people have been concerned about Atlantic City as a threat. They have been concerned about the gasoline shortage, they have been concerned about inflation, about recession. I won't bore you with very many numbers today, but I must say that before I came over here I looked at the June figures. In this I think it surprised me a little bit, but it may surprise you even more.

In June of this year which was in the middle of our worst gasoline problem, the United Airlines strike had just been settled, but there were 963,000 visitors in Las Vegas in June of 1979, last year, 947,000 visitors. That is a slight increase of 1.7%, and this in spite of the fact that the average week-end automobile traffic from Southern California was down 21% in June, and is estimated to be down another 15% in July. I think there has obviously been a disintermediation between the airline travel and the automobile travel into Las Vegas.

The deregulation of the airlines has had a significant effect on the number of seats. I think there are 20,000 new seats coming in from Los Angeles introduced in the last month or two, and of course, rates are way down. There are specials now into Las Vegas at $28.00 round-trip as opposed to the old $64.00 price. So that there has been a factor of gasoline becoming more expensive and airline travel becoming less expensive. This has helped Las Vegas and has overcome the problem of gasoline. At Caesars Palace, our figures also support the thesis that Atlantic City has not hurt what is going on there.

Our table game drop, for instance, in June is 15% ahead of last year and in July through yesterday was 31% ahead of last year. Drop, of course, being the only measure you could go by when you are talking about business, because that's the volume of business.

Slot take was up 6.3% over last year in June, and 25% over July of last year's figures. I must admit, during the time when automobiles were less in evidence in Las Vegas, the slot machines were the ones that were affected because obviously we rely on walk-in traffic at Caesars Palace for slot machines.

Hotel occupancy in June of last year was 89%. This year it was 88%; but we had a 13.8% higher room rate so that our room revenues were significantly higher than last June. In July, our occupancy actually climbed back above the 86% of last year to 89%, with a 16% increase in average room rate. Food and Beverage revenue in June was up 13% over last year, and 23% in July over last year, so that we have had a very healthy economic condition through this date in Las Vegas.

Caesars World entered the gaming industry in 1969, when, as Lums, we purchased Caesars Palace. Prior to that time Lums had operated about 450 fast food limited menu restaurants in the United States and overseas. They also operated a large chain of discount department stores in the southeastern part of the United States and owned their own meat packing operation where they provided about 35% of the protein requirements of the Lum stores. But in September of 1969, which I think was the watershed year for this corporation, although I must say that I might put Atlantic City in that category if I were trying to evaluate it, but in September of 1969 for $58,000,000, $3,000,000 of which was cash, Caesars Palace was acquired from a group of individuals, and we were in the gaming business. Since that time, the company has entered into a land development program in South Florida. It opened three honeymoon resorts in the Pocono Mountains of Pennsylvania. And it has involved itself in the organization of a computer manufacturing company on Long Island.

That essentially is the history of the company. It's encapsulated, but I think it puts the gaming business into perspective because our non-gaming activities today represent 10% of our gaming activities. It is important in order to understand our company, to understand how we are organized.

Each of our operating subsidiaries is set up on a thoroughly autonomous basis. In Los Angeles, our headquarters, we control the cash management of the corporation, we control the risk management, we control the banking relationships, the auditing in the intercontrols, we control security of our subsidiaries; and of course, all of our legal work and our stockholder public relations work, and all of that type of thing is done here. But each individual subsidiary operates as though it were a separate company and this has worked out very, very well for us. I notice in Terri Lanni's remarks to me when he is telling me how we are doing in New Jersey, he always likes to make comparisons with Caesars Palace. So we notice we are introducing a little competition into our family of companies today. I think healthy competition.

Of course, our main job at the headquarters is to make sure that the policies of the Board of Directors are effectively carried out. I would like to touch just for a minute on our management and our Board of Directors because I think we do have a strong and distinguished group of independent Board members.

This year we are probably going to spend about $17,000,000 to $19,000,000 on entertainment alone. That is the money we will be spending for our contracts for entertainers, and Harold Berkowitz, who is one of the senior partners of Kaplan and Livingston in Beverly Hills, a law firm that specializes in the entertainment and the theatrical field, has made a very valuable contribution to this important part of our activities. Peter Schweitzer is another outside director. Peter was formerly the Vice Chairman of Kimberly-Clark and a very large stockholder of Kimberly-Clark, and Peter is in charge of our Caesars World auditing. Manuel Yellen, another outside director who for many years was the Chief Executive Officer of P. Lorillard and Company, one of the largest tobacco companies, also serves on our auditing committee; and James Needham, who was formerly an SEC Commissioner and the Chairman of the New York Stock Exchange, is also on the Board and is Chairman of our Caesars New Jersey Audit Committee. So I think in our eight-man Board of Directors, four of which are inside and four of which are outside, we have eight very diverse and contributing and distinguished directors.

I think we are also very lucky at Caesars World in the way it has developed in the last few years with a lot of external financial support, because this is definitely a capital-intensive business. We have

$42,000,000 of unsecured lines of credit with banks across the country; in addition to that we are borrowing on a medium- and long-term basis from other banks and other institutions. We are borrowing on a long-time basis from insurance companies, but in the bank category, the Chemical Bank in New York is our lead bank, and we are very proud of our relationship with the Security Pacific, with the Crocker, with the United California Bank, Continental Illinois, and with the First National Bank of Boston, not to name a number of smaller banks in the country including the two largest banks in New Jersey: Midatlantic Bank and First National State Bank of New Jersey. So we feel comfortable as a company that needs money, to take advantage of the opportunities that we have; we feel comfortable with the kinds of people who are supporting us. Of course, we are very proud of the fact that the Aetna Life Insurance Company saw fit to make a $60,000,000 loan to our company last October, which was the second largest disbursement that Aetna ever made to one customer, and that relationship, of course, is a very comforting one. In the investment banking field, E. F. Hutton and Company has been our advisor and our chief investment banker, through five public deals as a matter of fact, going back to an exchange offer in 1974. And in New Jersey we have the two top regional firms, Janney Montgomery Scott and Butcher & Singer, who handled our rights offerings for the establishment of our market in the New Jersey subsidiary. So I think we have good support from outside.

I'd like just to take a second to touch very briefly on our non-gaming activities, because they represent a small part of what we are doing. Down in Florida, we have 303 acres of land, and a country club around which this land is located, and the country clubs, of course, a loss leader type of operation in order to develop a neighborhood and sell the land. We have disposed of, through sale or contracts to sell, about 95% of that property, and, of course, when we have disposed of it we will no longer be in the real estate business, for our company has no intention of re-entering that field. It has been a very unsuccessful part of our business over a period of years. But fortunately we are now in a position where we can see the light at the end of the tunnel; I would say that by 1983, all of this land will have been sold and paid for. As it is released, the buildings are built on it, and we will be in the process of releasing that land and reducing our long-term debt associated with that with about $20,000,000.

We have 489 rooms in the Poconos, three resorts. These are resorts that specialize in honeymoon business. The Poconos in Pennsylvania are the Niagara Falls of that area, and they attract a large number of honeymoon couples that drive from New York, usually the market of those people who cannot afford to get in an airplane and fly to more exotic places. We have three resorts: one is Paradise Stream, another is Cove Haven, another is the Pocono Palace. These are located on a total of about 450 acres of land—and represent a small part of what we do. But they are important in the sense that if slot machines were to become legalized, the counties in which these resorts are located happen to be counties that probably are going to become legal areas for slot machines. So they may turn out to be a very important part of our business at some point in the future.

We bought a little company in 1973 that was in Chapter 11, and renamed it, and reorganized it, and now we call it Ontel Corporation. It has had quite an outstanding record. It's doing about $20,000,000 of sales right now, making a good profit, and is on, as many companies in the distributing process in the computer business are, a very strong up-trend. We manufacture micro-processor based users of programmable intelligent terminals. These are sold by our company to the people who put their name on them. They are sold to the OEM market people, like Control Data, Lockheed, and Overseas Olivetti and Telefunken. These are some of our customers. Our equipment is interfaced with most other electronic information processing systems, and it is a small but important and very fast-growing part of our business. And perhaps you ask, how did we ever get into that business? It doesn't sound like the gaming business. Well, as it happens we have also developed quite a list of software which we sell. As a matter of fact, we sell software systems to the Disneyland Hotel, we sell them to 11 major hotels, and we essentially developed our computer operations using Caesars Palace as a laboratory, and now we are, of course, in the opening of our Boardwalk Regency Hotel. What we essentially did was to clone our system at Caesars Palace and move it right in, so we know it works, we know it works for our businesses. It is a very, very important helpmate to be able to extend into this business. That is the Ontel Corporation. That pretty well takes care of what we do outside the gaming field.

Caesars Palace is the best known resort hotel in the world. That, I think, we have proven to ourselves by various reports that I have seen. It is referred to as the "Miracle in the Desert." It's an incredible history of a hotel that has been nothing but profitable since it opened. It opened in August 1966 and has 400 rooms, seven restaurants, tennis courts, pools; it's a little city on seven acres of what I consider to be the best hotel corner in the world. The hotel corner where there are well over 10,000 first class rooms. We have been continually expanding Caesars Palace, almost from the day we acquired it, and in 1978 we added some 15,000 square feet to our casino, increasing the casino from 20,000 to 35,000 square feet. We added a very beautiful boutique shopping area which we call the Appian Way, in which we have as a center piece, in the rotunda, an exact replica of the statue of David which stands in Florence, carved out of the same marble for us as the marble that Michelangelo used, so the David stands there among the great Italian statues of other people which we have in our Appian Way shopping center.

We have built a new gourmet restaurant, we have also added a moving walkway, one way toward our casino, a moving "people mover." And incidentally it has been a very, very successful marketing tool for us. We have been averaging 6,000 people per day entering into our casino on our moving walkway, we are building another one at the other end of the property now. Since we have a good thing, we might as well try to duplicate it. So that was the 1978 expansion which cost us about $11,000,000.

In 1979, which we are at now, we are still under way with a very large expansion of Caesars Palace, primarily financed by the Aetna mortgage. We are adding a 590 room "Fantasy Tower" to Caesars

Palace which has been topped off as of two days ago. We expect to open this in late November. The "Fantasy Tower" is so named because we have created some suites in this tower, from ten to twelve suites which we call "Fantasy Suites," which defy my powers of description. The "Fantasy Tower" is going to bring our room inventory to over 1,800 rooms. It is absolutely essential, because we were beginning to feel, based upon our market studies and what we were told, that we would be losing our position as one of the prime convention hotels if we did not have the kinds of rooms that we have now.

The convention business has grown in Las Vegas to the point where you have to carve out 1,200 rooms for a major convention, and we could not do that with our present hotel. So this was really forced upon us. We are also introducing into Las Vegas, for the first time, what will be the terminus of our second people mover, an Omnimax theater. If you have ever been to Washington to the National Space Museum, you would have experienced in the Motion Picture theater that which is totally different than anything I have seen, or anything else anyone has ever seen. This is a 380 seat theater which we will be essentially making available on a very inexpensive basis. The first film is going to be the same film as they are showing in Washington, we have the exclusive in Las Vegas, and we also have it in Atlantic City. We were able to make that kind of a deal with the developers and that will be part of our expansion. We are having additional restaurant facilities, we are adding to our casino, we are adding to our slot machines, we are totally changing the front part of the hotel so that we can deal with these larger groups in a more efficient way.

We are in the middle right now of the agonizing process of totally relocating our front desk, but nothing seems to interfere with our building new business. I've been asked, "What do you think is the ingredient in your company that sets it apart from other people in your competitive area?" I think that the single ingredient—I feel our most valuable contribution to this business—is marketing. I think that is the vital difference in this business. You have a large number of rooms, you have a certain number of square feet in your hotel, but marketing is the key, and we have focused very, very aggressively in that area.

More television emanates from Caesars Palace than any place in the United States except the three major networks, and this is because we have had a whole series over the years of very, very visible sports promotions. I think we are the originators of heavy-weight, one-on-one big-name tennis promotions. Caesars Palace is now being referred to as the "Carnegie Hall of Boxing." We have been doing so much in the boxing field, which, of course, is a kind of promotion where we can tie into not only casino activity but also prime time television.

We have had some TV specials. As a matter of fact, last November we introduced in the house a two-hour commercial really for Caesars Palace which Procter and Gamble financed. It was called "Cinderella at the Palace." You may have seen it. It had all of our stars. It was the story of a new star who acted out the Cinderella story in Caesars Palace. That of course is advertising promotion. That's marketing.

Merv Griffin is a tremendous marketing tool to our company. The kinds of people that come to Las Vegas, whether they stay at Caesars Palace or not, all wanted to see Merv Griffin when he taped at Caesars Palace. Of course, he does give us many credits on his program. We have been the location for a number of feature films that encourage people to come to Las Vegas. The last film was kind of a bomb called "Pleasures" with Ali McGraw. The only thing that concerned me about that film from reading the reviews is that the star of the show, and the star that stole the show, is our own Pancho Gonzales. So I have a feeling it may be that Pancho's services will be a little more expensive in the future.

Films are another way we market. We have been marketing locally on this very important hotel corner with our people movers. Slot promotions, which are really new to our company, have become a very important part of increasing our casino win. Our convention business is solvent, we are booked for large groups through 1984, and we are booking now for 1985 to 1990.

We are focusing on off-shore marketing, have foreign offices in many, many countries, and do a great deal of promotion to try to get people in from South America, from Europe, from the Middle East. We like to feel that we are recycling petro dollars in some small way, and we have foreign language people in our casino that have badges that indicate what languages they speak. We want our foreign visitors to feel very, very much at home. They are in the high roller category, the ones that are our best casino customers. We have a very, very extensive casino host system. All this ties in to marketing, and I think we have to say to ourselves, with all of this expense and the dedication of marketing, what does it result in? I think it results in, as I said earlier, in the amount of utilization of your facilities as compared to our competitors. I won't go into any direct comparative figures, but I will say that from 1971 to 1978 Caesars Palace growth in table game revenues grew 16% a year versus other strip hotels' 5% a year. Slot machine revenues have grown 21% a year on the average in that period, an average of 14% for the strip. We have been able to get the highest room rates, we have been able to achieve the highest restaurant prices, and this translates itself to our return on investment capital, and also gives you an immunity to things like gasoline shortages, because I am sure that so many of our customers fly in, our figures are better than we would have expected if we were in a different category from a marketing point of view. So it is that same marketing approach that we had hoped to be able to use to maintain our competitive position as Atlantic City becomes more competitive over the years.

Atlantic City is our newest and most exciting venture. It has consumed practically all of our management waking hours in the last five months. We have two prime locations down there. We have moved very aggressively in Atlantic City. In June, 1977, hours after Governor Byrne signed the enabling legislation, we just put our name on it with a 90-year lease at the old Howard Johnson Motel, which is just a 100% location on the Boardwalk.

Our second hotel in Atlantic City, as you know from reading our prospectus, is located on the site of the old Traymore Hotel, and we took the first step toward completing a rather large and complicated financial layer cake for that company by selling 750,000 shares three weeks ago through our national underwriting group headed up by

E.F. Hutton. We have a long way to go, the project will cost in the neighborhood of 200 million dollars. It will have a thousand rooms, a very very large casino, and of course it has to be subject to all of the regulatory contingencies, and also to the financing climates of that outside project. The initial planning is well advanced, David Hanlon, who is here to answer any questions, has been designated as the chief executive officer of that project. He is putting that staff together, and we are very hopeful that it will be as successful as we were in moving ahead on the Boardwalk Regency.

In conclusion, I would like to be somewhat presumptuous and put on my security analyst hat for a moment and suggest those criteria that I think are important for analysts to consider when they look for an opportunity to invest in our business.

I think that it is very important that the company that is chosen have a strong independent Board of Directors. I think that an experienced professional management is important, and I guess the key word there is "experience" because this is an industry with a tremendous potential with very little in the way of management, because there are so few companies in the business. The casino resort hotel has characteristics that require special know-how to operate successfully, not a hotel type operation. I think that it is important that the company that you chose have proven controls and proven security systems. As an example: We are in the money handling business, where huge amounts of money are handled and carried in our casino cages. During our Christmas and New Year's promotion—December 26th until January 2nd of last year—we processed 96 million in cash through our cages in Caesars Palace and when the dust had settled our shortage was $700.

According to all those bankers that watch our affairs very closely, they were very proud of us for the kind of control that is absolutely essential. If you don't have the control and proven security systems, the leverage working against you with the kind of money floating around the business could be disastrous. I think that another example of controls is this: We happen to be the largest credit house in the world. We have issued about a billion two hundred million dollars' worth of markers or accounts receivable since the hotel opened, and have collected 96% of those markers. I think that again is something that should be recognized, keeping in mind that as far as Nevada is concerned a game debt is not legally enforceable, even in the state of Nevada.

I think that financial strength and external support is important because I read in the newspapers almost on a daily basis that this company or that company is going into Atlantic City and they are budgeting forty, sixty, or eighty million dollars to get open. All I can tell you is, there are going to be an awful lot of disappointed people because this is a business that requires a great deal of money, and it's a business that you *cannot* always determine from a political point of view exactly when reverse flow will occur. We were disappointed that we were not able to get the number of individuals licensed in our hotel in Atlantic City when we had hoped, and this of course set us back from the point of view of not having a full complement of casino employees until hopefully later this week.

I think that marketing expertise, as I said before, has got to be very important. When you are really competing in a kind of atmosphere that Atlantic City will present to us in four or five years, you have to be able to get people with the right profile into that casino, into that facility, to maximize the use of the facilities. I think that you have to go with a company that has had a highly successful record in the casino business.

Atlantic City is a huge market. With one full tank of gasoline you are in within 25% of the population of the United States. It is a very affluent market where the ethnic profile suggests an even higher level of casino play than Nevada's traditional market.

It is a market that is much more accessible to European, South American, and Middle Eastern customers. It is an industry that is recession proof, inflation proof. I think that the fact that not very many people play a five-cent slot machine makes that point. But it is an industry where investment decisions should be made on a highly selective basis, so if you will remember McElnea's three rules for investing in this industry—the three M's: Management, Marketing, and Money.

Thank you very much. I have appreciated the opportunity to be with you.

JENKIN LLOYD JONES
Editor, *The Tulsa Tribune*
The Thirst for Information

Gentlemen:

Last week in New York, instead of joining the high and pleasant wassail of the convening newspaper publishers, I spent some hours in the statistics section of the New York Public Library, and the research rooms of the Magazine Bureau and the ANPA Bureau of Advertising.

Normally, I am neither this studious nor this holy. But I wanted to test the validity of a feeling that has been growing in my bones for some years. It is a feeling that is shared by a steadily increasing number of my editor colleagues. And that is that there is, among the American people, a growing thirst for solid information, and the newspaper that ignores this trend is heading for circulation malnutrition and, if we must be crass about it, advertising anemia.

We have all long known, of course, that public and privately endowed education is being disseminated to more and more young Americans each year. Some of this education is pretty terrible. Some of our schools are still wading around in the Dismal Swamp of "progressive education." Many of our children have never been handed an honestly objective report card. Many of them have played at "keeping store" instead of learning abstract mathematical principles. Our high school graduating classes are thronged with ladies and gentlemen who move their lips as they read their comic books. Eccentricities in spelling have been looked upon with benign tolerance. And we are staggering into the space age leading a lot of normally smart and normally eager young people who never got closer to real science than raising pollywogs in the second grade window.

But this is not the subject of my speech. Let's dismiss it with a hopeful truism. Even a bad high school disseminates more information than a good grade school. Even a miserable, superficial college or university will turn out graduates more capable of grasping more ideas in this complex world than if they had never gone to college at all.

Thus it is that the wide expansion of secondary and advanced education in America, good and bad, is beginning to have an immense effect upon America. We in the newspaper business had better pay some attention to it. The theories on which we may have successfully edited newspapers 20 years ago are under question. The old maxims no longer hold. Something very big is happening to our country.

There are almost as many American youngsters in high schools today as had ever completed high school up until the year 1940. There are nearly as many persons enrolled in college right now as had ever attended institutions of higher learning in America in the 247 years between the founding of William and Mary College and the year 1940. While the population of our country has increased an estimated 38 percent since 1940, high school enrollment is up about 60 percent and college enrollment has increased about 115 percent.

What is this doing to the reading habits of the American people?

As a first step toward finding out, I went to the Magazine Bureau to check the ABC circulation figures of specific magazines in 1940 against 1960.

Listen to this:

The leading detective magazines, i.e., magazines devoted to both fictional and purportedly factual accounts of crime, had risen in circulation from 1,561,000 to 1,584,000—an increase of one and one-half percent. Mind you, during the same period the population of the country had gone up 38 percent.

This, I think, does not mean that the appetite for crime and murder stories has substantially decreased. But what it may mean is that such diversion is now receivable painlessly via the TV screen. The viewer can be lazier and more passive than the reader. He doesn't need to spell out words or turn pages. He is visually roared down Wilshire Boulevard behind screaming sirens and he is permitted to look over Lieutenant Friday's shoulder at the body on the slab. Thus it is that crime magazines seem to have fallen on evil days.

The leading "confession" magazines—*True Story, True Confession, True Romance*, etc.—had gone up from 5,007,000 to

6,153,000—a rise of 23 percent, or 15 percentage points below the population increase.

Here, again, the television detergent opera ladles out sentimental corn with more sniffle power than the old radio soap opera. And magazines aimed in the same direction are having a harder struggle.

But the top home and hobby magazines, the magazines devoted to homemaking, sports, and recreation, have leaped from 7,257,000 to 15,173,000 in the same period—a boost of 108 percent. The three leading national business magazines have grown by 120 percent.

And, finally, the three great "information" weeklies—*Time, Newsweek,* and *U.S. News & World Report*—have risen in circulation since 1940 by a staggering 257 percent.

We are still, of course, some light years short of becoming a nation of eggheads. The circulation of *True Story* is 11 times that of *Saturday Review.* But 20 years ago *True Story* had 70 times the circulation of *Saturday Review.* That's a substantial change. Since the war the circulation of *U.S. News* is up about 700 percent, and the latest figures show that at 1,149,000 it is running 1,000 copies ahead of *Modern Romances.* This may leave you with only moderate awe at American intelligence, but don't forget that 20 years ago *Modern Romances* outsold *U.S. News* by five to one.

Well, maybe the magazine appetite is improving in sophistication, but what about all this slush and gunk that leers at you from the pocket book racks in every drug store, railway station, and airport? The number of disheveled young ladies on the covers of these opuses is as overwhelming as it is intriguing. Some are being carried off by handsome musketeers. Some are battling for their virtue on the canyon's rim. Some are engaged in loading zip guns and hypodermic syringes. A recent phenomenon is the rash of low-bosomed novels that purport to describe certain phases of American history. One closes them with a sense of wonder that our pioneer ancestors could have built such a splendid country while spending practically all their time in the hay.

But when I brought this subject up in conversation with an eminent professor of history recently his answer surprised me.

"More power to these bum historians," he said. "They may be

sketchy on research and they spice their stories with heavy sprinklings of sex and violence. But by these devices they trap hundreds of thousands of persons who never read any history at all into some understanding of our past. And someday a lot of these readers are going to pick up something better. Out of this primitive and even furtive search for vicarious thrills will certainly come an enlarged audience for Bruce Catton and Bernard DeVoto and—who knows?—maybe even a few for Toynbee!"

Charles D. Lieber of Random House commented to me last week as follows:

"Let us not forget," he said, "that a trashy book is still a book. Reading a book is not like thumbing through a magazine. You cannot change the subject every 60 seconds. You must concentrate on the story line, keep the characters identified, and remember what went on 100 pages ago. This is a new experience to very many people of low intellectual traditions and little education. Yet vast numbers of them are now deep in the pocket books. That, undoubtedly, is where many of your old 'confession' readers have gone. And it's a step upward."

According to Mr. Lieber's figures some very long steps are being taken. *The Lonely Crowd*, a critique of the growing middle class, originally appeared in *The Yale Review*. Yet it has sold 100,000 copies in paperback. Reprinted classics are steadily invading the drug store racks. Books like Walt Whitman's *Leaves of Grass*, Harold Lamb's *Genghis Khan*, Louis Untermeyer's anthologies, and *Doctor Zhivago* are now big items. Science is hot. Fred Hoyle's *The Nature of the Universe*, Alfred Hooper's *Makers of Mathematics*, and a spate of biographies of great chemists, biologists, and astronomers are now being carried home in staggering numbers.

Cheap literature with a small "l" for the first time in American history is running into real competition with inexpensive literature with a large "L." The results are wonderfully encouraging. Millions of Americans are beginning to stretch their minds and extend their horizons.

So what of the newspaper business?

At the Bureau of Advertising I sat with the *Editor and Pub-*

lisher Yearbooks for 1940 and 1960. I picked out 13 large American cities where there remains lively competition between separately owned and operated newspapers. The list might have been longer, but not much longer, for the number of nonmonopoly towns has shrunk rapidly during this 20 years.

Out of these 13 cities I picked those newspapers which have a reputation for factual and informative news reporting somewhat superior to their competitors. This list is locked in my safe. I will never show it. For some of my most cherished friends are editors who, through conviction or presumed expediency, practice what I regard as rock-and-roll journalism. If my research has any validity, you must simply take it on faith. Or you can draw up your own list and see how close your results come to my conclusions.

This is what I found:

In 12 cities, excluding New York, 21 newspapers which in my opinion have had the best records for sound and complete reporting had a combined circulation in 1940 of 4,673,000. In 1960 these same newspapers had a combined circulation of 7,617,000. That's an increase of 63 percent.

In the same 12 cities, 23 newspapers which leaned toward more frivolous and more sensational news reporting had, in 1940, a combined circulation of 4,015,000. In 1960 these newspapers, now reduced to 16 in number as a result of suspensions, have a combined circulation of about 4,270,000—an increase of 6 percent.

It's worth noting that all of the suspensions took place among newspapers that were doing a relatively poor job of informing.

The New York City picture was cloudier. There the three soberest dailies posted an increase of only 13 percent, and one of these three showed a loss. But the four jazzier chronicles showed a gain of only 8 percent. Still, it seemed pretty much of a stand-off.

Then two thoughts occurred to me. First, the heavy influx of Negroes and Puerto Ricans during the past 20 years represents people who have had little tradition of newspaper reading. Many of them either through incuriosity or the inability to read English still do not buy any New York newspaper. But it is natural that as they are introduced to the newspaper habit they will first move toward the large type and plentiful pictures. Nobody fresh from a cotton or cane field is likely to pick up *The New York Times*.

Secondly, I had overlooked the tremendous increase in New York's suburban dailies, most of which compete fiercely with the 10-cent New York evening papers. These were of little consequence 20 years ago. But such has been the growth of suburbia that four papers, two on Long Island and two in Westchester, have increased in circulation from 125,000 to 664,000 in these 20 years.

Thus the pattern holds, even in New York. For most of the major suburban journals are making a real effort to cover international and national news in addition to the doings of the school board and the problems of the waterworks. The bedroom cities are becoming more like independent western American cities, with newspapers that trade on local loyalties but which are catering at the same time to growing middle-class curiosity toward affairs in the world outside.

Therefore, gentlemen, it is plain to me that the handwriting is all over the wall, and up on the ceiling, too.

Information is both our challenge and our opportunity. This doesn't mean we have to be stuffy. I still read our comic pages before I even look to see whether my lead editorial is in rightside up. There is nothing wrong with being at least as interested in "Dear Abby" as in the weather. Good feature writers will always be more precious than blood rubies.

But in an age when Man sits on an atomic bomb while he carefully draws a bead on the planets there is too much of legitimate excitement in the world to justify repetitious headlines week after week about the sexual misadventures of Miss Aadlund.

We now navigate by a manmade moon. We photograph the earth's cloud cover from 800 miles in space. Our understanding of our religious traditions has taken a great leap forward with the discovery of the Dead Sea Scrolls. Evidence supporting the virus theory of cancer and the physically-correctible origins of many hitherto mysterious and dreaded mental diseases is flooding in on us. Nuclear analysis of campfire ashes has rewritten whole chapters in human history. We are on the threshold of synthesizing life itself.

Two months ago I was deep in the Guatemalan jungles watching archaeologists map out the central square of the 1,700-year-old Mayan city of Tikal. As one of my newspaper friends watched this fascinating reconstruction of a mighty past he turned to me and remarked, "Somehow I just don't seem to care what happens to Jack Parr!"

We editors should take the hint. As a medium for titillating citizens who seek only diversion, television has us backed against the wall. If we only do badly what TV does well we are headed for trouble.

But why play the other man's game? Why not perfect our techniques for recording the swift march of history, for explaining the new world of science, for reducing complicated political issues to plain and clear dimensions. The public wouldn't understand? Baloney! Look at the circulation figures once again, contrasting broadly two classes of newspapers. Sixty-three percent increase against six percent. Look at the magazine figures, the swelling Niagara of dimes and quarters that go for magazines that inform. Look at the galloping invasion of the double-dome volumes on the pocket book racks.

Time is with us, gentlemen. The growing thirst for information fits our business perfectly. It is only if we cling to obsolete theories of what the public wants, theories that sickened with the elder Pulitzer and died with the elder Hearst, that American journalism will decay.

It's a brave, new world in which the most promising and exciting nation is a question, searching, eager America. Let's get with it!

INDEX